D1766401

Vikings in America

Dr Graeme Davis is a specialist in the mediaeval North Atlantic, its languages, literature and culture. Recent books include studies of mediaeval Germanic languages, of Early English settlement of Orkney and Shetland, and dictionaries of English dialects. He is lecturer in English Linguistics at the Open University and previously a British Academy researcher at the University of Iceland.

VIKINGS

IN

AMERICA

Graeme Davis

BIRLINN

First published in 2009 by
Birlinn Limited
West Newington House
10 Newington Road
Edinburgh
EH9 1QS

www.birlinn.co.uk

Reprinted in 2011

Copyright © Graeme Davis 2009

The moral right of Graeme Davis to be identified as the
author of this work has been asserted by him in accordance
with the Copyright, Designs and Patents Act 1988
All rights reserved. No part of this publication may be
reproduced, stored or transmitted in any form without the
express written permission of the publisher.

ISBN: 978 1 84158 959 6

British Library Cataloguing-in-Publication Data
A catalogue record for this book is available from the
British Library

Typeset at Birlinn in ITC Galliard with headings in ITC Tiepolo

Printed and bound in Great Britain by
CPI Cox & Wyman, Reading

Contents

Maps

Illustrations

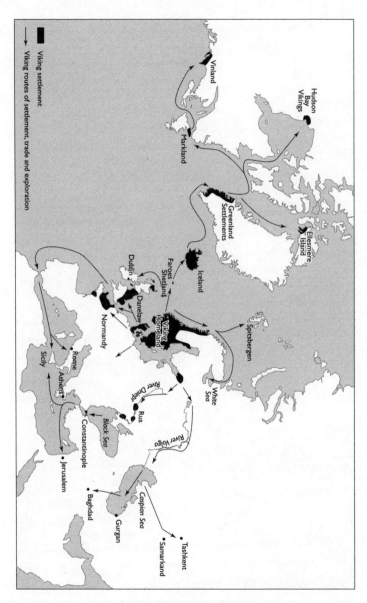

1. THE VIKING WORLD

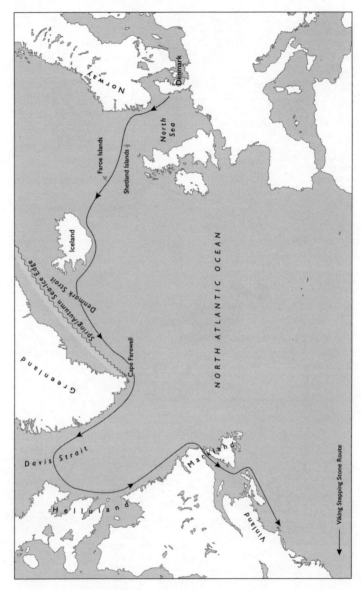

2. NORTH ATLANTIC STEPPING STONES

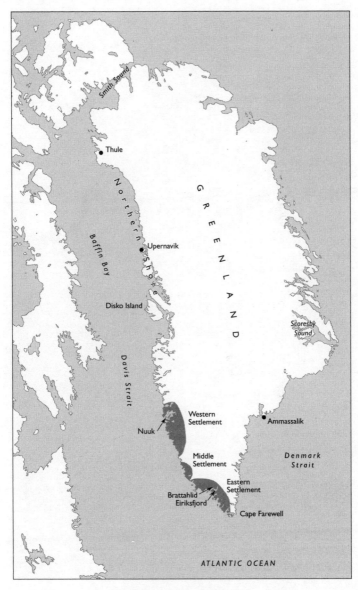

3. VIKING GREENLAND

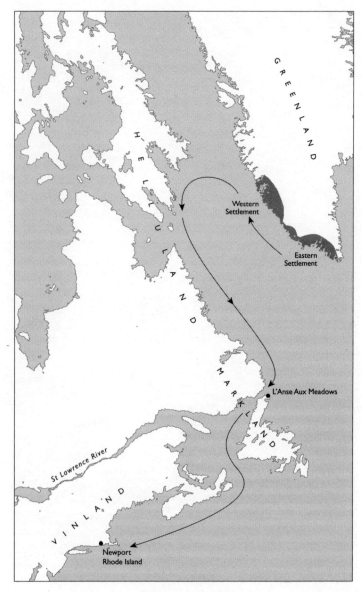

4. Viking Vinland

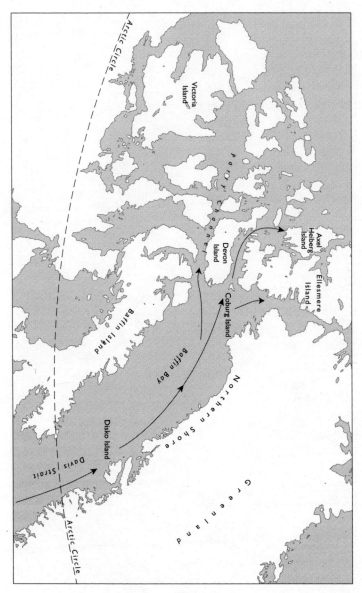

5. VIKING HIGH ARCTIC

6. VIKING HUDSON BAY

Vikings in America

1
Vikings to America

In fourteen hundred and ninety-two
Columbus sailed the ocean blue.
He had three ships and left from Spain:
He sailed through sunshine, wind and rain.

So goes the school-room jingle, and so most people today perceive the dawn of European exploration and settlement of America. Yet it is not Columbus but the Vikings who should be credited with the first significant European exploration and settlement of America.

Around five centuries before Columbus, the Vikings both explored and settled in America. The archaeological remains at L'Anse aux Meadows in Newfoundland leave no doubt that they established a substantial presence on the American east coast. Today we know for sure that the Vikings were there. Yet in popular perception the story of the Vikings in America remains at the margins of history. As a result the Vikings and their exploration of what they called Vinland is now presented as little more than a footnote in world history. The implicit assumption is that their remarkable achievement had no lasting impact on the history of either Europe or America.

The picture is changing. In recent years academics working in many different disciplines have been finding fragments of evidence which taken together tell a far bigger story of the Vikings in America. This is the story presented here.

For the Vikings did a lot more than just visit a few places in Newfoundland or elsewhere on the American east coast. From their base in the Viking colony of Greenland – itself strictly part of the American continent – we now know that the Vikings explored in three different directions. A thousand miles south from Greenland is the archaeological site of L'Anse aux Meadows, a staging post on the journey to what they called Vinland, east-coast America. A thousand miles north from Greenland the Vikings reached the High Arctic. Here Viking archaeological remains have been found in some of the most unlikely locations, in lands no-one would have dreamed the Vikings could ever have reached. Today we must accept the evidence of that the Vikings, against all expectations, in fact reached the High Arctic. Furthermore, 1,000 miles west from Greenland in Hudson Bay and its vicinity we have evidence of Viking presence, and can place the Vikings at the centre of the North American continent. Viking Greenland emerges as the starting point for exploration of three widely separated areas of the American continent: the east coast, the far north and Hudson Bay.

The Viking presence in America was no brief interlude, but something that lasted as long as the Viking Greenland colony – a little short of 500 years. Most of the voyages to America were made to bring back to Greenland and Europe cargoes of raw materials – but some resulted in over-wintering and some in settlement. Today we must accept that the Vikings played a noteworthy role in the exploration and development of America.

Stories of America came back to Europe. Yet for a variety of reasons – largely a mix of commercial sensitivity and bad conscience – Europe turned its back on these stories. This virtual conspiracy of secrecy is the canvas on which was written the fiction of the Columban discovery of America. Yet at a time when Mediterranean Europe was promoting the Columbus myth, northern Europe, particularly Britain, was demonstrating a continuing tradition of sailing directions that went back to the Viking explorers, as shown in the British search for a north-west passage. Without the Vikings, the post-Columban re-exploration of North America would have been very different in its character.

In researching *Vikings in America* I found a great mass of firm evidence, but also an almost equal volume of what may best be described as fiction.[1] Ideas that the Vikings reached California or were somehow linked with the Templars or any other Masonic group are, in my view, without any justification, and have not been considered here.[2] I have, however, looked at a whole range of doubtful evidence which may or may not give information about Vikings in America. In all cases I have sought to be clear that there are doubts, but also to avoid the temptation to discard theories out of hand. At least some of the disputed materials will, in my view, come to be accepted as reliable.

The most controversial legacy of Viking America presented in this book is that the name 'America' is of Viking origin. The old view that America takes its name from the explorer Amerigo Vespucci is a tired idea now so totally discredited that it cannot be maintained today – though still taught in many American schools. It may be that in discarding the Amerigo Vespucci hypothesis we should simply say that we do not know where the name 'America' comes from. Yet we must also note that 'America' is a regular phonological development of a name we know the Vikings used in their Old Norse language for this part of the world. Either the Vikings named America, or by some strange coincidence America gained from an unknown alternative source a name which resembles that used by the Vikings. The Vikings are certainly the first European settlers of America; they may also be the people who named the continent.

The Columbus Myth

The established view of history sets out that in 1492 Christopher Columbus set out from Spain with three ships, sailed across the unknown ocean with his sailors in fear of falling off the edge of a flat world, and discovered America. Today we may note that he didn't know he had discovered America, but thought instead that he was many thousands of miles away in India. For that matter, he failed to establish trade with the lands he visited, or to found any lasting settlements there. Surprisingly – if his role as first European discoverer were to be maintained – the New World is named not after him but supposedly after his contemporary, Amerigo Vespucci. All these limitations on Columbus's achievement are well known, but do not detract from the central role that history has given him as the discoverer of America. American history pretty much starts with Christopher Columbus – and because we were taught about Columbus in our early school years, we tend to hold to the story almost as an item of faith. In 1492 Christopher Columbus discovered America.

Yet today we know for sure that this is wrong. If we stop for one moment to think about it we realise that no European is the first discoverer of America. Rather the Americas were discovered many thousands of years ago by the Asiatic peoples who crossed the Bering Strait from Asia and made their lives in the Americas, the ancestors of the Native Americans who still inhabit the continent. At the very most, the role of Christopher Columbus is that of the first European to reach America.

Yet even this more limited role for Columbus we now know is simply not true. For 50 years or so there has been a popular awareness of academic evidence that many Europeans saw America before Columbus. No-one today can reasonably doubt that the Irish made it across the Atlantic and back to

Ireland nearly a millennium before Columbus, and told plenty of stories of finding a land to the west across the Atlantic. There is now widespread acceptance that the story of the Irish St Brendan's voyage in a coracle from Ireland to America and back again is a record of an actual voyage. Probably other peoples made their way across the Atlantic well before Columbus. For example, the supposition that the Basques, in search of Atlantic fishing grounds, ventured ever further west and found America is persuasive. They certainly reached the rich fishing grounds of the Grand Banks in the north-west Atlantic, just a few hundred miles from the American shore, and it beggars belief that in the hundreds of years that they fished the Grand Banks no ship was ever driven by storms those extra few miles to sight the coast of America. Yet neither the Irish nor the Basques seem to have settled in the new world of America, and their voyages there were sporadic. It is reasonable to conclude that the Irish and the Basques visited America before Columbus, but that they did little more than see the land from the sea, or at most just step ashore. They had no real impact on America.

As well as voyages by the Irish and the Basques, we now also know that some Vikings made the journey to America around five hundred years before Columbus, and since the 1950s and 1960s we have had conclusive archaeological evidence of their presence on Newfoundland. The Viking voyages to America have now become a staple of history books. There are no grounds whatsoever to dispute the central idea that the Vikings reached America. As well as the archaeological evidence from Newfoundland and now from elsewhere in North America we have a rich body of stories about the first Viking explorers, preserved in the Icelandic sagas. From these sagas we hear of the Viking adventurer Leif Eiriksson leading a ship of Vikings from Iceland to Greenland to Vinland. Exactly where Vinland might be is a matter for debate, but it is certainly somewhere on the east coast of North America, and equally certainly not Newfoundland. The Vikings established some sort of settlement in what they called Vinland as well as in Newfoundland.

This popular perception of Vikings in America is correct as far as it goes, but marginalises the Viking contribution to American history. The conclusion that is drawn is that the Vikings visited America, but did not alter the course of history of America, nor was their discovery much known in Europe so it didn't influence European history either. Therefore the Viking discovery of America scarcely matters. With a few footnotes for the voyages by the Irish, the Basques and the Vikings, the great myth of both European and American history can be reasserted – in 1492 Columbus discovered America.

It is time for the myth to be demolished. Evidence for Viking discovery and settlement of North America has been stacking up, but has not previously been presented in a popular book in a unified form. This book does just that. Archaeology, genetics, Icelandic literature and the archives of Europe give a coherent picture which contradicts the myth. The Viking voyages to North America were not the footnote to history that would signify an occasional visit by tiny groups of Vikings. Rather, tens of thousands of Vikings made the journey to America before Columbus, and some of them settled. American goods moved to Europe centuries before Columbus – and European goods to America. Much was known about America before Columbus visited – indeed the voyages of Columbus and his successors show detailed knowledge of the Viking discoveries. Instead of a Columbus myth, we should have the real story of the Vikings in America.

That the Columbus myth has developed and become accepted should be a cause for concern, as it is a substantial falsification of history. The evidence for a Viking presence in America before Columbus has been expanded in recent years through archaeology and genetics, but even without these sources there have always been overwhelming documentary materials. The knowledge that mediaeval Europe had of America was fuzzy – but so was its awareness of Asia or Africa. The merchants and seamen of ports on the west coast of Europe certainly knew America existed, just as they knew of Asia or Africa, though they rarely visited these continents. The Vatican knew of America – through the Middle Ages the Popes appointed 17 bishops to Greenland *and lands to the west of Greenland*, all well before Columbus. Our continuing credence in the story of Columbus as discoverer of America perpetuates a fifteenth-century deception. For when Columbus described his first voyage to the king and queen of Spain, and through them to the Pope, all the key players knew that this was not a new discovery. Columbus had previously spent the winter of 1477–78 in Iceland with Icelanders who had been to America – as recorded in local 'parish' records from Olafsvik, Iceland – and he was as aware as anyone that his discovery was not new. The king of Spain was aware of the stories of Basque fishermen. The Pope knew that his predecessors had ministered to Greenland and the lands to the west as part of the diocese of Hamburg, and had appointed bishops and collected taxes. All Columbus could truly report was a successful voyage from Spain to America and back again, one building on hundreds of years of transatlantic voyaging. Yet such an unremarkable achievement would have been of interest to no-one. By treating this voyage as a new discovery, Spain was able to lay claim to America. The Pope supported this claim. Spain was then the bastion of Roman Catholic orthodoxy, the darling of the papacy, riding high on its success in the crusade against the Moors in Grenada; by contrast, Hamburg and northern Europe were at the edge of the Roman Catholic world, doctrinally suspect, and within a generation to be sundered from the Roman Catholic church by the Reformation. Spain and the popes benefited from claiming Columbus as the discoverer of America, and in doing so chose to forget the Vikings and the part played by seafarers of northern Europe.

Two sorts of stories need to be told. The first story is of the great extent of Viking exploration of North America, and their settlement there. Alongside this is the equally remarkable story of the European conspiracy to cover up their role, a fabrication which even today is reflected in European and American school curricula, and in popular belief in the Columbus myth.

The Viking Achievement

So what really happened? What is the story of the Vikings in America, and how can the cover up be exposed?

The context for the Viking voyages to North America is a part of the much larger history of the Viking exploration of the North Atlantic, Europe and western Asia. This Viking Age took the world by surprise. Before it, Europe hardly knew of the Vikings, inhabiting as they did a remote location and a tough environment in the far north of Europe, right up as far as the Arctic Circle. They were farmers in an environment where farming was marginal, where agriculture and animal husbandry could only just sustain a settled lifestyle, a little-known people struggling for survival in a harsh environment. They lived alongside the fjords of what is now Norway, on the coast and lake-land of Sweden, and on the marshy islands of what is now Denmark, in small communities never far from the sea. The Viking Age started abruptly in the late eighth century AD, when an unremembered craftsman made a breakthrough in shipbuilding that produced the most seaworthy ships the world had ever seen. With these magnificent ships began an expansion which amazed the world. In the centuries that followed, Vikings travelled far to the east and the south. They moved down the great rivers of Russia, founding the first Russian kingdom as they went. They reached Baghdad and Constantinople, served as crack mercenary troops to the Byzantine emperors,[3] visited Jerusalem, carved runic graffiti on a statue in Athens. To the west the Vikings moved into what is now France, creating the North-man's-land of Normandy. In England they were checked for a generation by the English hero King Alfred, but went on to conquer all England, and rule first through the Canute dynasty, then through the dynasty of the Viking duke of Normandy, William the Conqueror. In Ireland they created the great Viking city of Dublin, where Viking power and Celtic art coalesced to create the Irish nation. Their expansion continued north and west, across the Atlantic. First the islands of Orkney and Shetland were settled by the Vikings, then the Faroe Islands and Iceland, as the Vikings marched across the stepping stones of the North Atlantic. From Iceland it is but a short hop to Greenland, itself part of the North American continent, and the Vikings established their settlements there around 1,000 years ago. From Greenland they voyaged yet further west.

The Greenland colony, created in AD 986, was no settlement at the edge of the world. Greenland flourished. The land the Vikings discovered was then unpopulated – the Inuit Greenlanders who live there today arrived after the Vikings. For nearly 500 years Greenland was the place to be. Skeletons of colonists excavated in Greenland show they enjoyed excellent health and remarkable longevity compared with Europeans, and grew an average two inches taller than their Viking cousins in northern Europe. Greenland had a vibrant culture, both as shown by the high culture of church ornament and the low culture of the form of dress of the people – the latest European fashions, no less. The two main settlements, both well south of the Arctic Circle, supported agriculture and husbandry. The population was scattered in around 500 farmsteads, and would have totalled no more than 5,000 people – fortunate people enjoying a level of health and political stability unmatched by their relatives in Europe. The Greenland the Vikings found was – and is today – a magnificent land. Viking Greenland prospered.

The one thing missing from Greenland was timber. Even the best efforts of our age have scarcely produced in Greenland trees more than six feet high in experimental plantations, while for the Vikings, trees were confined to the knee-high scrub of dwarf birch and dwarf willow. Driftwood does sometimes float onto beaches in Greenland, and while it is of use as firewood, its condition is such that it is not suitable for building houses or ships. The Viking Greenlanders had an enormous need for wood, and finding this resource drove their expansion.

It is a short voyage from Greenland to Canada's Baffin Island, a short voyage from there to Labrador, a short voyage from there to Newfoundland. The Vikings made it to Newfoundland and beyond by about the year 1000, just fourteen years after establishing their colony in Greenland. There they found the timber they needed in abundance. From Iceland we have sagas which tell of some of the first voyages to this new land. The Vikings explored what they called Markland – Forest Land – which is usually identified with southern Labrador and the island of Newfoundland. The land is therefore named after the resource that the Vikings were seeking. Further south is the land they called Vinland, usually regarded as New England. L'Anse aux Meadows, the most remarkable American Viking archaeological site, is in Newfoundland; not in Vinland as often suggested, but rather in Markland.

Over the years the Greenland colony developed. There were two major settlements there – both on Greenland's mild west coast facing the Davis Strait, and called simply the East Settlement and the West Settlement. Between them a smaller settlement later developed – the Middle Settlement. These settlements comprised farmsteads that were widely scattered, each farming many square miles of the coastal strip between sea and ice cap. They had their religious institutions provided through several dozen churches, the appointment of a bishop, and the development of both a monastery and a nunnery. Politically Greenland functioned as a commonwealth. Each farmstead appointed a representative – usually the head of the household – to periodic local meetings, which in turn appointed representatives to a yearly parliament. The system is an early democracy, a style of government shared with Iceland and some of the more isolated Viking settlements in the Faroe Islands, Shetland, Orkney, Scotland's Western Isles and the Isle of Man. Contact with Europe was maintained, with Greenlanders taking part in the Crusades, and European ideas finding expression in Greenland. Trade from Greenland brought the resources of the Arctic – furs, ivory, oil – to the countries of Europe, while ensuring that the Greenlanders kept abreast of the latest European fashions, and received the manufactured goods of the European High Middle Ages. Ultimately Greenland became a part of the Norwegian kingdom, and later the Danish kingdom. This distant rule appears to have done Greenland little good. The decline of the colony and its fifteenth-century extinction occurred while the colony was part of the kingdom of Denmark.

East Coast America

Almost from the start of the Greenland colony the Vikings were exploring and settling the eastern coast of America. A Viking ship could manage a distance of up to 125 miles on a good day – a day when the wind blew steadily in the right direction as a stiff breeze but not a storm. Against the wind their progress was negligible. As a rule of thumb, taking into account good days and bad days, the Vikings seem to have managed about 1,000 miles in two weeks to a month. In a summer sailing season of around three months they could comfortably manage a journey out and back of 1,000 miles on each leg, perhaps a little more. The American east coast was therefore within easy reach of Greenland.

A thousand miles south of Greenland took the Vikings to the northern tip of Newfoundland. Here is L'Anse aux Meadows, where excavations in the 1950s and 1960s uncovered a substantial Viking settlement. About 200 people lived at L'Anse aux Meadows at any one time. They arrived about the year 1000, built their shelters, and abandoned the settlement around 1025. Curiously, the settlement was not a village. It is best regarded as a travellers' inn, a staging post for people on their way somewhere else. L'Anse aux Meadows offered accommodation, in what we would regard as barrack blocks. Most importantly, it offered a boat-building yard, and a smithy and workshop. This was the place to get boats repaired. Here there was wood, and copious iron available from the local bog-iron to make the essential rivets that held Viking ships together. L'Anse aux Meadows was the service centre of the Viking Age: not only could boats be repaired here, accommodation and over-wintering were also possible for Vikings who had left it too late to get back to Greenland. But L'Anse aux Meadows was never regarded as home by its population. Thousands of Vikings passed through, but not a single body was buried there. In an age where every settlement had its graveyard, the absence of even a single skeleton at L'Anse aux Meadows is striking. The Vikings believed it important to take their dead home, and clearly L'Anse aux Meadows was not home. The dead were taken back to Greenland or on to Vinland.

There is evidence of Viking travel south from L'Anse aux Meadows. Butternut squash, which grow nowhere north of New Brunswick, have been found at L'Anse aux Meadows, demonstrating travel further south. With L'Anse aux Meadows as a sound base-camp, travel another 1,000 miles south is plausible, and seems required if the Viking name of Vinland – whether it means 'Fertile Land' or 'Grape-Vine-Land' – is to be seen

9

as truly descriptive. In Maine, a Viking coin has been found within a pre-Columban Native American site. The Vikings were clearly on the east coast of North America for centuries before Columbus.

Yet the Vikings struggled to establish permanent settlement on the fertile east coast of America. The reason for their problems in maintaining settlement was simply the North American natives – a people the Vikings rather rudely called Skraelings, meaning 'wretches'. North America was fully settled by the Native Americans millennia before the Vikings arrived, and they did not take kindly to the newcomers. In contrast with Greenland, North America was not an empty land. The Native Americans were hunter-gatherers, living from the resources of the land but not farming. Their lifestyle created a mobile population which at certain times of the year could collect together into large, well-armed groups. These are the Red Indians who resisted the much better armed later European colonists who sought to settle the American continent. Faced by such a mass of numbers the Vikings did not have a chance. The small numbers that could settle in a farmstead would be overwhelmed by the Native Americans. Colonisation of the whole American continent was just not possible, though some settlement was practical and did happen.

The American High Arctic and Hudson Bay

The Viking expansion from Greenland led also in another direction. One thousand miles north of the Greenland settlement is the coast of Ellesmere Island, in the Canadian High Arctic. This is the northernmost land mass in the world, almost as big as the British Isles, and with its northern tip just a few hundred miles from the North Pole. It should come as no surprise that Ellesmere Island has a most severe High Arctic climate. Summer temperatures do manage some days above freezing point, but the long winters have the full vigour of the High Arctic cold and wind. Today Ellesmere Island is populated only by a handful of hardy souls, for example at the military listening station of Alert, part of the United States' DEW-line early warning system. As recently as the nineteenth century, Ellesmere Island had a tiny Inuit population, though even the Inuit found it unrewarding and moved to Thule in northern Greenland, where their descendants still live. Yet before even the Inuit were in Ellesmere Island, the Vikings were there.

Viking archaeological finds on Ellesmere Island have been made sporadically over the last 30 years, for example in a series of digs by the University of Manitoba from 1998 to 2002. Finds have included the round bottom of a barrel, a piece of chainmail, fragments of swords and knives, and the ever-present iron rivets that Viking ships seem to have dropped whenever they were hauled out onto a beach. A clear 1,000 miles north of the northernmost Viking settlement in Greenland we have firm evidence of Viking occupation with at least occasional over-wintering and probably year-round settlement. Seven to eight hundred years ago the Vikings were living in a land now uninhabited, which we had supposed unvisited by Europeans before 1818. That the few archaeological studies that have so far been made in this enormous land have already yielded some amazing finds gives hope that there is much more to find. No-one could have guessed at Viking visits this far to the north, while settlement of any sort is staggering.

From Greenland the Vikings voyaged 1,000 miles and more south to Newfoundland. They voyaged 1,000 miles and more north to Ellesmere Island. In both these areas they established settlement of which we have archaeological traces. They also explored at least as far to the west. West from Greenland is the Hudson Strait, leading through to Hudson Bay and the heart of the North American continent. The climate is characterised by the extremes of a mid-continental location. Hudson Bay experiences winters far more severe than those of Greenland, but also summers that are much warmer. Hudson Bay was no place to spend a winter, but was an ideal summer destination, for wood, for hunting, perhaps simply for the experience of weather warmer than Greenland. Archaeological remains of Vikings in the Hudson Strait are persuasive, though not without their detractors; those in Hudson Bay itself and further south, controversial. Enough has been found to demonstrate that the Vikings were present in Hudson Bay.

As Greenland declined in the fifteenth century, its off-shoots in Vinland, Ellesmere Island and Hudson Bay failed. Vinland and Hudson Bay presumably did not survive the end of the Greenland colony, though there are some who would argue otherwise. The Ellesmere Island presence is puzzling. There is some slight evidence that it or a settlement near it still existed in the 1570s, well over a century after the Greenland colony had failed, which suggests that the settlement was self-supporting. When Europeans visited in 1818 there was no sign of a Viking presence, though the Inuit of nearby Thule have stories of European people living there no more than a generation before the 1818 rediscovery.

America was reached by the Vikings; parts were explored, and parts were settled. This furthest reach of the Vikings was dependent upon Greenland as the key link in the stepping-stone route across the Atlantic, and Viking America failed when Viking Greenland did. This is no footnote in history – the Vikings have a long and important history in three widely separated locations in America.

2
Stepping Stones to America

THE sea routes created the Viking identity. It is on voyages first across the North Sea and later across the North Atlantic that the character and values of the Vikings developed. From Norway a series of short voyages, rarely out of sight of land, led to the Shetland Islands, the Faroe Islands, Iceland and Greenland. While Christopher Columbus and sailors that followed him went straight across the Atlantic in one leap, the Vikings crossed in a series of short voyages from stepping stone to stepping stone. From Greenland, itself part of the North American continent, the stepping stone principle took the Vikings to Baffin Island, Labrador, Newfoundland, New England and, perhaps, New York's Long Island. The American voyages were the Vikings' furthest reach, and their exploration of a distant land a demonstration of what courage, skill and the Viking ideals of democracy and personal independence could do. The North Atlantic, with its island stepping stones all the way from Norway to America, was the world of the Viking.

The Peoples of the Viking World

The Vikings didn't at first call themselves Vikings. Rather the name they used was *Northmonna*, meaning North-men, or Norse-men, or just Northerners. Their identity was that they lived far to the north in Europe. Indeed they even made this a boast. We have on record a Viking adventurer, Othere by name, who appeared at the court of the English King Alfred with the claim that of all the North-men he lived the furthest to the north. The coast of the land in which they lived they called *Norway* – the north shore – while the language they spoke they called *Norrona* – north speech, literally north rune-ing – the language we today call both Old Norse and Old Icelandic, closely related to Old English, Old High German and several other old Germanic languages. These people of the north were proud in their claim to be North-men. Just about everyone else lived south of them. Furthermore they had a simple system for dividing up the world between four great races, corresponding to the four quarters of the heavens.

The North-men were first of all the peoples of Scandinavia, the people whom today we call Norwegians, Swedes and Danes. The term was applied more widely than just to Scandinavia, to include people who spoke dialects of the North Speech – the English in England, the Germans in Germany and the Low Countries, and the Goths in Eastern Europe. When the North-men invaded part of France they called it Normandy after themselves, and the people of Normandy were treated as North-men. To the people of the north, North-men meant simply 'our people'. So when the Norwegian Othere from the furthest north of Norway appeared at King Alfred's court he readily ac-knowledged King Alfred as his *hlaford*, his lord and protector, a title that no northerner would give to someone who wasn't also a northerner.[1]

After the North-men were the East-men. These were the Slavic speak-ing peoples of eastern Europe. The North-men travelled extensively in the east using the network of rivers which run through European Russia, com-plete with well-established haulage routes where ships were dragged across watersheds between a north-flowing and a south-flowing river. These are the routes which took them to the Caspian and Black seas. For the North-men the lands of the East had a special draw. In their legends the home-land of their people was in the East, somewhere in the steppes of Russia. Somewhere in the East was the mythical city of Asgard, the city of the Norse gods. Many of the North-men who adventured east found wealth and power in Russia, in the Eastern Roman Empire and in the Middle East. In Russia, where they found unorganised tribes, they created the first Rus-sian kingdom, with Norse rulers, so that today even the very name 'Russia' is a Norse word, meaning the kingdom of the red-haired North-men.

Russia was by no means the limit of their eastward spread. From the Caspian Sea the Vikings moved south to the great trading city of Babylon, today Baghdad, as well as to Astrakhan. The Black Sea gave access to Con-stantinople, the city previously known as Byzantium and now as Istanbul. The Norse called it simply *Mikligathr*, the Great City. With a population of around half a million people, Constantinople was by far the largest city in Europe, and far removed in grandeur from the isolated farmsteads and tiny villages from which the North-men had come.

In the *Mikligathr* of Constantinople and further to the south, the Vikings encountered the citizens of the Eastern Roman Empire: Greeks,

Romans, Jews, Arabs and many other groups. All these the Norsemen called by one name: South-men. Beyond Constantinople through the straits of the Bosphorus and Dardanelles the Norse reached the Eastern Mediterranean basin, where they took a prominent part in the Crusades to recapture the Holy Land for Christianity, reaching the Holy Land and Jerusalem. The South-men lived in an area of fabulous wealth – yet they employed the North-men as mercenaries to fight their wars for them, and in these wars the North-men were victorious and became wealthy. Northern peoples came to rule much of today's Italy: Lombardy, Naples and Sicily; while the establishment of the Crusader kingdom of Jerusalem was under a mixed Norse and French dynasty.

Finally there were the West-men. These are the speakers of Celtic languages whom the Vikings encountered in Scotland, Ireland, Wales and the Isle of Man, and whom by marriage and conquest they made part of their world. Scotland was for long a battlefield between Vikings and Celts, with the north of Scotland firmly in Viking hands, and the northern isles of Orkney and Shetland for centuries acknowledging a Norwegian king as overlord. In the Isle of Man the Vikings established a long-lived kingdom with its own parliament and institutions, creating a sense of identity for the Isle of Man such that even today it remains outside the United Kingdom and the European Union, though it is a British territory. In the west, in Ireland, the Vikings established the greatest truly Viking city: Dublin.

This was the world of the North-men. Those North-men who visited other lands took part in the great adventure of the age. Certainly they went for trade and plunder, or the chance to serve as mercenaries to a Greek emperor in Constantinople, or to rule a territory in Russia. But most of all they went for adventure, and the chance to make their name and reputation. A band of 20 or so men, usually from one village and of about the same age, left for the journey of their lives east to Russia, and south to the Mediterranean or the Middle East. Before leaving they swore an oath of unquestioning loyalty to their group – a *varang* in their language. The oath was absolute, to last through the years of the journey until they came home. In years of travel the Norse were continually threatened by hostile peoples, or tolerated on the basis of uneasy alliances. For survival they were utterly dependent on their comrades and on the integrity of their *varang*. They became the people who had sworn an oath – Varangians. Thus the Norse who formed the personal guard of the Greek emperor in Constantinople were called Varangians, and the shock-troops who fought in the Holy Land were likewise Varangians.

While the movement to the east and south was an adventure for men only, the voyages to the west were more often a family matter. The defining factor for a group of North-men setting off on a voyage to the west was that they were all from one location, one *Vik*. *Vik* means both a dwelling place and also a bay or creek – a term which reflects the fact that in Norway human settlement is usually on a bay or creek. From a *Vik* came a group of *Vikings*, people of the *Vik*. The Vikings were the Norse explorers and settlers of the lands of the North Atlantic.

Viking Ships

The westward expansion started a little later than that to the east and the south. The key development which made it possible was advances in the area of ship building.[2]

The Vikings had had ships for many centuries, but they were flat-bottomed, really suitable only for rivers or sheltered, coastal waters. While the occasional Viking boat had doubtless made the journey over the North Sea to the British Isles, such voyages were very much the exception.

It is the ship that is the key to understanding the success of the Vikings. Before the Viking Age the hulls of all European ships had been constructed around a wooden frame, with timbers fastened to the frame. This produced a heavy ship that was also structurally weak. Mounting a mast produced more strains on the frame, and prevented large masts and sails. Pre-Viking ships could be rowed – with great effort – or could sail in the direction of the wind. The system of building a ship in this way was the style of all European ships both in the classical age and the early Middle Ages, and at the dawn of the Viking Age it had a pedigree of around 2,000 years, with little evolution. The ships so produced could not develop as there were intrinsic limitations in the design.

In the late eighth century an unknown Norse craftsman made a spectacular technological breakthrough that transformed ship design, creating the style of vessel that enabled the Vikings to visit four continents. In a nutshell, Viking ships dispensed with the frame. Instead of fastening timbers to the frame they were all fastened directly to the keel and to one another. Planks overlapped one another in the clinker technique, and this became the basis of all shipbuilding until iron hulls were developed. The mast, the flooring and the rowing benches were likewise all fastened directly to the keel rather than to the hull, allowing the hull far greater flexibility.

Viking ships were built usually from oak, on occasion from other hard wood. The keel was a single timber, stressed so that it bent upwards fore and aft, and cut from an oak tree using axes alone. An axe cuts with the grain and ensures that the resulting timber has maximum strength and flexibility, and this tool is therefore preferable to a saw. In building a Viking ship everything depended on the strength and integrity of the keel. While the keel remained intact the ship could scarcely founder, but if the keel broke the ship was certainly lost. The need for the keel to be of just one timber imposed a maximum size on Viking ships, in that they could not be bigger than an oak tree can grow. The timbers of the hull were likewise of oak, and likewise created by use of an axe alone, with no sawing whatsoever. Both keel and timbers were produced by eye rather than measured, and the process was such that the ships could be built very quickly. Seasoned wood was preferred, but green wood was used when a ship was required at short notice. Bonding of the timber was achieved through thousands of iron rivets which nailed the timbers into place – the rivets were produced in such great numbers that today they are one of the most frequent metal-detector finds from the Viking period. The result was a lightweight but strong vessel of shallow draft which flexed with the sea. The contrast between Viking ships and the heavy, structurally weak and deep draft vessels previously known is enormous. The Norse had made a technological breakthrough that set the standard in shipbuilding for the next millennium. Steering was by means of a single steering board on the right (steer-board, or starboard) side of the ship, and which did not pierce the hull, which would have created a weakness. The single square sail enabled the ships to sail before the wind, and gave some ability to cross or even tack against the wind. The strength and stability of the Norse ships was such that masts and sails much larger than those of earlier ships could be used, giving a great increase in speed.

The ships that the world today most closely associates with the Vikings are the Dragon Ships, also called Long Ships. These were the war ships which terrorised the British Isles and the Baltic, fast troop-carriers that could cross from Norway to Britain in around 36 hours at speeds of up to 14 knots per hour. The combination of sail and oars for speed in all conditions, and a flat bottom for coastal waters and beaching, made these the perfect troop landing ships. They were brightly painted in order to strike terror into the enemy, often with stripes on their sail, and usually with a prow that was shaped as a dragon head. These were large vessels, typically around 90 feet in length, with the largest discovered measuring 119 feet. Able to carry up to 100 armed men, just one of these ships could destroy any small coastal settlement, be it a monastery or a village. Their drawback was that they had little space for a cargo, no provision whatsoever for shelter from the elements for the crew, and very little space for food and water. The most frequent use for these ships was in the endless quarrels of the Norse in Norway and Denmark, and for raids across the North Sea. It is unlikely that a ship of this construction ever made a voyage as far as Iceland, and certainly not to America. We can be sure that no dragon ship ever sailed into the bay at L'Anse aux Meadows.

Dragon ships must have been an impressive sight. A contemporary account of the Danish Royal Fleet is given by a monk at St Omer, France:[3]

> When at length they were all gathered, they went on board the towered ships . . . On one side lions moulded in gold were to be seen on the ships, on the other birds on the tops of the masts indicated by their movements the winds as they blew, or dragons of various kinds poured fire from their nostrils . . . But why should I now dwell upon the sides of the ships, which were not only painted with ornate colours but were covered with gold and silver figures? . . . The blue water, smitten by many oars, might be seen foaming far and wide, and the sunlight, cast back in the gleam of metal, spread a double radiance in the air.

No wonder these magnificent ships have been remembered as the symbol of the Viking Age.

Alongside the dragon ship, and using the same fundamental construction technique, was the *knarr*, or merchant ship. This was first of all a cargo ship, broader than the dragon ship, with higher sides, and with cargo space fore and aft. The *knarr* lacked the very high prow of the dragon ship, and was without most of the decoration. Inevitably these broader ships were slower than the dragon ships, and they were less manoeuvrable in coastal waters, but they were much better suited to open seas, and may be regarded as the first wooden ships with the ability to withstand the storms of the North Atlantic. The *knarr* came in many different sizes. A small *knarr* might be 40 to 50 feet long and could be crewed for short voyages by as few as four to six men. Such a ship was almost exclusively a sailing vessel, as the ship would be too heavy for so few men to row, though oars would have been used for short distances within harbours. A larger version of a *knarr* might be 60 to 70 feet long and carry a larger crew, typically around 20 men, which was an adequate number to row such a ship, though not at any great speed. These should be regarded as sailing vessels which could at need be rowed for short distances. The *knarr* rather than the dragon ship was the vessel that enabled the Vikings to expand out of Scandinavia, and these were the ships that took the Vikings to America. Used as migrant ships, they are known to have carried about 40 people, a combination of crew and passengers, as well as livestock and belongings.

The triumph of the design of the *knarr* is demonstrated by its long usage. Even in the mid twentieth century, ships which the Vikings would have recognised were in use in many places as a lightweight and functional cargo row-boat that was seaworthy in the North Atlantic. In Scotland's Isle of Lewis until the 1960s a boat based on the design of the *knarr* was used every year to cover 50 miles of open North Atlantic from Stornoway to North Rona to harvest gannets there. Its design reflected an unbroken pedigree of well over 1,000 years. Many of the grand nineteenth-century ships built from wood reflect directly the achievement of Viking design. For example, the Viking square sail principle was utilised even by the nineteenth-century tea-clippers, the last and greatest of the line of Viking-inspired sailing ships.

Viking Expansion

The first stage in the Viking westward expansion was across the sea to Britain. Historians point to the year 793 as a convenient starting date for the Viking Age, for in this year a group of Viking looters in their new dragon ships landed at the monastery of Lindisfarne, and sacked it. And the target could not have been more shocking!

Lindisfarne is the 'Landward-Farne', the nearest to land of a group of small islands off the North Sea coast of England's Northumberland, and closely linked with the Christian culture and art which had arrived in England. In the eighth century the English kingdom of Northumbria had flourished as the very font of the English nation. The kings of Northumbria had created peace and prosperity, with a growing population supported by the fertile land of the Northumbrian coast, and by trade with Celtic kingdoms to the north and east. At Yeavering they built a royal palace from which Northumbria was ruled, along with a tiered hall for discussion, which may be regarded as a form of parliament and the earliest example of English democracy.

Alongside these regal and democratic institutions, now excavated, Yeavering has the distinction of being a key location in the spread of Christianity, for this is where in AD 627 Paulinus, Bishop of York spent 36 days baptising converts in the River Glen. It is at Yeavering that many English people – rather than just their rulers – accepted Christianity. Yeavering epitomises the achievement of Northumbria – a strong kingdom, a nascent democracy and a Christian country. Northumbria is where England started, and where eighth-century England saw its great flourishing. Just ten miles away, off the coast of Northumberland, was the great Christian monastery of Lindisfarne.

Lindisfarne is an island at high tide, but at low tide a causeway three miles in length links the island to the coast. The site was perfect for the first Christian missionaries. They came by sea – from the Apostolic Celtic Church of St Patrick in Ireland, to St Columba's Iona on the west coast of Scotland, through the Forth–Clyde Valley of central Scotland to Inchcolm – Columba's Island – in the Firth of Forth, and from there under St Aidan to the new Christian site of Lindisfarne, known to many people since simply as the Holy Island. Lindisfarne Christianity was Celtic, claiming an Apostolic mandate which pre-dated the Catholicism of Rome. It is this Church to which the scholars of the English Reformation looked for authority in creating the Anglican Church. This is the Church of the Venerable Bede, greatest worthy of the early Middle Ages, and the Church which produced the magnificent Lindisfarne Gospels, the single greatest artistic achievement of the English early Middle Ages. This is the environment that produced the poet Cynewulf, author of some of the greatest poetry in English. This is the Church that produced its own saint, St Cuthbert. Yet probably what is best remembered today of this beacon of civilisation and culture is its sack, when fewer than 100 Viking adventurers in a dragon ship destroyed it in one brutal raid.

The sack of Lindisfarne shocked England. It represented the end of the first English cultural flowering. The monks fled with their treasures, and even with the bones of their saint, so that after many adventures St Cuthbert ended up buried in Durham Cathedral. They fled with their most precious book, the *Lindisfarne Gospels*, now in the British Library in London. Generations of historians have reported that the English prayed 'from the fury of the Vikings, Good Lord deliver us'. Whether this prayer was ever used in quite this form is open to question, but the sentiment is correct. For 200 years after the pirate raid on Lindisfarne, the Vikings attacked England in more and more locations, and with ever greater bands of fighters. English national pride is enhanced by the story of King Alfred, who against the odds fought to defend his part of England from the Vikings. The storytellers forget that Alfred's work was undone in the generation that followed, and the Vikings came to rule the whole of England. The pinnacle of Viking rule was reached under King Canute – King of England, King of Denmark, King of Norway. Under Canute the Vikings demonstrated their power as sea-kings of the North Sea, able to rule wherever the sea-road took them. All of England was ruled by the Vikings; the north and the east was settled by them. The indigenous people of the British Isles today are, in terms of their genetic heritage, as much Viking as they are English, and the descendants of European migrants around the world who claim British ancestry likewise carry Viking genes.

The Viking expansion also took in the islands of Orkney and Shetland, the northernmost islands of the British Isles. Today they are frequently perceived as bleak, windswept and poor, yet to the Vikings they offered everything that was wanted for comfortable living. The climate discourages tree growth, leaving the islands clear of the obstruction of woodland, exactly the sort of landscape the Vikings wanted for meadowland and grazing. Clearing well-established forests to create meadows and pastures was a massive undertaking, ongoing in more southern parts of Britain even into the twentieth century. By contrast the naturally cleared lands of Orkney and Shetland were exceptionally desirable. The islands also offered bird cliffs, a ready source of food exploited until the 1940s, though now out of fashion as tastes have changed. The seas provide rich fishing, as well as seals and whales. Despite modern perceptions, Orkney and Shetland are rich lands. Indeed in the eighteenth century, Orkney was judged the second most prosperous county in Scotland; only Lothian, the county of Edinburgh, was richer.

Orkney and Shetland were not empty lands. Archaeologists have struggled to sort out the layers of civilisation from some of the world's densest archaeological remains, and are still without firm conclusions. Shortly before the Vikings came, a people called the Picts[4] had been living in both groups of islands. They had built around 100 brochs, apparently fortified towers which served almost as villages, providing accommodation, village industries, and perhaps emergency corralling for sheep. The Picts remain one of history's mysteries. We don't know their ethnicity, nor do we know their first language, though later generations spoke Celtic, and though they were a literate people, very few decipherable inscriptions have survived. Nor do we know when they died out. At the time of the Viking arrival in Orkney and

Shetland – conventionally given as around 800 – the majority population was Pictish. Alongside the Picts were the Irish. The expansion which had taken the Irish up the west coast of Scotland had taken them also to Orkney and Shetland, and in these islands they had reached an accommodation with the Picts which saw Irish settlers living alongside the Picts in brochs, and the Pictish writing system transmitted back to Ireland as the enigmatic Ogham script. And there was one other, the English. The English migration from the continent of Europe to England in the century and a half following AD 449 is well recorded; what is often overlooked is that the late Roman historian Claudius Claudianus states that the English were in Orkney in AD 363.

Into this ethnic melting pot the Vikings entered. They dominated, ruling both archipelagoes, and making Orkney the jewel of their British possessions. Orkney and Shetland together were rich in grazing land, in the food resources of the bird-cliffs and the sea, but also they were the 'Grand Central' of the Viking world. East was the shortest crossing to Norway. South was the coast of Scotland, just a dozen miles across the Pentland Firth, to the Vikings simply the Southern Land, today the county of Sutherland. Further south the coast led along the North Sea littoral, to the rich lands of Scotland and England. West was an easy voyage along Scotland's north coast, to Cape Wrath. To today's romantics the name implies storms and angry weather, which are frequent enough in these northern latitudes, but the name has a prosaic meaning given by Viking navigators – Cape Turning. Here the Vikings turned south, to the Western Isles of Scotland, to the Isle of Man and, most of all, to Dublin.

In Dublin the cultures of Viking and Celt came head to head. Dublin was a Viking city in foundation and rule, but sitting on the edge of a Celtic Irish kingdom. Its reason for existence was trade. The Vikings brought in gold and silver, originating in the eastern Mediterranean and transported through the rivers of Russia, across Scandinavia, then to Orkney, and finally to Dublin. In exchange they bought slaves, Irish men and women who were destined to labour on the farms the Vikings were establishing in Scotland, Orkney, Shetland – and in their Norwegian homeland.

Perhaps this might have been the limit of Viking expansion if it were not that from the northernmost hills of Shetland, or from a boat fishing the rich seas just north of Shetland, the massive cliffs of the Faroe Islands can just be seen. The Irish settlers they encountered in Shetland had already been there. Inevitably the Vikings explored these neighbouring islands.

Vikings to the Faroe Islands

The Viking settlement of the Faroe Islands is recorded as a coherent story in a manuscript dated about 1380 – the *Flateyjarbok* – and in fragmentary form in a few other manuscripts from around this period. These historical sources are hundreds of years after the Viking settlement, but there is no reason to doubt the broad outline of the story they tell. The very first Viking settlement on the Faroe Islands was made by Grimur Kamban in or just after the year 800. Like the Vikings who sacked Lindisfarne in 793, Grimur Kamban was exploiting the new designs in shipbuilding which made long voyages practical. Like those Vikings he was presumably driven by the hope of gain, driven from Norway by a lack of land to farm and a need to seek his fortune overseas. Tradition has it that he travelled to Dublin, before heading north via Cape Wrath, Orkney and Shetland to the Faroe Islands. His ship would have held at most two dozen men and women, and the bare necessities needed for building shelter and getting a subsistence living from the land. He landed at Funningur on the island of Esturoy, and there set up his farm. Grimur Kamban is treated by the Faroese people today as their common ancestor, and it is likely that all Faroese people today are descendants of this one man, a true nation founder. Curiously, his name is a hybrid of Norse and Celtic. His first name, Grimur, is the familiar north European Grim, one of the names used by Odin in his guise as 'the masked one', and a thoroughly Viking name. His second name however is not a Norse patronymic but rather an Irish–Norse hybrid. *Kam-* is an Irish root meaning crooked; *ban* appears to be the Old Norse for bone. The name means something like 'the crooked' or even 'hunchback'. Grimur appears to have spent long enough in Ireland to have picked up an Irish nickname.

The Faroe Islands were not an empty land. The Irish had certainly visited.[5] Their discovery of the Faroe Islands dates from the mid sixth century, around 250 years before Grimur Kamban's landfall. But while the Vikings arrived in family groups, the Irish migration is usually asserted to have been a male-only matter. In contrast to the Viking wooden ships capable of carrying two dozen or more people, the Irish were using coracles made of leather over a wooden frame, typically requiring a crew of less than a dozen, and Irish custom dictated that the crew of such boats should be men only. The Irish had reached the Faroe Islands, and brought their sheep, which ran wild over the islands, but they had not established permanent settlements there. Indeed, the Irish appear to have regarded the Faroe Islands as a form of religious retreat rather than a land to be settled. Grimur Kamban and his settlers soon swamped these Irish ascetics. Faroese tradition has it that the Irish left of their own accord.

For several years in the late 1990s the Faroe Islands led the UN league tables as the most prosperous country per capita in the world, their wealth based on fishing supplemented by husbandry. This has always been an area abounding in natural wealth, and the Vikings were quick to see the economic value of the Faroe Islands with their magnificent natural resources. There is abundant sheep pasture, Europe's biggest bird cliffs providing an almost endless supply of food, and the seas offering what were then some of the world's richest fishing grounds. The Faroe Islands flourished in Viking times, as they do today.

It is possible to travel from the Faroe Islands to Shetland, Orkney and the Scottish mainland and thence to almost anywhere in Europe without losing site of land. Yet the reality of travels in these northern latitudes is that fog and rain means that the sailor will often be out of sight of land. Additionally there is the human tendency to take short cuts. The shortest route from the Faroe Islands to the old Norwegian capital of Nidaros is not via Shetland, but to sail due east across the open sea. Similarly a voyage due south is the shortest route to Cape Wrath and Ireland. Settlement of the Faroe Islands gave a stimulus to this sort of traveling, where navigators deliberately set a course out of sight of land. Faroese ballads have almost as a theme the calm and unemotional acceptance of the perils of long journeys out of sight of land. Thus in the *Ballad of Sigmundur Brestisson*[6] we hear:

> He was two nights and three days at sea
> Before he sighted the Faroe Islands.

This is a punishing journey in an open boat with no shelter made at latitudes north of 60°. The distance is perhaps 250 miles – a straight run from Cape Wrath perhaps. The Vikings made their voyages both summer and winter, so a voyager might face the very long nights as well as the cold and damp of the North Atlantic in winter.

Grimur Kamban and his fellow Vikings had no technology to help their navigation. They had neither compass nor sextant. The navigational limitations they faced are common to all North Atlantic Viking voyages, and a feature of subsequent voyages to America. When possible they remained in sight of land, navigating by sightings of conspicuous headlands. Without the pollution of the modern world, visibility was significantly greater than is usual today. Thus, for example, the 21st-century visitor to Greenland, one of the few accessible truly wild northern locations, is amazed at the clarity and distance of naked-eye vision, which is frequently in excess of 80 miles; in Viking times this sort of visibility would have been possible everywhere. Nonetheless, there are limits to the possibilities of naked-eye vision. Where sight of a distinctive coastal feature was not possible the Vikings made intelligent use of the sun and the stars – though they were without calendars or star charts, and were therefore using the heavens only as a rudimentary direction guide. Knowledge of the weather patterns created by land masses over the horizon is recorded as a guide used by Vikings. Additionally, at least sometimes, they took ravens on their voyages. As a land bird, a raven set loose from a ship will fly up until high enough to see land, then fly towards the nearest land, which helped the Vikings to identify which direction to go in. The final navigational aid open to the Vikings was fleas. Humans in the Middle Ages habitually had fleas, and the Vikings spent much of their time plucking these annoyances from their hair and clothes. It seems that human fleas have a use – as a crude direction finder. The Vikings discovered that if the fleas are placed in a box, the fleas hop towards the north side of the box. The phenomenon has recently been confirmed by the Smithsonian Museum, though as far as I am aware no explanation has been advanced as to why fleas should act in this way.

Grimur Kamban and his Faroese Vikings had these basic means of navigation. These tools were useful, yet not sufficient to give certainty to the location or direction. Sailing on the Atlantic searching for the rather small targets of the three island groups, Orkney, Shetland and Faroe, was in the most part an act of faith. Mistakes in navigation inevitably happened. Indeed, Viking voyaging was a series of best guesses, with efforts to correct navigational errors once land had been sighted.

Vikings to Iceland

It is not far from the Faroe Islands to Iceland. The sagas tell us that the first sighting of Iceland was made in 850 by Nadd-Oddur. Nadd-Oddur had no intention of discovering a new land; indeed he probably wished himself at home in Norway. Born in southern Norway, at Agder, Nadd-Oddur had got into trouble in his homeland, with the result that he was sentenced to outlawry. What he had done is not recorded, though usually killing someone, in a duel or otherwise, was the crime that led to this punishment. The exiled Nadd-Oddur set his course for the Faroe Islands. Perhaps because he did not know the route, perhaps through bad luck, he missed his way and was storm-driven to the south-east coast of Iceland. He made a landing there, and even named the land – Snaeland, in English 'Snowland' – but he was not sufficiently encouraged by what he saw to stay, and back-tracked to the Faroe Islands.

The Faroese Vikings gradually became aware of the existence of Iceland. Nadd-Oddur made his home in the Faroe Islands and doubtless told the story of his chance sighting. The Irish who had been on the Faroe Islands before the Vikings arrived would have known about Iceland – and presumably communication took place between these Irish ascetics and Grimur Kamban's Vikings. Grimur Kamban and many of his companions must have had some knowledge of the Irish language through time they had spent in Ireland, and probably also had Irish brides, so communication was practicable.

A few years after Nadd-Oddur's voyage, Garthar Svavarsson became the leader of the second Viking voyage to Iceland. Garthar was deliberately following Nadd-Oddur's route. Crossing from the Faroe Islands, he made landfall, as Nadd-Oddur had, on the south-east coast and confirmed that this shore was uninviting. There are few harbours, none of them good – indeed, even today the only passenger ferry to Iceland, which is from the Faroe Islands, is forced to use an anchorage in the East Fjords at Seythisfjordur, far removed from the closest Icelandic landfall, as there is no usable anchorage on the closest shore. Almost the whole of the south coast of Iceland is comprised of glacial sands, producing sometimes poor-quality pasture but more frequently no usable land at all. Garthar made the voyage along the south coast, where the narrow strip of ice-free land fringes one of Europe's biggest glaciers, Vatnajokul. Today we know that Vatnajokul contains more ice than all other European glaciers combined, and to Garthar and his Vikings, even if they had seen the glaciers of northern Norway, this massive ice-sheet was an awe-inspiring site. This is the glacier that later caused the land to be known as Iceland. Garthar was looking for good farm land on which to settle, and did not find it on the south coast. The south-east he found a little more attractive, though still without proper anchorages.

He also discovered that the land was not empty. There is a lively debate as to who reached Iceland first, but it certainly wasn't the Vikings. Plausibly Iceland was visited by the ancients, both the Romans and the Greeks. An account of a voyage made in the years 330–325 BC and described by Pytheas of

Marseille[7] contains remarkable details which have long convinced scholars that the voyage really happened. The voyage followed the established trade routes from the Mediterranean through the Pillars of Hercules and then north to Cornwall in Britain's south-west. Cornwall provided tin, which the Mediterranean world lacked, and which was required for the production of bronze. This trade route is well documented. What surprises today is Pytheas's claim that his informants voyaged north to the northern extremity of Britain, then a further six days north to what he called Ultima Thule, now most often identified as Iceland. Here he describes a land where the summer sun does not set, but rather dips to the horizon and skims the ocean before lifting again. Pytheas's informants travelled north again, and a day north of Ultima Thule encountered a dense fog, and a place where the sea congeals to ice. All this is a fair description of Iceland, a land just south of the Arctic Circle where the sun at midnight in midsummer does indeed skim the horizon, and where there are 24 hours of daylight. North of Iceland is found the multi-year sea-ice, which in most summers extends across the ocean from Greenland to Jan Mayen Island and to Spitsbergen. Pytheas gives an accurate account of the midnight sun and the sea-ice, which is hard to explain unless his informants had actually been there and seen them.

Archaeology has produced unexpected evidence of Roman presence in Iceland, in the form of two Roman coins in an archaeological context which suggests their antiquity. While some post-Roman transmission of these coins to Iceland cannot be absolutely ruled out, perhaps as someone's good-luck token, their presence does suggest that at least one Roman galley made it to Iceland.

The Greeks and Romans were hampered by their ships. They could only sail effectively with the wind; they were not able to sail across the wind, or to tack into the wind. Within the Mediterranean basin, waiting for a wind in the right direction is usually possible, but in the North Atlantic this is entirely more problematic. While winds can and do come from any direction, the prevailing wind is from the south-west, and may blow in this direction for days or weeks. Oars were practical only over very short distances, and even with oars the progress that could be made against the wind was negligible. In short, the Greeks and Romans did not have ships with the characteristics needed for North Atlantic voyaging, and their exploration north of the British Isles was minimal. While an informant of Pytheas of Marseille appears to have made a return trip to Iceland his voyage is exceptional, and there is no record of another Greek emulating his achievement. Roman presence is just about explicable in terms of the fourth-century drive to explore the islands, with at least one Roman circumnavigation of Britain, and the possibility of a ship venturing north by plan or accident, but any visit they made was occasional, and has left no written record. No-one has ever suggested that the Greeks or Romans established any sort of toe-hold on Iceland.

But after the Greeks and Romans had come the Irish. The Irish breakthrough, like that of the Vikings, had been in the area of boat-building. The boats were coracles,[8] and are unique in Europe in being made of leather.

Coracles are still occasionally used today by fishermen in the creeks and bays of western Ireland. As used today they are tiny craft, designed for carrying just one man, and while practical for the coastal work they do could never be taken across an ocean. Even leaving aside their tiny size, there is the insurmountable problem of the leather perishing. After several days' exposure to salt water the leather becomes weakened, and the boat must be taken out of the water, dried out, and the leather oiled in order to keep it strong and supple. If this is not done, the leather quickly rots and tears. But the Irish of the early Middle Ages made two innovations. First of all they discovered that if the leather was cured in an oak-bark solution it gained a durability that would enable it to stand up to many months, even several years, of exposure to the sea. And second, they discovered that it was possible to sew many dozens of hides together to produce much larger coracles that could transport up to a dozen men. The coracle of mediaeval Ireland was a functional, sea-going boat, on occasions even an ocean-going boat. It conveyed men along the indented west coast of Ireland, and from Ireland across to Scotland and through the labyrinth of the Hebrides, to Orkney, to Shetland, to the Faroe Islands and to Iceland.

When Garthar reached the south-east of Iceland, where there is soil in places that may be cultivated, he found not the empty land he sought, but rather the Irish living there already. Garthar continued his voyage, travelling to the north of Iceland, when the onset of winter made him decide to overwinter, choosing Husavik as his winter quarters. In the spring that followed he left some of his men in Husavik, and with the remainder of his crew continued onwards. Later saga writers suggested that the men who stayed were not volunteers, but were abandoned there because of arguments. Given the treeless nature of Iceland and therefore the impossibility of building a boat to leave, this abandonment was virtually a death sentence. Ultimately Garthar circumnavigated Iceland, encountering Irish people wherever he went. He returned to the Faroe Islands.

Garthar's exploration encouraged many others. In 860 Floki Vilgerthar-son decided to make a new life for himself and his family in Iceland. He therefore loaded his ship as a pioneer, with seed, sheep, wood and tools, and set off from his home in Norway. He chose to sail direct to Iceland – perhaps because he felt his wife and children were safer at sea than risking the doubtful hospitality of the inhabitants of the Shetland and Faroe Islands – and we have an account of him using the Viking navigation technique of releasing ravens.[9] The story is that the first raven he released flew south-east back towards Norway, the second flew high, circled, then returned and perched on the mast of the ship, while the third flew north-west, guiding him to Iceland. Floki earned himself the nickname in later sagas of Ravens Floki, because his use of a direct route meant that he was reliant on ravens for navigation.

Making landfall in south-east Iceland, Floki chose to sail to the north-west – the opposite corner of Iceland – to establish a farm at Vatnafjorthur. The location is puzzling, as this is not good farm land, and the farm was not a success. After a few years a disenchanted Floki took his family back to Norway.

After Floki, voyages to Iceland become increasingly frequent. In the Faroe Islands in AD 870, the grandson of Grimur Kamban, Torolvur Torsteinsson, took a ship and explored the corner of Iceland that faced the Faroe Islands. It seems that he didn't like what he saw, as no settlement followed.

The first Viking settlement that lasted is credited to Ingolfur Arnarson, who came to Iceland in 874. Ingolfur had had the bloodthirsty past which drove so many of the Viking voyages. Born in Norway, he had been forced to leave because of some unspecified crimes, and with his blood-brother Hjorleifur had acted as a pirate around the coasts of Britain and in Ireland. In time, the blood-brothers became sufficiently unpopular in this part of the world for them both to seek a new start at the edge of the Viking world, in Iceland, though both acted independently. Hjorleifur set up his farm at what he called Vik, meaning simply 'the creek', on the south coast of Ice-land. During the first winter he quarrelled with and was murdered by his slaves, and his colony fell apart. Hjorleifur has become just a footnote to Icelandic history. It is rather Ingolfur who has been remembered by history and today's Icelanders as the founding father of Iceland, with many stories told of him. Ingolfur is portrayed as a devout pagan. He came to Iceland intending to settle, and properly equipped. Knowing that there was scant wood in Iceland he brought with him the timbers that would form the structure of his farmhouse. Nearing land, he threw overboard the two chief timbers, asking the gods to direct him to where he should set up his farm. The timbers came ashore at an area where geothermal steam was vented from the earth, and for this reason we are told Ingolfur named the place Reykjavik – 'smoky bay' (though it is steam, not smoke, that vents) – establishing his farm there. While with the passage of 1,000 years we can scarcely speculate on Ingolfur's religious beliefs, we can suspect that there was a far more prosaic reason for casting timbers into the sea and seeing where they washed up. In Iceland the flotsam and jetsam that the sea brings ashore has always been a source of resources for the inhabitants, and particularly important when a new settlement is being set up which doesn't have the benefits of a previous harvest to feed it. Ingolfur was, in fact, seeing where the sea would deposit its bounty.

Following Ingolfur, Iceland was settled remarkably quickly in the next 60 years. Most settlers came from Norway, driven by land shortage and tyrannical government there, and attracted by the prospect of land for the taking in Iceland. Many came in family groups, many were driven by family problems. So we hear, for example, of Aud Ketildottir, nicknamed the Deep-minded, a Norwegian lady living in Scotland, who came on hard times after the death of her husband. Captaining her own ship, she brought her family to Iceland, and laid claim to a large tract of farmland. Laying claim to land was what mattered, and this act of land-taking is recorded in exhaustive detail in one of Iceland's earliest books, the *Landnamabok*[10] or 'Book-of-the-Land-Taking', which sets out who settled where, and what the bounds of their farm were.

Although Iceland was not an empty land, for the Irish were already there, Icelandic sources give us a version of events subsequent to the arrival of the Vikings which is remarkably peaceful. According to the Icelanders, the Vikings encountered only a few priests, living lives of solitude and contemplation. These priests were banished – or even went voluntarily – to certain islands off the shore of Iceland where they lived out their lives without troubling the Vikings. Thus Papey, a most unattractive island off the southeast coast, became inhabited by the Irish priests – the name means 'Island of the Monks'. Similarly a group of islands off the south coast was settled by the Irish – called the Westerman Islands, or Islands of the West Men. This benign account of peaceful co-existence was for long unchallenged.

But the challenge did come from three separate areas, and three different disciplines – history, genetics and military strategy.

The historical account of the Irish expansion suggests that the Irish reached Iceland in the sixth century, and had therefore been living there for around 300 years. The earliest remembered voyage is linked with the name of St Brendan, who is credited with a voyage to the Faroe Islands and Iceland and further west, then back to Ireland, during a period usually given as 565–73. While the account has been garbled by later retelling, there would seem to be at least a kernel of truth in the story of the St Brendan voyage. The Church in Ireland put great store on asceticism, and established many monasteries in Ireland – and indeed in Scotland and northern England. It is in keeping with this convention that Ireland should send out to Iceland men who wished to lead the lives of hermits. However, the implication of many later writers that individual hermits travelled to Iceland is simply not tenable. Single-person coracles could not make the journey to Iceland. Rather, voyages were made by groups of six to twelve men, who are likely to have lived together after their arrival in Iceland. The priesthood of the Celtic Church was not celibate – indeed it encouraged its priests to marry. In three centuries of Irish voyaging to Iceland it seems incredible that some women did not make the journey, and that a permanent Irish settlement did not become established if this is the case. So far archaeology has found some scant remains of habitation prior to the Viking Age, which would lend credence to the idea of Irish colonisation.

The second area of evidence comes from genetics. In 2002–03 the DECODE[11] genetics project, based in Reykjavik, looked at evidence for the ethnicity of the Icelandic people. An island population with excellent genealogical records along with a liberal attitude towards access to personal health records had encouraged the selection of Icelanders as the key population for DNA study for the human genome project. Looking at the ethnic origin of the Icelanders was the logical next step. The results were published in two reports a few weeks apart during the summer of 2003. The first report looked at mitochondrial DNA, which is passed from mother to children, and which indicates the ethnic origin of the original women who made up the Icelandic population. The findings, expressed in broad terms, were that 60 per cent of the first women who settled in Iceland were Irish, and 40 per cent were Norse. The results were greeted with shock in Iceland. Iceland prides itself on being a Viking nation, perhaps the only true surviving Viking nation. This finding at one stroke appeared to demolish that claim. Yet within weeks the findings for the study of the Y-chromosome – transmitted from father to son – were released and produced a very different result. Of the male population of Iceland, in broad terms 90 per cent of the first settlers were Norse and 10 per cent Irish. For the combined male and female population, around two-thirds of the first settlers were Norse, one-third Irish.

Interpreting these results is problematic. The male distribution is most easily explained. The migration we know was from Norway, or of ethnic Norse from the Faroe Islands, Scotland and Ireland. The 10 per cent Irish males might perhaps represent slaves bought in Dublin and transported to Iceland as farm labourers. The result as far as the male composition is concerned is susceptible to ready explanation. By contrast the female split was completely unexpected. Immediately after the announcement explanations were advanced on the following lines: that the Norse who settled Iceland were predominantly men who arrived with scant provisions, struggled for a few years to found a farm, then made a voyage to Dublin to find an Irish wife. Yet this explanation simply doesn't hold water. It is not at all clear that the Viking migration to Iceland was predominantly male – indeed the accounts we have speak of family groups. Voyages from Iceland tended to be to Norway rather than to Ireland, Norway being the homeland of most of the settlers, suggesting that single men would have found Norse brides. Dublin was a Norse city; the Irish who were there were slaves. In Norse society there was a taboo against taking a slave as a wife, and while it doubtless happened, it was presumably not common.

An alternative and much simpler explanation is that the Vikings who arrived in Iceland found an established Irish population and intermarried with them. The gender balance suggests a marked male Viking dominance, suggesting that Irish men in Iceland were killed.

Military strategy gives a third insight into the fate of the Irish in Iceland. Accounts are precise in terms of the locations where the first explorers overwintered, and the locations of the first settlements. Most of these sites can be identified today. They can be seen to have certain features in common:they are rarely the site of major later settlements, and frequently locations where no-one lives today, they are almost never close to good quality farm-land; usually they are by the sea and have a place where a ship could have been drawn up, but only rarely are they the best anchorages of the region. Typically it is found that the Vikings chose to establish their first settlements on barren headlands far from good land. In military terms they were taking up defensive positions. Looking at Viking military advances elsewhere, particularly in Scotland, we can see that they were carrying out a process of 'ness-taking': seizing headlands which they could easily defend, and use to sally out from and harry the population in the surrounding countryside. The settlement on the ness continued until Viking numbers increased, and they could move to a new farm or group of farms surrounded by richer land.

The Iceland that the Vikings settled was not an empty land. The comfortable story of just a few Irish priests living there who fled to islands off the coast has to be dismissed – rather, the Vikings invaded a populated country just as they had done in Orkney and Shetland and Scotland and Dublin.

Iceland provided two necessities the Vikings sought: land and freedom. That said, the land is not particularly rich. Much of Iceland is covered with lava fields from recent flows, which are of no value for farming whatsoever, and create the additional problem of hindering travel overland as it is not practical to walk or ride over a lava field. The remainder of the land is covered by typically thin soils, often glacial sands, which are difficult to work and not particularly rewarding. Even so, crops can be grown, aided by the long days of summer. The climate is far milder than the name Iceland suggests. While summers are cool, rarely exceeding a daily average of 10°C, winter temperatures only just drop below freezing point, with the result that Reykjavik, just below the Arctic Circle, has warmer winters than the cities of northern Italy or the cities of Canada. Given sufficient land per family – and at the time of the settlement there was plenty – Iceland provides adequate farm land. Even today most of the food eaten in Iceland is produced in Iceland. Freedom was also available in Iceland. While mediaeval Europe sank into the tyranny and barbarism of the feudal age, Iceland provided an environment in which the Viking ideals of self-determination and personal liberty could flourish. The basic settlement unit in Iceland in the years following the settlement age was the farmhouse. This would be isolated, as the low fertility of the land did not permit the clustering of farms to form villages. Typically a farm would comprise around 20 people. There was the head of the household – usually a man, though occasionally a woman – the householder's family, and a group of farm workers. The workers comprised both farm labourers, predominantly men, and weavers and dairy workers, predominantly women. In the years following the settlement these labourers would have included slaves, but within a couple of generations most slavery had ceased, and workers sold their labour to farms. Each farm was represented by the householder at local meetings, called *Things*, which provided basic justice, and a forum to debate and resolve matters of local concern. The principle was equality of power for all householders,

33

making the system a basic democracy. Each local *Thing* acted as an electoral college appointing its representatives to an annual all-Iceland parliament, the *Althing*. Representatives travelled long distances to attend, living for the duration of the *Althing* in temporary shelters, and meeting in the open on the parliament plains – *Thingvellir* – to enact their business. Iceland can boast that it established one of the earliest parliaments in post-classical Europe, and while the system was very far from perfect it did serve to offer a basic level of democracy, with a legislative and judicial process that strove towards openness and justice.[12]

The Vikings required wood, which Iceland rarely supplies. Confusingly, early accounts speak of Iceland being forested from the sea to the central ice, though today we understand this word 'forest' to be a description for the scrub of dwarf birch and willow that covered much of the land. The climate is characterised by variable spring and summer weather, alternating mild weather, which coaxes trees into growth, with freezing spells which kill them. In Reykjavik gardens today, trees are grown by keeping them for the first few years of their life in greenhouses, and planting them out only when big enough to withstand the cold snaps. Curiously, there are a few outdoor-grown trees in the far north of Iceland around Akureyri. Though temperatures here are on average cooler, the area is less prone to the spring warm–cold alternations in temperature of the Reykjavik area.

The Vikings had three crucial uses for wood: firewood, the timber frame of their houses and ships. The absence of wood in Iceland created very real problems. In Orkney, Shetland and the Hebrides, where wood is also lacking, the abundant peat could replace wood on domestic fires. Driftwood and the scrub of dwarf willow and dwarf birch were among the materials used for fires throughout the Middle Ages, but the labour involved in collecting sufficient quantities even for a modest fire is prodigious. In time, a building style for farms was developed using ever-thicker turf walls to offer more insulation, and even building into the ground, which went some way to compensating for the lack of material to burn on a fire. However, the timber frame for farms proved problematic. Viking buildings in Iceland usually used turf walls as well as roofs, but in order to support the roof a number of substantial wooden beams were needed. The first settlers solved this problem by bringing their timber with them – a heavy cargo for a small ship. Problematic also was the timber needed for building and maintaining ships. Driftwood is not the solution for these various requirements for wood. While sometimes found washed ashore in Iceland, it is rarely found in large quantities, and the quality of driftwood is usually poor, certainly inadequate for weight-bearing beams in farms or for the strength and suppleness required by ships.

The need was satisfied by trade, mainly to Norway. For this purpose every area of Iceland maintained ships, enabling voyages to be made every year to buy timber. Norway was the nearest major market, and well able to supply the timber required, as well as being the homeland of the majority of the first settlers. From Norway the Icelanders bought first timber, then a variety of luxury goods, often traded from the Mediterranean to Norway. In return, the Icelanders sold wool. Icelandic wool is still regarded as being of superb quality, and found a ready market in Norway. The trade was, however, unequal. While Norwegians were content to buy Icelandic wool, they had no absolute need for it, and could take the wool they needed from other sources or produce it at home. By contrast, the Icelanders did have an absolute need for timber, which forced them to trade on any terms. As a result, while trade from Iceland to Norway was considerable in volume it did not make the Icelanders rich. Rather, it created a dependency culture, where Iceland was unable to exist without the support of Norway. For Icelanders there was pressure to find different goods to trade; for Norwegians there was an expectation that their culture and values should be exported along with the timber to their Icelandic brethren. In time a broadening of Icelanders' trade goods happened, but not before Norwegian pressure resulted in an export of Norway's culture.

The conventional date for the conversion of Norway to Christianity is 1030, though in fact there had been some penetration during the reigns of Olaf Tryggvason (995–1000) and Olaf II Haraldsson (1015–30), both Christian kings, though both baptised outside Norway. Norwegian Christianity therefore post-dates the Vikings' settlement of Iceland, and Christian penetration of Iceland was far from universal. Throughout the Middle Ages and well into the modern period, Christianity and paganism lived side-by-side in Iceland, with the people worshipping the gods which make up the Norse pantheon, a complex group of gods and their myths which provide a way of understanding the world.[13] Thus Thor, in origin a thunder god, had developed into a representation of the values of strength, honesty and hard work, and became a favourite of the Icelandic farmers. He embodies their values, and is commemorated in many hundreds of place names, and the enormous popularity of personal names with the element Thor. Odin too, the All-father, was popular, associated with the heroic ideals of personal independence and personal responsibility, as well as the god of war and magic. While Thor is the god of the farmers, Odin is very much the god of the Viking seafarer. These two sets of values around Thor and Odin are key to understanding the value system of the Icelanders: strong, honest, hard-working farmers who valued independence and were prepared to fight for it. A thousand years of Christianity have demonised the Norse pagan religious system, yet there is much in its values that is commendable, and much that should be applauded in the ethical values of the society the Vikings created in Iceland. In Iceland, the Viking way of life demonstrated its ultimate potential.

In the late Middle Ages, Iceland went on to produce a northern renaissance of learning and literature built around a society which valued democracy, justice and peace. This North Atlantic island is a key stepping stone in the route from Europe to America, and also a key in the development of the values which prompted the Viking expansion to America.

Vikings and Greenland

Iceland is the last truly European stepping stone of the North Atlantic. It is a short step from Iceland to Greenland.

The discovery of land to the west of Iceland must have been contemporary with the first settlement of Iceland. From a ship at sea it is possible on a clear day to see at one time both the glacier-clad peak of Snaefell in Iceland, and the central ice cap of Greenland. In exceptional weather conditions it is even possible to glimpse Greenland from Iceland, from the top of Snaefell. Cloud patterns and the flight of birds make it clear that there is land west of Iceland, and even the very first Icelanders must have been aware that a land mass existed. Yet the sea between is one of the world's most dangerous. The Denmark Strait has a strong, cold current from the north which in summer brings down a constant stream of pack ice, and frequently icebergs, while in winter the sea freezes out from the coast of Greenland, in a particularly cold winter forming an ice sheet right across to Iceland. The Denmark Strait is a very major challenge for navigation. For the coracle-using Irish living in Iceland it was an absolute barrier, for coracles cannot withstand ice. Whatever westward movement the Irish may have managed – and there is little doubt that they voyaged further west – was accomplished without a stop in Greenland. For the Vikings, the Denmark Strait was challenging, but just passable. Their route was not straight across through the pack ice, but took them well out to sea. Out of the way of the pack ice they sailed south along the coast of Greenland until its southernmost point, Cape Farewell, was reached. Here the ocean breaks up the pack ice, and they were able to round the cape and land on Greenland's western coast.

Icelandic sources record the name of the Viking credited with the first landing on the coast of Greenland – Gunnbjorn Ulfsson. A Norwegian bound for Iceland, he was blown off-course in 900 and made landfall on some islands off Greenland's east coast around present-day Tasiilaq which, with a view to preserving his name, he called Gunnbjorner Skerries. This coast had little to offer, and Gunnbjorn corrected his error and sailed to Iceland. Indeed, even today the east coast of Greenland is the most marginal of human habitation, supporting only a few hundred East Greenlandic Inuit along well over 1,000 miles of shore. There is a strip of land between ocean and ice cap which is free of snow for the summer, but the resources it offers are exceptionally meagre. The problem is compounded by the navigational difficulties presented by the pack ice and icebergs which are pushed close into shore and prevent access by sea. There can be no surprise that Gunnbjorn was keen to head to Iceland.

There is no record of another voyage to Greenland for 78 years. In 978 Snaebjorn Galti became entangled in the endemic Viking feuds, committing a revenge killing which left him and his companions liable to a death penalty at the *Althing*. Snaebjorn and his companions fled Iceland for Gunnbjorn's land to the west. A saga passage records a dream by one of Snaebjorn's companions on the eve of their departure: 'I can see death in a dread place, yours and mine; north-west over the waves, with ice, and cold, and countless wonders.' Snaebjorn nonetheless set out, retracing Gunnbjorn's steps to Gunnbjorner Skerries, and establishing a homestead nearby on the fjord at Blaeserk. Winter fell, effectively confining the men to the shelter they had built, and in this claustrophobic environment they turned first to arguing, then to murdering one another. In the spring a handful of survivors made the return voyage to Iceland, concluding the first attempt at the settlement of Greenland.

The attraction of Greenland as a refuge for an outlaw was not lost on its next settler. Eirikur Thorvaldsson, known to later generations as Eirik the Red, either on account of his red hair or his bloodthirsty ways, established the first permanent settlement. Eirik was a Norwegian, forced to flee Norway 'on account of some killings' as the sagas tells us, who sought his fortune in Iceland. In Iceland he pursued a similarly bloody career, murdering the killer of two of his slaves, with the result that he was outlawed from Iceland, too.

Eirik stands at the head of so many Icelandic genealogies that he is in effect the progenitor of the Icelandic nation. It is probable that all Icelanders today are his descendants. His house in west Iceland has been painstakingly excavated, and a faithful replica built close by. To many in Iceland and beyond, Eirik is simply the archetypal Viking, a figure of his age.[14] However we wish to judge his murderous career, he was a remarkable character. Following the sentence of outlawry passed in 982, Eirik and a tiny band of followers took refuge over winter on an islet in Breithafjordur, a tiny scrap of land. They were literally in hiding, as men with a price on their heads who could be killed by any bounty hunter. Return to Norway was not possible for Eirik as he was an outlaw there, too, while even the stepping-stone islands of Faroe, Shetland and Orkney were effectively closed, as the local chiefs would not have been willing to risk the displeasure of both Norway and Iceland to shelter a man twice outlawed. Dublin would have been a possible destination, but also a high-risk strategy. When it suited the Vikings in Dublin so to do they acknowledged the overlordship of the king of Norway, and delivering Eirik to him – or making him a slave – would have been tempting to them. The winter of 982–83 therefore finds Eirik and his band in hiding and with nowhere to go. The islet they chose reflects their fear and desperation, for it has a deep bay with its entrance obscured from open water by another islet, providing a genuine place of concealment. Presumably the men subsisted on whatever winter stores they had been able to steal, and the marine life of Breithafjordur.

From Breithafjordur it is a short crossing to Greenland. Rather than emulate Snaebjorn in settling on the coast opposite Iceland, Eirik instead explored the coast to the south, rounded Cape Farewell, and realised that the lands on the west coast of Greenland were suitable for both sheep grazing and for agriculture. Eirik and his band staked out land-holdings for themselves, with Eirik himself settling at Brattahlith at the head of Eirik's Fjord.

In 986 Eirik returned to Iceland with a view to finding settlers to establish a Greenland colony. Though still a man with a price on his head, it seems that the passage of a few years and the good news he brought of available land made his visit possible. In seeking colonists, he found he was pushing at an open door. After a century of Viking settlement, Iceland was effectively full. The land-hunger that had pushed the Vikings west from Norway had caught up with them in Iceland, and stories of vacant land to the west were attractive. It was Eirik who christened this new land Greenland. He is credited with saying that he thought people were more likely to come if it had an attractive name, in contrast with Iceland, which he said many early settlers had found an unattractive name. Many modern writers have seized on this to suggest that Eirik was fibbing, and that the name was no more than a scam. Clearly these writers have not been to Greenland. The summer pastures of Greenland have an unrivalled vitality in their brilliant green, un-equalled anywhere else. Greenland is certainly an attractive name; it is also an accurate name.

In Iceland, Eirik found enough colonists to fill 25 ships – a number reported as little less than 1,000 people. In 986 they set out from Iceland as pioneers bound for a fertile land where they could carve out farms for themselves.

Of the 25 ships that set out, 11 sank en route without survivors. There can hardly be a better demonstration of the dangers of the Denmark Strait. Doubtless the ships were overloaded, both with people and the materials they needed to start their new homes. Perhaps there was particularly bad weather. Yet even considering these factors, Viking ships were sea-worthy, Viking mariners aware of what they could reasonably carry, and losses at this terrible level – perhaps 400 deaths – are nowhere else recorded. It is likely the Denmark Strait produced conditions which the Viking ships were scarcely able to withstand. The crossing from Iceland to Greenland was dangerous, and as there were no significant developments in ship design in the centuries that followed, it remained perilous throughout the Viking Age. It is the Denmark Strait that is the true barrier between Europe and America, and from the outset Greenland, which is geographically part of America, had to function largely independently of Iceland and Europe.

Maps of today correctly include Greenland as part of the American con-tinent. The boundary between Europe and America is set by geologists as the mid-Atlantic ridge, with the result that Iceland, the only part of the ridge which rises above the sea, might be regarded as sitting on the bound-ary. Culturally Iceland is European, and no-one would seriously wish to argue the contrary, though Icelandic tour guides are prone to assert that one side of the Thigvellir rift valley is in Europe and the other in America. Greenland is open to discussion. Politically, the land is part of the Kingdom of Denmark, and in terms of its recent history is bound to Europe. Yet its Inuit inhabitants are an American people, tied by blood and culture to the

Inuit of the Canadian Arctic. For the Vikings the decisive boundary was the difficult crossing of the Denmark Strait, the sea that their ships were scarcely adequate to sail. Greenland represents not an off-shoot from Iceland, but a new continent. For the Vikings this was the start of a whole new world.

From the development of sea-going ships to the settlement of Greenland had taken the Vikings around 200 years. The islands of the North Atlantic had provided stepping stones, and the Viking expansion along this route may be regarded as inevitable. From Norway it was certain that they should reach Orkney and Shetland, island groups but a couple of days' voyage with a favourable wind. Once there it was sure that they would reach the Faroe Islands, visible from a little distance off the shore of Shetland. Iceland and Greenland were just as certain. Driven by an expanding population and a need for arable land, the expansion had to happen. Just as the European settlers of North America pushed at their wild-west frontier until within a few generations they had crossed the continent, settling from ocean to ocean, so the Vikings pushed at their sea frontier.

Yet Greenland was not the end of the road, just the last and biggest stepping stone. After Greenland was the continent of America, its northern lands just another short sail west. Driven by population growth and land-hunger, discovery, exploration and settlement of America was simply inevitable.

3
The Greenland Base

THE base for all Viking exploration and settlement of America was Greenland, and this expansion can only be understood within the context of Greenland. In Greenland we find a prosperous nation, one of the world's first democracies, which flourished for approaching five centuries, before failing for reasons still not fully understood.

To the Vikings, Greenland was a land of plenty. While winters were severe, they were little worse than in many parts of Norway or Iceland, and the Vikings' style of farmstead met the challenge of keeping people warm through the Greenland winter. The country offered ample farmland, abundant food and a good quality of life. Greenland to the Vikings was as California to the pioneers who crossed the American continent. Skeletal remains of early Viking settlers in Greenland show them growing around two inches taller than their ethnically identical contemporaries in Norway, while there is much evidence of robust health and longevity.[1] Whatever the myths about Greenland in Europe and America, to the Vikings it was a good place to live.

Green Greenland

Today Greenland is perceived through an accretion of myth. Two hundred years ago the hymn-writer Reginald Heber told of 'Greenland's icy mountain',[2] a single phrase which has done much to colour the world's perception of Greenland, while children's books have presented Greenland as a world of perpetual snow. The reality of Greenland as a land where people may live warm and well-fed lives still surprises. In contrast to popular perception, most of Greenland is without polar bears. Parts of it are free from snow and ice for much of the year. The people who live there today are part of the Kingdom of Denmark, enjoying the comforts and prosperity of a first-world country. Greenland does not conform to popular perception, at least not those parts that are populated, for there is a contrast to be made between the inhabited parts and the ice cap of the interior and the isolated north and east coasts. The Greenland of human habitation is a strip of land between the west coast and the central ice cap. Typically, this strip is 20 miles wide; in a few places the ice cap pushes as far as the sea, where it calves icebergs; in a few places there is as much as 80 miles from the sea to the ice cap. With a coast many thousands of miles long, this thin strip of land comprises a habitable area roughly equivalent in size to the whole of the British Isles. This is a substantial area of land. While snows cover Greenland for a long winter there is also a summer which provides a growing season. Even the winters are not as severe as many would think – much of the west coast of Greenland has winters milder than, say, Ottawa, milder even than Chicago, though Greenland lacks the warm summers of these more southern locations. Wheat will grow in Greenland, along with a range of root vegetables, while the meadows produce a season of berries. Agriculture in Greenland was marginal in Viking times; while possible today, it is rarely practised by Greenlanders, whose heritage is that of hunting rather than farming. The weathered landscape of Greenland means that in many places there is a good depth of soil, and that soil is often fertile, a marked improvement on Iceland with its thin soils. The Vikings practised animal husbandry as well as agriculture, and added the resources which could be found through fishing and hunting. Along the shores seal and walrus were then plentiful, alas sadly depleted today by excessive hunting, while the seas offered, then as now, some of the world's richest fishing and the cliffs teemed with seabirds.

The Greenland that the Vikings settled was not at the margins of habitation, but rather a land that gave them a lifestyle far healthier than their cousins in Europe. It was also an empty land. Though North American people had lived in Greenland many centuries before, when Leif Eiriksson and his pioneers arrived, no-one was there. Greenland offered that great rarity for migrants of any age – a truly uninhabited country.

Having crossed the barrier of the Denmark Strait and reached Greenland, the Vikings encountered one major problem. Greenland shared with Iceland the limitation of not having any trees for the timber essential for the main beams of houses and for boat building. Like Iceland, Greenland has only dwarf trees, rarely exceeding three feet in height. While in Iceland it has proved possible to grow some trees with careful nurture, twentieth-century experiments in Greenland have been disappointing, and it is not possible that the Vikings could have found any trees. Greenland is simply too far north of the tree-line. A partial solution to the problem was available through driftwood, for the west coast of Greenland is washed by the West Greenland Current, a warm current coming from far to the south, from Newfoundland and even further, which brings driftwood in reasonable quantities. As in Iceland, the driftwood had value as firewood, but rarely had the suppleness or strength for building houses or ships. From the beginning of the Greenland colony, timber had to be imported.

The distance which had to be travelled for timber is substantial. All the stepping-stone islands – Iceland, the Faroe, Shetland and Orkney islands – are virtually without timber. The nearest good European source of timber was Norway. Almost from the start of the Greenland colony trade was direct between Greenland and Norway, and predicated on the need for timber. A voyage via Iceland was many additional hundreds of miles, and putting in at an Icelandic port would have incurred costs and inconvenience for a Greenlandic ship. The sailing directions have been recorded, and are almost comically simple: sail west from Nidaros in Norway so as to pass midway between Shetland and the Faroe Islands, so that the top portion of the cliffs of each island group may be seen over the horizon; set a course due west from there. The south coast of Iceland may be seen to starboard; continue until Greenland's Cape Farewell is sighted.[3] This direct route took ships south of the worst drift ice obstacles of the Denmark Strait, offering a voyage that was actually safer than the short crossing from Iceland's Snaefelsness to east Greenland. While this route was clearly followed by hundreds, even thousands of ships, it was a major undertaking to cross the whole of the North Atlantic in one leap, and there can be no minimising the achievement of these mariners. A trade was established whereby the Greenlanders supplied at first wool, and later walrus and narwhal ivory and Arctic furs, and traded this for timber and some European luxuries. In the ivory and furs Greenlanders had a valuable, low-weight cargo for trade, something their cousins in Iceland largely lacked, and giving Greenland the potential for prosperity and even wealth.

Settlements in Greenland

The Vikings created around 200 settlements in Greenland, of which around 160 have been identified, and many have been excavated. These settlements were not villages, but individual farms. A typical farmstead would have accommodated 20 to 30 people. At its centre was the house, often called a hall. The building material was usually stone, sometimes stone and turf, with a turf roof supported on timber pillars. All of these halls have a similar ground plan. The sole door was situated at one end of the structure, entering into a small room sometimes described as a store – and doubtless often used in this way – but in effect a porch. The cold winters of Greenland discouraged direct entry from the outside to the living room. From the store or porch a door led into the hall proper. This was an all-purpose living room, with wooden platforms on either side that were used for sleeping at night, and for seating and as work-space by day. A double row of wooden pillars supported the roof. In the middle of the floor, in an open hearth, a fire was kept burning continually, providing both light and heat. There was no chimney; the smoke found its way up to a hole in the roof, though even this could be closed in bad weather with a wooden trapdoor, leaving the smoke to circulate within the roof space.

The hall was identical with those found in Iceland, and elsewhere back across the stepping stones to the Faroe, Orkney and Shetland islands. Further south turf was more often replaced with stone as a building material. Viking halls were both functional and comfortable – a style of building that has withstood the test of time. Indeed, the Viking style of building offered a greater level of comfort than was offered in some areas of Britain even in the second half of the twentieth century. For example, as recently as the 1960s Scotland's Western Isles had many families living in 'black houses', single rooms with an open fire in the centre, and this one room divided by a wattle screen to provide a living space, and a byre into which they brought their livestock, perhaps a cow and a few sheep, into one end of their living room. Such poverty, requiring animals to be housed alongside people, was unknown to the Vikings. Reconstructions of long-houses in Iceland show the hall to be a functional room which can reasonably be imagined as comfortable.

The hall room itself was where the men worked and slept, and where the whole community prepared food and ate. Often there was a social distinction between one side of the hall, which was occupied by the farm owner and his male relatives, and the other, occupied by the hired farm labourers. From the far end of the hall a door led to another room, usually called the women's room. This provided sleeping space for the women of the farm, as well as space for a vertical loom. Weaving was a year-round occupation, necessary to manufacture the cloth needed for clothing, for sail cloth and for export. Another room opening off the hall is usually called the kitchen or the dairy, though its primary function was not the preparation but the storage of food, the cooking taking place on the fire in the hall. One final room opened from the porch. Writers have often chosen to call it a bathroom; yet in most cases it was simply a latrine. The Vikings in Greenland had indoor toilets 1,000 years ago; in Britain, outdoor latrines persisted into the 1970s.

In close proximity to the hall were other farm buildings. In Greenland a byre was a requirement to over-winter sheep and to stable horses, as well as to house cattle and pigs when they were kept. Frequently a farm would have had a workshop, and therefore had a specialised industry associated with that specific farm. Farms might, for instance, have a forge and work metal. They might specialise in the production of a specific household artefact, perhaps as potters. Or they might have a special role in fishing or shipbuilding. While farms were self-sufficient on a day-to-day basis, trade between farms was needed to exchange specialist goods, while trade with Norway was carried out by groups of farms that between them could equip and crew a ship, and assemble a cargo for trade. Farms in Greenland needed to co-operate, and they did this despite the considerable distances that frequently separated them. The distance between farms was too great for them to coalesce into villages, but there were groups nonetheless to which the term 'settlement' is conventionally applied.

The 200 or so farms supported up to around 5,000 people, widely scattered over many hundreds of miles of coast. The indented nature of the coast encouraged travel by sea; indeed there is no evidence that pathways became established between the farms, and even today in Greenland there are no two modern settlements with a road joining them. Despite the logistic difficulties for travel, Greenland established a basic democracy on the Icelandic system, with each farmstead sending a representative to a *Thing* or parliament. These annual meetings helped to forge a sense of identity for Greenland.

Settlement in Greenland from its inception was in two main areas. In the south, just around Cape Farewell, was the Eastern Settlement; while around 300 miles to the north around the present-day capital of Nuuk was centred the Western Settlement. Both were on the west coast, despite the misleading name. The Vikings' use of the points of the compass differs from ours. In Britain John o' Groats is established as the northernmost point, while Land's End is the westernmost coast. To the Vikings a journey from anywhere in Britain in the direction of John o' Groats would also have been a journey north; one towards Land's End a journey west. Thus a traveller could leave Land's End and go north to John o' Groats; however, the return journey to Land's End would be described as a journey west. When the Vikings named their settlements they had this sort of logic in mind. For the Vikings the Eastern Settlement was en route to the east; the Western settlement en route to the west.

The Eastern Settlement was where Eirik the Red settled, and where the best grazing land was to be found. It was also a little closer to Iceland and Norway, and throughout the Viking period tended to be a little more prosperous. By contrast the Western Settlement had better access to hunting grounds, which in the Arctic environment improve the further north one goes, but its grazing land was somewhat poorer than that of the Eastern Settlement. The two settlements complemented one another. Between them a smaller settlement developed, called simply the Middle Settlement. As the colony developed, these settlements virtually flowed into one another, so a Viking making the 300-mile voyage between the Eastern and Western Settlements would have found farmhouses at the head of almost every bay and fjord along the coast. North from the Western Settlement stretched around 500 miles of coast that was inhabited in the summer, and where Vikings sometimes over-wintered. This is the Nordresetr or North Shore.

It is from the North Shore that the northernmost example of Viking runic writing has been found, on Kingiktorssuaq Island in Upernavik District. In 1832 a party of Inuit visiting the island dismantled part of a cairn and found within it a stone with a clear inscription in runic. The style of the runes is widely accepted as fourteenth century. The inscription reads: 'Erlingur Sigvatsson, Bjarni Thordarson and Enridi Oddsson built this cairn the Saturday before Rogation Day.'

The names of these three Viking adventurers are otherwise unrecorded. Rogation Day is not generally observed today. To the mediaeval church there were in fact four rogation days – the Major Rogation, which was a fixed day (25 April), and the three days of Minor Rogation, which were the three days before Ascension Day. Major Rogation is a seventh-century adoption by Pope Gregory the Great. Presumably this inscription with the singular form for Rogation Day refers to the Major Rogation, 25 April. This is too early a date by which to have reached Upernavik by sea in that season, as the sea ice is still present in April, and suggests that the Vikings had over-wintered in the location, perhaps trapping animals for their valuable winter coats.

Viking Greenland in History

The ultimate violent demise of Viking Greenland means that there are no surviving Greenlandic archives with which to trace the history of this nation. What information has survived is from European sources, and is fragmentary. Notwithstanding this, there is enough to provide an outline history of this Viking nation.

Of the years immediately following Eirik the Red's settlement there are glimpses from the Icelandic *Saga of the Greenlanders*. A culture is revealed which is based upon belief in the Norse religion, with the concomitant set of ethical values. Christianity is found in Greenland from the beginning – and some of the most impressive Viking remains from Greenland are in fact churches – but Christianity exists alongside the old beliefs, rather than as the sole faith. Christianity is supported by contacts with Europe, and was a necessary requirement for those contacts to exist, but there is little to suggest that it was more than a veneer. Important decisions were made under the advice of pagan soothsayers. Thus we hear that one Thorbjorn takes advice from a seeress called Thorbjorg – presumably a relative, in view of the similar name – before moving his home. This stands in contrast with a voyage made by Leif Eiriksson to Norway in 999–1000 when he overwinters with the king of Norway, Olaf Tryggvason. Olaf had converted to Christianity in the course of an expedition to England eight years before, and nominally converted his own country; he now encouraged Leif to convert. Leif returned to Greenland with a mission from King Olaf to bring about the conversion of Greenland, presumably as a precondition of trade with Norway. This is part of the process by which Christianity was sweeping through the whole Viking world. Thus in 1000 Iceland adopted Christianity by means of a vote taken at the *Althing*. While the old beliefs still continued in Iceland, Christianity was in the ascendant. In Greenland the religious position seems comparable, with growing adherence to Christianity. Many of the records for the centuries that follow are related to the Church, and may seem to suggest that Greenland was fully converted. Yet personal names in Greenland, as in Iceland, remain predominantly Nordic, honouring the gods of the north.

The early years of the eleventh century saw rapid exploration, both to America and within Greenland. Greenland voyaging included visits to the inhospitable east coast of Greenland. One Thorgils Orrabeinfostre was wrecked with his crew at an unknown location on the east coast. Here they encountered people they described pejoratively as 'witches'. Earlier Icelandic exploration of the southern section of the east coast made no mention of people living there, and the archaeological record has not found evidence of settlement there at that time. It is likely that Thorgils had travelled further north than previous Vikings, to the region of Scoresbysund. Here it is possible that Dorset Culture people may have been encountered – indeed, it is hard to imagine who else these people might have been. Thus, the Vikings encountered a last remnant of an American people who had once flourished in parts of Greenland, but who had largely vanished before the Viking arrival. Thorgils and his crew took three years to walk from the scene of their shipwreck south to Cape Farewell and north to the Eastern Settlement – a truly epic feat of survival, and one which demonstrates the resilience of the Vikings. The food resources of the southern portion of the east Greenland coast are meagre, and for the most part inadequate to support a settled population either of hunters or farmers. However, a band of men passing through can find food to support them for a short time in each area, though at the price of seriously depleting the resources there. The survival of Thorgils and his crew must be a story of endurance, and it is only because of their achievement that we have a mention in the sagas of an encounter with the very last of the Dorset Culture people in east Greenland, a people fast facing extinction in this location as a result of the warmer climate leading to a reduction in their food resources.

Trade with Europe was a prime concern for Greenland. Around the middle of the eleventh century, Greenland furthered its trade with Denmark by the gift of a polar bear to the king of Denmark. It is most unlikely that the Greenlanders were able to capture an adult bear; far more likely that they killed the mother and took a cub. Much of Greenland, including the area of both the Eastern and Western settlements, is not part of the range of polar bears, and only very rarely are polar bears encountered in the area of the central west coast. For example, the modern community of Kangerlussuaq – further north than either settlement – records just two polar bears in the period 1945–2005, both starving (and therefore particularly aggressive) adults that seem to have got lost on the central ice cap. That the Greenlanders could capture a polar bear cub suggests that they were visiting a breeding area, presumably the north-west of Greenland, and there acquired their gift. The polar bear survived the long sea voyage, and lived for a time in Denmark. One of the stranger items of trade is described in the *Saga of the Greenlanders*: a ship's figurehead carved from New World wood – probably maple – which was sold as a curiosity to a man from Bremen, for one gold mark.

In 1053 Greenland received its first 'official' mention. Pope Leo IX defined the archbishopric of Hamburg-Bremen to include alongside its north German heartland all the Nordic lands, which are listed by him as Denmark, Norway, Sweden, Iceland and Greenland. It took a further three years to appoint the first bishop for Greenland, Isleif Gizuerarson, himself a Greenlander. From this time on Greenland was a part of European Christendom, at least in name – part of an archbishopric, with its own bishop, and paying tithes to the Church. That within two generations a settlement founded by a band of outlaws and extolling the Viking virtues of independence had been persuaded to pay taxes to a very distant Rome indicates both the power of Christianity, and the absolute necessity for the Greenlanders to conform with the culture of Europe in order to trade. Further European recognition is accorded to Greenland by a history book, *Gesta Hammaburgensis ecclesiae pontificum*, written by Adam of Bremen and describing the lands of the Archbishopric of Hamburg-Bremen. Greenland is here, along with Iceland and Vinland. And at the end of the century, *c*. 1100, Saxo Grammaticus includes Greenland in his *History of the Danes*.

Some time in the mid to late eleventh century, the Greenland Vikings must have first encountered the Inuit. This people was undergoing a rapid expansion. Many centuries previously they had expanded from Siberia across the Bering Strait to Alaska and the Barren Grounds of Northern Canada. From the eleventh century another wave of migration led them north and east, through the Canadian Arctic Archipelago and on to northern Greenland. Where the Vikings and Inuit first met is not recorded, though as archaeology comes to understand more about both Viking and Inuit expansion a location may one day be identified. Within Greenland the Inuit continued their expansion, and by the early twelfth century had reached as far south as Disko Bay. From this time on the Viking and Inuit populations lived alongside one another within Greenland. Perhaps surprisingly there seems to have been peaceful coexistence. It seems that as farmers and hunters respectively the two communities made different demands on the resources of the vicinity, and were able to trade to their mutual benefit. The two groups were not in direct competition. That said, the peaceful coexistence of two peoples in one land is a sufficiently unusual human achievement to be worthy of comment. The first written record of the Inuit is from around 1150, and from a most unexpected source. This is in the *World Geography* written by a Sicilian Arab, Al Idrisi. He provides very little information, but confirms that by the middle of the twelfth century not only had the Vikings met the Inuit, but that descriptions of the Inuit had been passed back to Europe and through European Christendom to the Islamic lands beyond.

The century and a half from roughly 1100 to 1250 was a golden age for Viking Greenland. This period coincides with a warm period, which made farming easier, and provided more weeks of ice-free seas for travel. Bishops were appointed to the diocese of Greenland and Vinland, and trade with Europe was fostered. There is a record of another live polar bear being sent to Europe in 1123, with King Sigurd of Norway the recipient. Around this time the Greenlanders appear as a part of a wider world. For example in Denmark they heard stories of crusades as far as Jerusalem, including one which King Sigurd himself had taken part in, for which he was nicknamed *Jerusalemfarer*, the *Jerusalem-traveller*. Inspired by such stories, Greenlanders themselves took part with their Viking cousins in the Crusades. We know that Greenland was then seen as a good place to live, and was attracting more settlers. For example, three ships of Icelanders and Norwegians arrived in 1131. Notwithstanding the prosperity of the golden age, Greenland continued to find trade with Europe problematic. The stretch of Atlantic east from Cape Farewell was always exceptionally dangerous, and ship design did not in any significant way develop to compensate. An account of a wreck survives from 1130, when a ship on this passage was wrecked on the east coast, and all its crew killed. We know of this wreck because there was a particularly messy dispute afterwards as to who owned the salvage rights. The reality is that there must have been very many wrecks. Another wreck, again on the east coast, is recorded for 1189; a ship named the *Stangarfoli* from Bergen was shipwrecked, with one of the bodies recovered eleven years later in 1200, when it was found in a cave. Presumably a sole survivor of the wreck had sought shelter there, yet perished perhaps long after from cold and hunger.

Greenland built its first cathedral in the year 1200 at Gardar, dedicated to St Nicholas. Bishop Jon, Greenland's bishop at this time, set out in 1203 for Rome, returning to Greenland a few years later. He died in Greenland in 1209, and is buried at Gardar. This trip emphasises Greenland's position as a bishopric firmly established within the Roman Catholic Church giving its allegiance to Rome, and as much a part of Christendom as any other country in Europe. Bishops were expected to act as liaison between Greenland and Rome, and were expected to travel. In 1234 the Pope consecrated the first man who was not a Greenlander as Bishop of Greenland. At this time Bishop Nicholas, a Norwegian, was appointed. He appears to have been most reluctant to make the trip to Greenland, delaying in Norway for six years, and his contribution to Greenland may well have been small, for he died within two years of his arrival. However, his appointment demonstrates that Greenland was considered by the Church as a bishopric to which any appropriately qualified person might reasonably be appointed, not a preserve of Greenlanders. Europe was becoming ever more aware of Greenland, as is shown by its inclusion in another world geography, the *Speculum Regale*[4] of 1245.

As it became better known in Europe, so Greenland found itself subject to closer control from Europe. The trend was set not in Greenland, but in Iceland. In the early thirteenth century, Iceland experienced a flourishing of learning unknown anywhere in Europe since the classical age.[5] This northern renaissance was fostered by the democracy of Iceland, and reached its zenith under the direction of Snorri Sturluson. Snorri was in effect Plato's 'Philosopher King', being both the most powerful noble in Iceland and also its greatest scholar. Born in 1179, Snorri was heir to vast estates in Iceland which he increased by marrying an heiress. Within the Icelandic democracy he reached the top position of Law-Speaker at the *Althing*, in our terminology prime minister, and in this guise represented Iceland overseas, particularly in Norway, seeking a balance between co-operation with Norway and a robust assertion of Icelandic independence. His scholarly output is prodigious. His massive *Heimskringla*[6] is in effect an encyclopaedia of the knowledge of the day, starting with the resounding assertion that 'the world is a sphere', a truth not then fully recognised in continental Europe. The culture he fostered in Iceland included a remarkable degree of comfort. His own spacious home at Reykholt had as an amenity a circular pool fed with geothermal hot water, providing comfortable bathing. Snorri's bathtub still exists and is still occasionally used, a marvellous reminder of the level of civilisation that was created in Snorri's Iceland. Sadly, the northern renaissance was brutally extinguished. Haakon, King of Norway, demanded that Snorri should be killed, and in 1241 sent 70 men to carry out this task. They reached Reykholt and found Snorri hiding from them in his cellar. There, they murdered this unarmed 62-year-old. The subsequent suppression of the democracy, scholarship and prosperity of Iceland was completed in 1262 with the formal annexation of Iceland to the crown of Norway, from which date Iceland declined through extortionate taxes and decades of civil wars promoted by Norway. This suppression and its aftermath put back the progress of European civilisation.

Records from Greenland are not complete enough to reveal a character such as Snorri. It is clear, however, that the suppression of democracy and independence in Greenland was as effective there as it was in Iceland. In 1261 Greenland acknowledged Norwegian sovereignty over the Eastern and Western Settlements and the Nordresetr – a curiously wordy designation which seems to be a deliberate avoidance of the name 'Greenland', and perhaps to imply that other territories associated with Greenland were excluded. In 1262 Greenland was forced to agree to a Norwegian monopoly on all trade. Both the annexation and the trade monopoly were impositions striking at the heart of Viking Greenland. In addition to the Church tithes that Greenland had been paying to Rome since at least 1053, Greenland now had to pay national taxes to the king of Norway. Additionally, it was subject to impositions such as the 1274–82 'Crusading Tithe'[7] levied on all Christians by the Council of Lyons and used to fund a crusade to Jerusalem. Ties to Europe were such that a meeting of the Church of Rome in a town in the south of France to fund a campaign in the eastern Mediterranean impacted on the pockets of the Greenlanders. It seems that the Greenlanders were tardy in paying this last imposition, for in 1278 the archbishop of Nidaros – who had taken over responsibility for Greenland from the archbishop of Hamburg-Bremen – sent men to collect by force the crusading tithe. Records show from this time a reduction in the number of ships sailing for Greenland. Pope Nicholas wrote that Greenland was 'visited infrequently because of the cruel ocean' (1279), and there are accounts of wrecks of ships that attempted the journey. While in previous years Greenlanders had owned the ships that sailed for Europe, now the monopoly dictated that all the ships should be Norwegian, and Greenland was dependent on Norway deciding to send them. The ships came to trade, but they also came to collect taxes, even to announce what the increased taxes were and to demand immediate payment, and they must have become increasingly unwelcome. In such circumstances it would be reasonable to expect that the monopoly would be broken by Greenlanders. With Iceland, as well as the Faroe, Orkney and Shetland islands, all owned by the king of Norway, the practical alternative was trade direct with the British Isles, particularly with north-west Scotland. There is every expectation that such harbours as that of Dunvegan on Skye were used by Greenlandic ships, and perhaps one day evidence will be found.

Greenland was further taxed in 1282 when the archbishop of Nidaros, Jon the Red,[7] stated in a letter to the Pope that the Greenland luxury goods (in which the taxes were paid) were selling in Europe for lower prices than had previously been the case. Whether Jon the Red's claim is true is doubtful, as there seems no obvious reason for the price of furs and ivory to fall at this time. He was later found guilty of embezzlement of Church money and forced to go into exile, so his claim about the low values of Greenlandic goods should surely be treated with caution. Even so, the impact on the Greenlanders was simply a demand for more goods, as they were now deemed to be of lower value in Europe.

In the fourteenth century there is evidence that Greenland was carrying out trade in breach of the imposed monopoly. It would be very strange were this not the case, as Greenlanders needed trade for their survival. There is a curious Icelandic record from 1347 of a Greenlandic ship driven off course and forced to put into Iceland. The record – which occurs in three sources, the *Skalholt Book*, *Gottskalk's Book* and the *Flateyjar Book* – states that the ship, with a crew variously set as 17 or 18, was bound not for Europe but for America, specifically for Markland. The obvious interpretation is that under duress from the Norwegian trading monopoly, Greenlandic ships were voyaging to Markland for essential timber. With timber from Markland the Greenlanders had the ability to build the ships they needed for survival. Supply of wood from America was one obvious response to the monopoly. Another was trade with European countries not under Norwegian–Danish control, effectively with the British Isles.

Greenland's Decline

Greenland's fortunes were on the wane. Plague in Iceland in 1306 and 1309 may have spread to Greenland, though there is no direct evidence of this, while from 1308 Greenland experienced a decade of exceptionally cold winters. Europe at this time seemed to see Greenland as no more than a place from which to extract taxes. Records are particularly fragmentary in this period. In 1325 the bishop of Bergen in a letter to the archbishop of Nidaros complains about the behaviour of the Trondheim merchants who were on a previous ship from Norway to Greenland. A plausible interpretation is that the Norwegian monopoly ships had become little better than pirate vessels plundering from the Greenlanders. Yet by one route or another, Greenland products were certainly finding their way to Europe. For example, in 1327 a Flanders merchant bought from Norway 2,000 pounds of walrus ivory at a price of 28 pounds of silver. We have a record dated 1341 of a Norwegian priest, Ivar Bardarsson, sent to Greenland to re-register the churches and claim the king's rights – that is to ensure that taxes were paid. Ivar spent 20 years in Greenland, finally returning to Norway in 1362, and provided one of the last accounts of Greenland.

It was Ivar who gave notice that something was seriously wrong with the Greenland settlements. He arrived in the Eastern Settlement in 1342, and travelled on to the Western Settlement in 1349, which he found abandoned. This was a settlement of perhaps 2,000 people which had flourished for well over 300 years, and was suddenly deserted, seemingly in 1349, and without that information being brought back to the neighbouring Eastern Settlement. It appears that the destruction of people and buildings was sudden and total. The Western Settlement's termination has left archaeological traces. Some farmsteads appear to have been abandoned suddenly, leaving for example a stock of unused wood, others show signs of having been burnt. Yet others seem to have undergone an orderly evacuation, with almost all possessions removed. There seems to be evidence of two sorts of end to the farmsteads: some attacked by an enemy, others abandoned, perhaps threatened by an enemy.

The final years of the Eastern Settlement have left scant records. The Black Death which swept through Europe reached Norway in 1349 and Iceland in 1350. There is no indication whether it reached Greenland, but as it had received no check anywhere else in its spread, most probably it did. Following the devastation of the Black Death, Norway was preoccupied by domestic problems and in effect lost interest in both Iceland and Greenland. An Icelandic source notes that in 1350 Mass could not be held in churches because that year no ships had arrived from Norway, with the result that communion wine had run out. If Iceland received no ships, we can be sure Greenland didn't either.

There are brief records from 1354 and 1355 that Norway's King Magnus gave permission to Powell Knutsson to take a ship to Greenland to 'protect' the Christians, though why they needed protection is not explained. Greenland was subjected to another calamity in 1362. A massive eruption in Iceland by the volcano beneath the glacier Oraefajokul created a dust cloud which reduced daylight and caused failed harvests in Iceland and all the lands around the North Atlantic.[8]

The end of formal contact between Greenland and Europe occurred in 1367, as this is the year of the last official royal ship from Norway to Greenland. The ship presumably over-wintered en route, perhaps in Iceland, as it arrived in 1368, bringing Greenland's last bishop, Bishop Alf. A Royal Ship was sent out in 1369, but was shipwrecked – not in Greenlandic waters, but in Norwegian waters just outside Bergen, her port of departure. The ship seems not to have been replaced, and from this date Norway appears to almost forget Greenland. Subsequent records of Greenland are exceptionally fragmentary. The king of Norway sent a representative to Greenland in 1374, though how he travelled and even whether he made the journey as instructed is not recorded. In 1378 Bishop Alf died, leaving the Church in Greenland without a head.

The last sure record from Greenland is a marriage which took place 14 September 1408 between an Icelander and a Greenlander. The marriage was in the bride's church of Hvalsey in the Western Settlement; the couple sailed for Iceland and made their lives there, and it is there that the record is preserved. This record suggests some repopulation of the Western Settlement had happened since its abandonment in 1349. There are uncertain records in the years that follow. In 1448 Pope Nicholas implied in a letter that he believed the Greenland colony still existed, and might be in need of help. The information available today suggests that by just after the middle of the fifteenth century both the Eastern and Western Settlements had been abandoned, and Viking Greenland was completely finished before 1500.

The End of Viking Greenland

Many reasons have been put forward for the demise of the Greenland colony. Most of them do not withstand scrutiny. The reasons suggested are as follows:

1) The Vikings were defeated by a worsening climate, and starved to death.

2) The Vikings were killed by plague; alternatively their crops were destroyed by a pestilence.

3) The Vikings were swamped by the Inuit, and became Inuit.

4) The Inuit killed all the Vikings in an act of genocide.

5) The Greenland Vikings emigrated.

6) Pirates or other Europeans killed the Vikings.

The climate of the North Atlantic region did indeed cool in the fourteenth and fifteenth centuries. The average change was in the region of

2° C cooler both summer and winter, which in areas of marginal agriculture can be significant. In Iceland this deteriorating climate caused years of poor harvests and times of famine. Nonetheless the Icelanders survived, and continued to live in all parts of Iceland including the most marginal. If they could survive it is very hard to see why the Greenland Vikings could not. Indeed the Icelanders, who were almost entirely dependent on husbandry for their food, were more vulnerable than their kin in Greenland, whose diet was supported by hunting – and while the cooling climate caused difficulties for agriculture it also created a proliferation of the fish, birds and sea mammals that were a major source of food. Climate change alone cannot explain the demise of the Greenland Vikings, and probably was not even a contributory factor. In view of the Arctic paradox whereby colder temperatures result in more wildlife as food, the cooler temperatures may actually have helped the Greenlanders.

Nor can plague be the explanation. The Black Death may well have come to Greenland, as it did to Iceland, but in all plagues there are survivors. The isolated nature of farmsteads in Greenland would have acted as a barrier to the spread of infection, while the climate created an environment largely free from animals which spread plague. Greenland has no rats, the animal that spread the plague through Europe. The presence of plague in Iceland, another country without rats, argues for an infection route other than rats and the fleas they harbour, though this transmission route has so far not been identified. Even with this proviso, Greenland, with the isolation offered by its vast distances, was not a country that should have suffered substantially from plague. The concept of crop blight is similarly unrealistic. The Vikings in Greenland grew a range of crops, and while the failure of one crop through pestilence is possible, the failure of all, and in all locations, is most unlikely. As with plague, the distance between farms provided a barrier for the spread of pestilence. Plague and pestilence, like climate change, cannot explain the disappearance of the Greenland colony after over 400 years. At the most these factors somewhat weakened the population, though even this is speculation.

The idea that the Greenland Vikings were swamped by the Inuit is again problematic. Greenland had a mixed population. In their west-coast settlements the Viking population numbered in the region of 5,000; the Inuit population for the whole of Greenland was in the region of 5,000, but distributed throughout the ice-free areas of Greenland, including a population on the north-west and north coasts. In south-west Greenland the

Inuit were a minority. Perhaps intermarriage between the two groups occurred, but the balance in numbers between the two groups is such that the result would not be that the ethnic Norse would vanish, subsumed within an Inuit population. Later Europeans visiting Greenland discerned no trace of European characteristics in the Inuit they encountered there. This supposed process, which has been termed 'Eskimo-isation', cannot explain the disappearance of the Greenland Vikings. Indeed, were the process to have happened at all it can even be suggested that the direction would have been for the Inuit to be swamped by the Vikings, for relative numbers in the areas of Greenland that both Vikings and Inuit inhabited were such that the Inuit were in the minority.

The idea that the Inuit carried out genocide against the Greenland Vikings has to be considered as there is at least some evidence to support the idea. The Icelandic sagas make it clear that the writers believed the Western Settlement was destroyed by people. The term that is used is 'skraelings', a term certainly sometimes applied to the Inuit. However 'skraeling' is not a racial description, but rather a term of contempt, meaning something like 'wretches', applied to many different races, and the sagas cannot be taken as stating specifically the Inuit killed the Vikings – rather that a people the saga writer held in contempt killed them. Notwithstanding this, Hans Egede,[9] the first missionary to Inuit Greenland, believed on the basis of the Icelandic sagas that the Inuit had killed the Vikings. He asked the Inuit about this, and believed that he gained confirmation from their answers. A researcher today would say that his methodology was suspect in that he asked leading questions; additionally, he was struggling to communicate in a language he understood imperfectly. The Inuit in recent years have been observed to have a cultural tendency to give answers they feel are those wanted by the person they are speaking to, irrespective of whether they are correct. Whatever the Inuit may have told Hans Egede cannot be regarded as safe evidence. It is also doubtful how much Inuit oral history could be expected to remember of events that took place hundreds of years previously. There have been claims for long folk memories among the Inuit, and some of their stories do seem to be centuries old. Yet there must be doubts as to the validity of claims that folk history extends over many hundreds of years, and it is hard to prove that the Inuit of the eighteenth century would have known anything about events in the fourteenth and fifteenth centuries.

The Greenland Vikings and the Inuit had coexisted for perhaps 400 years. Their lifestyles were complementary. The Vikings were farmers, seeking land at the head of fjords, while the Inuit were hunters, making their settlements by open water, frequently close to headlands. The two groups were not in direct competition for the same resources. There was no inevitability of conflict, but rather a history of centuries of tolerance and trade. Each group gained benefit from the other. If conflict should have arisen, the Vikings were better armed, for they were metal users, while the Inuit, despite centuries of contact with the Vikings, were still predominantly a Stone Age culture. In theory the Vikings could have been attacked farmstead by farmstead, with the Inuit forming a large party for the purpose of destroying each farmstead one after the other. In practice, it is hard to see how they could have completely destroyed all the Viking settlements. The Vikings were not outnumbered by the Inuit in Greenland, and in the southwest it was the Vikings who had the advantage of numbers. They should not have lost in a war.

The Inuit people throughout the Arctic have an exceptionally peaceable history. They are not prone to carrying out wars against other Inuit groups, nor against other peoples. If an aggressor is to be sought to explain the demise of Viking Greenland, then the Inuit are not likely suspects.

Emigration is an idea that must be taken seriously. As it happens, the very last sure record of Greenland is of a migration – of a couple who moved from Greenland to Iceland. Iceland at that time had suffered a substantial fall in population, and did have vacant land available for the taking. It was able to accommodate a population from Greenland. Similarly, Greenlanders could have migrated back to Norway, or elsewhere in Europe, or even, in theory, to lands to the west of Greenland. Emigration as a theory is possible – but we have no evidence that this took place. It is not clear that Iceland or anywhere else in Europe was a more attractive location, nor that Greenlanders whose families had lived there for up to 15 generations would have any wish to leave Greenland. While we are not in a position to say that emigration did not happen, it does seem implausible.

The root cause of the destruction of Viking Greenland is most probably that of pirate raids. The official 'royal ships' from Norway came primarily to extort taxes, and became little better than thieves. Over and above these state-sponsored raids, Greenland was increasingly subject to the attentions of pirates. Such ships were numerous in Europe, acting without the overt support of a nation state, trading where they could, and stealing with impunity. For centuries isolated communities on the European littoral feared the arrival of an unknown ship. The Greenlanders were especially vulnerable, for their tiny scattered settlements put them at the mercy of any visiting ship whose crew outnumbered them.

European Christendom condemned the activities of pirates, but only when they were directed against Christians. There were no restrictions imposed upon pirate activities against non-Christian people, whom the Church explicitly stated could be killed or enslaved, and their property seized. This was the way the Church recommended treating non-Christians. Proselytising zeal, a feature of the expansion of the early Church, and of the Church in the nineteenth and twentieth centuries, scarcely existed at the end of the Middle Ages. Christendom had reached an accommodation with European Jews, though one which was often breached. They had fought to a stalemate against Islam in the Middle East and to the south of the Mediterranean. These exceptions aside, to be a non-Christian was almost to be non-human. Within this context it is striking that towards the end of the Greenland colony the popes began to assert that the Greenlanders had returned to paganism and the worship of the Norse gods. The import of this view is that it justifies the actions of the pirates, giving papal sanction to the killing and captivity of Greenland Vikings.

Records of pagans sold into slavery certainly exist. In Bristol in 1429 five boys and three girls, all from Iceland, were sold into slavery, while in the same year in Kings Lynn the visiting Icelandic bishop of Skalholt dramatically rescued eleven Icelandic children who were on the point of being sold in a slave market. In 1448 Pope Nicholas V makes reference in a letter to an attack on the Greenlanders '30 years before' (1418) in which many Greenlanders were taken captive. Now, after 30 years of captivity, in Europe, they had been freed, presumably on an intervention from the Pope, and were returning home. The Pope commented on their 'fervent piety'. By becoming Christians – fervent ones – they had become unfit for the status of slaves. It is not recorded whether these survivors of captivity ever reached their homes in Greenland.

The balance of probability is that the Greenland colony in its last years was over-run by European pirates. They operated from Britain, Flanders, Denmark, and even, in 1453, a ship from Portugal. What we are seeing is the systematic destruction of a people by Church- and State-supported pirates through theft, through carrying the Greenlanders into captivity as slaves, through burning of farmsteads and through murder. This genocide was justified on the grounds that the Greenlanders had relapsed into the pagan faith, and were therefore considered scarcely human. Pirate raids do not seem recorded much after the middle of the fifteenth century, which might be because there was nothing left to raid. In 1492, the very year that Columbus set off to America, Pope Alexander IV repeated the papal view that the Greenlanders had sunk into 'heathen practices', which might possibly suggest that some Greenlanders at least were then left – or perhaps that the Pope's sources were old.

Pirate Voyages

The pirate voyages provided a conduit of sorts through which knowledge of Greenland and lands to the west could be transmitted to Europe. One such example is provided by the *Zeno Voyages*,[10] a confused narrative which is best understood as an account of such a voyage, though the text has in recent years been subject to much fanciful interpretation. In its day the *Zeno Voyages* was one of the most influential sources for fashioning views of the geography of the North Atlantic. The account, along with a map, are both found within a book published in Italian in Venice in 1558.

What we have in the *Zeno Voyages* is a poorly written and often confused account of voyages from Europe to Greenland in the late fourteenth century, written by a sixteenth-century Venetian, Nicolo Zeno, who claims as his source letters preserved by his family and which detail voyages made by his ancestors, the Zeno brothers. Nicolo Zeno's narrative based on these letters is muddled, as perhaps might be expected from a story written by a Venetian who knew little about the North Atlantic. When it was published it had a political purpose in asserting that Venetians – the Zeno brothers – visited America a century before Columbus, and this propaganda distorts the text throughout. While some today have been prepared to take at face value this story of an Italian voyage to America, a sober reading must discount it. Yet while a visit to America is fiction, there is at least some truth in part of the story set out. The Zeno brothers are known from numerous documents as Venetian merchants, and there is proof, for example, that one of the brothers, also called Nicolo Zeno, made a voyage to England and Flanders. At least some of the places they are supposed to have visited exist, though many do not. Much attention has been given to the name of the prince under whose authority the Zeno brothers make their voyage – an improbably named Zichmni. The name is so strange that Zeno is presumed to have based it on something in a source text, for if he were creating a name he would at least have come up with something pronounceable.

The credulous have sought to equate Zichmni with Prince Henry Sinclair of Orkney, an idea without a shred of support. More plausible is that from Zichmni we should remove the Italian ending in –i, and insert the essential unstressed vowel, giving Zichman. This much is sound philology; Italian is a syllable-timed language (which puts equal stress on all syllables) while the Germanic languages of northern Europe are stress-timed (they have stressed and unstressed syllables). Representing an unstressed syllable from a stress-timed language in the spelling conventions of a syllable-timed language is problematic; one method is simply to leave out the vowel, which is what the Italian seems to have done here. Philology also suggests that the use of Z in Italian suggests a sound that in English would usually be represented W. Zichmni is perhaps an effort to represent in Italian what would be spelt in English 'Wichman'. Brian Smith, a leading critic of the identification of Zichmni with Sinclair, suggests that a more plausible identification for Zich-mni is Wichmann,[11] a known North Sea pirate in the late fourteenth century – though Smith feels that such an identity cannot be proved. I suggest that Smith has understated his case – Wichmann and Zichmni are philologically identical, which is a significant finding, and the identification of Wichmann with Zichmni a credible one.

Smith has given a hint as to how the kernel of truth may be found within the story of the Zeno voyage. We know that the first Nicolo Zeno did make a voyage to England in 1380, and it is well within the bounds of possibility that he met Wichmann or another of the many pirates operating from English ports, and heard from him of voyages he had made to Greenland, and tales of lands beyond. Zichmni is identified in the account with the places Porlanda and Sorant, places which commentators have struggled to locate in the Orkney Islands, though they may readily be equated with Portland Bill and The Solent, both on England's south coast.

The description of the North Atlantic merges the Faroe Islands and Iceland as the fictitious Frisland, has scant reference to the Shetland Islands, leaves out the Orkney Islands, is sketchy in its account of Greenland, and gives only the haziest of accounts of a land further west. Possibly we are to imagine the first Nicolo Zeno in a south of England port hearing a tale of Wichmann's piratical voyage to Greenland, writing an account of what he had heard, and nearly two centuries later his namesake manufacturing from this a claim that Zeno had himself travelled to Greenland and America.

In the Zeno story and map we have a confused echo of a pirate voyage of the sort which most probably caused the demise of Viking Greenland.

Greenland – the Essential Stepping-Stone

Without Greenland there would have been no Viking America. Greenland is the lynch-pin of the transatlantic route navigated by the Vikings. Certainly they voyaged direct from Norway to Greenland, but there has never been a suggestion that they made the voyage direct from Europe to America. The distance between Europe and America is too great and navigation too difficult for the skills available to the Vikings.

Every story of the New World travelled back to Europe via Greenland. Every Viking visitor and settler to America travelled via Greenland. Greenland provided the mariners' supplies and the workshops to repair ships for the long voyages both east and west, and it offered an opportunity for trade.

Without Greenland there could be no Viking America, and no European knowledge of the New World. The failure of the Greenland colony, presumably at the hands of European pirates, also marks the end of a chapter of European exploration of America. As Greenland failed, instead of the sound knowledge of geography expressed in the mediaeval Icelandic sources we find confused texts like the story of the Zeno voyage. The end of the Greenland colony was more than just a tragedy for the 5,000 or so Vikings living in Greenland, but a tragedy that put back by centuries interaction, cultural and economic, between Europe and America.

4

Vikings to Vinland

THE name 'Vinland' appears on no modern map. Yet Vinland, part of the east coast of America, was the jewel in the crown of the Viking New World. Today we know of Vinland from two major sources which tell of Viking exploration and settlement of the American east coast: sagas written in Iceland, and the archaeological dig at L'Anse aux Meadows in Newfoundland, a way-station on the route to Vinland. Additionally, there are a host of minor sources. Vinland is not on the modern map, but is a real place nonetheless.

Adam of Bremen

The very earliest source for Vinland is one of the minor ones, the writings of an eleventh-century cleric, Adam of Bremen, who provides the first surviving account of Vinland. A mediaeval chronicler working towards the end of the eleventh century, his book is the *Gesta Hammaburgensis Ecclesiae Pontificum*, in English *Deeds of the Bishops of the Hamburg Church*. The Hamburg diocese – strictly the archdiocese of Bremen-Hamburg led by an archbishop, though Adam is careless in his terminology – had an enormous jurisdiction. The arch-diocese had been entrusted with the Roman Catholic Church's 'Mission to the North', and as such its jurisdiction included the whole of Scandinavia, the Faroe Islands, Iceland and Greenland, as well as north-western Russia. The Church's missionary activity was extensive, with all these lands having nominally accepted Christianity, and a process of conversion of the populace ongoing.

Adam of Bremen is an important source for the early mediaeval history of Scandinavia and Russia, and he also provides fragments about Greenland and Vinland. Very little is known about Adam himself. We can say little more than that he appears to have been born in the 1040s in Saxony, to have had the most extensive education available in his day, earning him the honorific title *Magister*, and to have died in the early 1080s. In 1068 he was invited by Archbishop Adalbert of Bremen to come to direct the cathedral school there, though his subsequent career shows him to be more than just the headmaster. Around 1069 he started his history of the arch-diocese of Bremen-Hamburg, a work he was still revising when he died. His sources for information on the north came from time he spent in Denmark at the court of King Svend Estridson, nephew of King Canute, including specifically information he was given by the king himself. Additionally, he heard accounts from merchants and missionaries who passed through the port of Bremen, and made use of numerous written sources in the library of Bremen, to which he had ready access.

What he has given us is an extensive history of the archdiocese from 788 up to his own days, a biography of his archbishop, Adalbert, and a geography of the north – this section of his book has the heading 'Descriptio insularum Aquilonis' and is sometimes referred to by this name as if a separate book. It is here that Vinland is described (IV, 38):

> Furthermore King Svend mentioned yet another island found
> by many in that ocean. This island is called Vinland, because
> grapevines grow there wild, yielding the finest wine. And crops
> grow there in plenty without having been sown. I know this
> not from fabulous report, but through the definite information
> of the Danes.

Adam, usually a careful scholar, makes important mistakes in these lines. Adam's mother tongue was what we today call Old High German, while King Svend Estridson spoke what today is called Old Norse, specifically the Old East Norse dialect of Denmark. These languages were close enough one to the other for speakers to understand one another, albeit imperfectly. During his brief visit to Denmark Adam would have spoken his Old High German, and been understood imperfectly. Similarly he would have struggled to understand the Old Norse of the king and of the Danes. One mistake is in his use of the word 'island', where he is translating an Old Norse word that has the meaning of 'shore'. Adam's sources are not saying that Vinland is an island, simply that it is a shore. The other mistake is with the name Vinland, where both elements of this name mean something different in Old Norse and in Old High German. In Old Norse *vin* means good, fertile land – land which may be cultivated – a meaning emphasised by the element *land*, which again means farmland. Yet in Old High German *vin* has a completely different meaning – it means wine and is a Latin borrowing – while *land* was beginning to be used to refer to a country. That Adam was told that grapevines grow in Vinland need not necessarily be doubted; his mistake is to link this fact with his wrong interpretation of the name. Vinland means 'fertile-farmland'; he understood it as 'wine-land'.

The Icelandic Sagas

The story of the Vikings in America is also contained within the Icelandic sagas. Taken as a whole, this body of writing is the greatest mediaeval literary survival of any nation and a magnificent contribution from Iceland to world civilisation. The sagas are a superb literary flowering, and we are indeed fortunate that these Icelandic masterpieces have survived the vicissitudes of history in considerable numbers – 1,666 manuscripts now in Reykjavik alone. By contrast England has just four manuscripts of literary texts from the early Middle Ages, plus a few fragments. The whole body of early mediaeval literary texts in English will fit one thick modern paperback. England has the curious story of the hero Beowulf, lyric poetry that is among the best offered by English of any period (but not much of it), finely crafted stories such as *Andreas*, the life of St Andrew, the comedy of riddles, love poetry as *Wulf and Eadwacer*, and the sublime power of *Caedmon's Hymn* or *Bede's Death Song*. England is truly fortunate to have such a superb literature from this period, a literature which ranks with the very best produced subsequently in English, yet sadly so very much has been lost. Regrettably Germany has only fragments from the period. Russia has just one significant poem, the *Lay of the Host of Igor*. There is nothing whatsoever from France or Spain, Italy or Greece, scraps only from Denmark. Yet from Iceland there are these many hundreds of literary manuscripts.

In Iceland the freedom of spirit which drove the Viking Age produced a literature which stands comparison with the very greatest of the European tradition. It is the independence of the Icelandic vision which ensured its survival. In 1235 the Vatican had its own library destroyed, then the most important library in Europe, and embarked on a programme of worldwide destruction of books which did not conform with the papal ideology. The four English manuscript survivals are accidentals which escaped the Church's bonfires. Thus for example the Vercelli manuscript was preserved in the library of St Andrews cathedral in Vercelli, Italy, described as an old book in an unknown language, and seemingly overlooked for destruction because no-one knew what it was. England once had thousands of literary manuscripts. In the poem *Widsith* we have what is virtually an index of stories, which gives us a hint of what was destroyed. England lost almost all of a great literature, and with it a history, a culture and even an identity. Thus to the English world of the Early Middle Ages tales of men like the hero Ingeld were part of the everyday currency, and known to everyone. Yet today we know Ingeld only as a name, and no longer know his story. We have no more than a record of a monk reprimanded for telling the story of Ingeld – asked *Quid Hinieldus cum Christos?* – What has Ingeld to do with Christ? In England, and throughout the continent of Europe, the writ of the Roman Catholic Church was obeyed, and literature which was not approved by the Church perished. In Iceland it was different. The literature of Iceland existed not in a library, but widely distributed around Iceland. Literacy was a relatively common accomplishment, in marked contrast to anywhere else in Europe. Most Icelanders would have known the runic alphabet, the northern alphabet of letters made up of straight lines that was so well suited for carving on wood, bone or stone. For example, a group of Viking crusaders returning to Iceland via Orkney broke into the ancient burial mound of Maeshowe,[1] and there many of them amused themselves vandalising the interior of this structure by carving their names and other snippets of grafitti. One even boasts that his knife was once owned by Gaukur of Stong, a famous farmer of southern Iceland who was killed in a duel fought over a woman. Icelanders knew their runes, and from this it was a small step to knowing the Latin alphabet, and using this to read and write the northern tongue, the language we today call interchangeably both Old Norse and Old Icelandic. Many farmsteads had manuscripts. For example on the tiny island of Flatey – Flat Island – in the middle of Breithafjorthur – Broad Fjord, a great bay on the west coast of Iceland – was preserved the *Flateyarbok*, one of the major sources of information for Viking exploration of Greenland and America. Were it not the case that every Icelandic farmstead had people who could read and write there would be no *Flateyarbok*, and no Icelandic source for Vinland.

It is the sagas that provide the human detail of the Viking voyages to America. There are two major sagas – known in English as the *Saga of the Greenlanders* and the *Saga of Eirik the Red* which together make up *The Vinland Sagas*.

In approaching them we need to remember that they are not histories. As their name states, they are sagas. They have the sort of accuracy that a

Hollywood film has when it tells a story of the Second World War. The Hollywood story is, of course, based on a true story – but changed to meet the artistic needs of the director and the sensibilities of the audience. Certain events become magnified as cameos illustrative of the war, while others are forgotten. Much of what people today in Britain or America know about the Second World War is filtered through Hollywood. In the same way Icelanders knew the story of exploration of Greenland and America through the Hollywood of their day, through the sagas. In these we hear of the brave deeds not of Greenlanders or Vinlanders, but rather of Icelanders who visited Greenland and Vinland. The two major protagonists in these stories are Eirik the Red, and his son Leif Eiriksson, nicknamed The Lucky, both of whom could be claimed to be Icelanders. In Iceland the character of Eirik underwent a transformation. This is the man who was exiled first from Norway and then from Iceland for his violent behaviour. Yet today in Iceland children play at being the hero Eirik the Red, while the Icelandic genetic record raises the intriguing probability that every single ethnic Icelanders living today is a direct descendant of his. The sagas recognise his achievement is discovering, exploring and colonising Greenland, and applaud his free spirit as a Viking; they gloss over his expulsion from Norway 'on account of some killings', and are similarly forgiving on his misdeeds in Iceland. His son Leif Eiriksson is remembered in Iceland today because he is an Icelander, and commemorated by an impressive statue outside Reykjavik's biggest church. The sagas tell stories of Icelanders, of the first Icelanders to visit Greenland and America, and they aim to tell a good yarn rather than a history, without worrying over-much about facts which might spoil the flow of their story. The emphasis on story-telling rather than accuracy results in contradictions in the sagas, and statements in the sagas which we know now must be wrong.

Understood in these terms the sagas can be given their proper worth. So, for example, they are specifically not a history of Greenland. Were our knowledge of Viking Greenland limited to the saga story we would have a picture of Greenland settled just by Eirik and his colonists, and assume that the colony vanished after a generation, when in fact we know Greenland continued for nearly five centuries. Our knowledge of Viking America would be similarly partial. We would have – indeed until recently we did have – a view that Leif Eiriksson and his companions visited America for a few years around the year 1000, and that that was an end to the exploration. Instead what we are seeing in the sagas is a loss of interest by Icelanders in the affairs of Vinland when the people involved are Greenlanders or Vinlanders rather than Icelanders. The audience of the Icelandic sagas wanted to hear about Icelandic heroes. Stories of Greenlandic and Vinlandic heroes were doubtless told – but in Greenland and Vinland. So far we have not discovered these.

The Icelandic sagas of Greenland and Vinland were never forgotten in Iceland. It was, however, as late as the 1830s before translations were made into Danish and English, and then in rather obscure scholarly books, and it was the 1880s before the stories reached a popular audience.[2] Suddenly Viking mania gripped America. Vikings were to be found everywhere from Newfoundland – where they certainly were – to California, where they certainly were not. Within this mania the real story told in the sagas is frequently lost.

A careful reading of their sometimes confusing narrative shows that the Icelandic sagas record six distinct voyages to America.

The first voyage and first recorded European sighting of mainland America is credited to Bjarni Herjolfsson and his crew. Their discovery was accidental, made as they were voyaging the Iceland–Greenland crossing. The year was 985, just after the Greenland settlements had been established. Through a combination of bad weather and simply not knowing where he was going – it was Bjarni's first voyage on this route – he sailed too far south, thereby missing Greenland's Cape Farewell, and instead sighting forested land, presumably in what is now southern Labrador. Bjarni is reported in the sagas to have made the decision not to make a landing, but rather continued first northward until the correct latitude was reached, then due east to his intended destination in Greenland, at Herjolfsnes, his father's farm. In making this voyage he sighted American land twice more, but again it is stressed that he did not land. This story has the mix of fact and fiction that is characteristic of the sagas. Bjarni has all the appearance of being a real figure. No-one has seriously doubted that he made the voyage described. Yet it is absolutely incredible that he did not land. When he sighted America he had been at sea for around two weeks, much of it fog-bound, and around another two weeks and two American land-sightings were to pass before the ship arrived in Greenland. Drinking water was an acute problem on any Viking voyage of more than a very few days both because of limited storage space and the difficulties of keeping water fresh. While Viking ships did make the direct passage from Greenland to Norway, these voyages were substantially shorter than Bjarni's marathon; furthermore, these ships were equipped with food and water for a long voyage. Bjarni was expecting a journey of about four days, and while as a prudent mariner he surely took more than four days' supplies it is unlikely that he took a month's supply. Add the problem of damp and cold endured by the crew of an open boat through days of freezing fog off south Greenland, the impossibility of lighting a fire on board ship for hot food, and the discomfort of overcrowding: all these point to an obvious conclusion: Bjarni landed.

In landing, Bjarni implicitly established a land claim to the land he had discovered, just as Eirik the Red had established a claim to the whole of Greenland by his landing there. In this can be seen the motivation in insisting that he did not land. The saga writers or their sources seem determined to deprive him of this claim. The reason becomes clear in the subsequent action of Leif Eiriksson. Leif visited Bjarni in Herjolfsnes, 15 years after Bjarni's voyage. In those years Bjarni had not returned to America, so any claim he had to that land, while legal in terms of Norse custom, was not being exploited. Rather he had worked developing his father's farm, and trading with Norway, both presumably more profitable than an unknown land further to the west. He still had his ship, and presumably this ship had now made a dozen or more annual return trips to Norway and was old. Leif negotiated with Bjarni, and according to the sagas he bought this ship. Doubtless this is correct; I suggest that in doing this he additionally bought out Bjarni's land-claim to America. The stated reason for wanting Bjarni's ship was that it was a lucky talisman and that the ship itself would know the way to America. This is fine as a saga story, but the Viking mariners of Greenland knew that navigation required more skill than luck, and were well aware of the limitations of a ship as old as Bjarni's.

The second voyage to America, and the first official European landing on the continent of America, took place in Bjarni's boat, captained by Leif Eiriksson, and with a crew of 35 Greenlanders, including two Irishmen. Leif's first voyage is usually dated 1000, though the sources allow for a year or two of flexibility either side. Leif deliberately retraced Bjarni's steps, and thus encountered the three lands sighted by Bjarni.

The first, west across the Davis Strait from the Greenland settlements, he called Helluland, or Slab Land. There is general agreement that this name applies to Baffin Island, whose slabs of exposed rock make this an obvious descriptive name. The second, a few days' sail to the south, is Markland, or Forest Land. This is described as a land with a low coast and extensive forests. The description fits southern Labrador and Newfoundland, and the identification of this land with Markland has again received general agreement. South again is Vinland, described as a fertile land with good pasture and timber, and where wild grapes grew. Countless scholars and amateurs have attempted to place Vinland, and with a remarkable range of different locations proposed.

Ultimately, attempts to locate Helluland, Markland and Vinland seem to work better on a modern map than they would in reality. The equation of Helluland with Baffin Island is too simple. Baffin Island has an east coast which extends around 800 miles, and that so deeply indented as to treble the miles of actual coastline. For the first Vikings there was no way of knowing that this was a discrete entity, one island. Indeed two indentations on the east coast of Baffin Island – Frobisher Bay and Cumberland Sound – are so vast that the land they divide appeared to later European mariners as if completely different lands. Frobisher Bay is named after the sixteenth-century explorer Martin Frobisher who believed it to be the entrance of the Northwest Passage. That Helluland was a name for a part of Baffin Island is a reasonable assumption; that it was the name for the whole of what we now know to be one island is not. The second name from the sagas, Markland, is plausibly identified with southern Labrador – though identification with the island of Newfoundland is equally possible. In order to follow the sailing directions set out in the sagas it is necessary to sail from Baffin Island across the mouth of Hudson Strait and along the coast of north Labrador. This intervening, treeless land could hardly have been called Markland, yet must have had a name which has not been remembered.

In the land he called Vinland, Leif established a series of booths – temporary shelters made with turf or stone walls and roughly roofed with whatever temporary roofing materials are available. The term is familiar from Thingvellir in Iceland, where the representatives attending the parliament set up booths as summer shelters for the duration of the parliament. Leif overwintered in Vinland, at a place he called Leifsbudir, noting that the winter there was exceptionally mild, and in the spring he set out for Greenland with a cargo of timber, as well as something which the saga writers identify as grapes. En route to Greenland Leif rescued 15 Vikings from a ship he encountered wrecked on a reef, a remarkable case of being in the right place at the right time which earned him the nickname 'the Lucky'. Perhaps the incident should indicate that even as early as 1001 the waters off the coast of Greenland were busy with many Viking ships, so that there was a realistic chance of shipwrecked mariners finding a passing ship to rescue them.

The third voyage was led by Leif's brother Thorvald, with a crew of 30. The sagas do not date the voyage, but the context makes the following summer – 1002 – seem likely. Thorvald went direct to Leifsbudir and set up his camp there, which was occupied for two summers and the intervening winter, presumably 1002–1003. During this time Thorvald undertook an orderly exploration both north and south, building on the exploration accomplished by his brother, Leif. It was Thorvald who first encountered the Native American people.

The encounter is a key moment in human history. Millennia of human dispersal had brought the ancestors of the Native Americans from Asia across the Bering Strait, possibly over a land bridge or more probably simply over the winter sea ice. From Siberia, Asiatic peoples crossed to America in three great waves, and colonised the whole of the American continent. Their eastward movement brought some ultimately to the east of the continent, the shore of the Atlantic. By contrast it was a westward drive from Asia that had brought the ancestors of the Vikings to Scandinavia, then in the Viking Age another westward drive had led across the stepping stones of the North Atlantic, until around the year 1002 east met west in America, a remarkable meeting which signified that the human race had circled the globe. The first encounter was unhappy. The Vikings felt they were being attacked – perhaps indeed they were being attacked – and killed eight of the Native Americans. Subsequently the Native Americans attacked Leifsbudir, and among the Vikings Thorvald was killed, according to the sagas the first European to die in America. As a convert to Christianity he was buried with crosses set up both at his head and feet, and the headland on which he was buried was named after these crosses Krossanes.

Following the return of Thorvald's crew to Greenland the fourth of the Vinland voyages was planned. This set out presumably the next summer, therefore in 1004, and was led by Thorstein, another of Leif's brothers. Thorstein attempted the direct route to Vinland which Thorvald had used, but because of storms and adverse winds failed to reach Vinland, instead returning to Greenland. He and his crew suffered from exposure, and he died in Greenland a few months later. His widow Gudrid married a merchant, Thorfinn Thordarson Karlsefni, and it is this Karlsefni who made the fifth Vinland voyage.

Karlsefni is no blood relative of Leif – rather he is Leif's brother's widow's new husband – and Leif does not accord him the same support he has previously given his brothers. The sagas record that Leif lends Karlsefni the Vinland property of Leifsbudir. These booths were of negligible value; rather in this gesture we should see that Leif is agreeing with Karlsefni a lease on the land of Vinland which Leif considers to be his property. Karlsefni travelled with 60 men, five women and livestock, with the intention of founding a colony. This is the model of the colonisation of Greenland begun a generation earlier, and in Karlsefni's day still ongoing. Attractive through Greenland was, the best farming sites were already becoming full, and a new territory in Vinland was of interest to colonists.

Karlsefni's voyage is not dated precisely, though it could hardly have been before 1005, and may have been a few years later. The colony was successfully founded at Leifsbudir, and the group over-wintered there. In the spring they had their first encounter with the Native Americans, which was peaceful. The sagas are not works of anthropology, yet they do give many scraps of information about the North American people encountered. The Vikings call them simply skraelings – literally wretches, perhaps in this usage cognate in meaning with Kipling's savages. There is enough information for us to make at least a tentative identification between the people described in the sagas and a tribe of the Algonquin Indians. Physically the people described have black hair and broad cheekbones, certainly correct for the Algonquin Indians. A staple of Algonquin diet was pemmican, while the sagas describe the skraelings as eating deer marrow mixed with blood, an accurate description of pemmican. The Skraelings have a weapon which appears to be the ballista of the Algonquins. The ballista is a heavy rock placed in a skin bag and tied to a pole. This device was used sling-shot fashion to catapult the rock at the enemy. Trade between Vikings and the Algonquins is described, whereby the Vikings gained furs, trading for them small strips of red cloth and measures of milk. Possibly the Algonquins regarded the exchanges as presents to establish friendship, for if this were truly trade, the Algonquins did very poorly from it.

The first meeting of Karlsefni's group with the Native Americans was peaceful, but it nonetheless prompted Karlsefni to build a defensive palisade. The brief description in the sagas suggests that Karlsefni was following a policy of 'ness-taking', the familiar Viking technique for establishing a bridgehead on a hostile coast which was to fortify the tip of a headland. Their ship would have been pulled up on a beach immediately below the headland. The palisaded area of the farmstead would have been tiny, for the intention was for the defensive wall to be held by the 60 or so settlers. Grazing for cattle and sheep was outside the wall, as were the farmed fields. This describes the very beginnings of what the colonists intended to be a permanent settlement. In the summer a son was born to Karlsefni and Gudrid, named Snorri, whom the sagas describe as the first Viking to be born in Vinland. There is no reason to doubt this story; around 1,000 years ago the first ethnic European was born on the American mainland.

In the autumn there were two further encounters with the Native Americans. At the first of these the Native Americans came to trade, offering furs. However something went wrong, and one of the Native Americans was killed. Shortly afterwards the Native Americans attacked, and a battle ensued. The Vikings had had sufficient notice of the attack to bring their bull within the palisade, presumably along with all their animals. The story told in the sagas is that the noise of battle caused the bull to bellow, and this huge and noisy animal terrified the Native Americans, who fled. While the attackers had been repulsed, the settlers were clearly unnerved by the encounter. It was too late in the year for Karlsefni to risk a voyage to Greenland so the colony overwintered at Leifsbudir, but in the spring they took the decision to abandon the settlement. They sailed first to Greenland, then to Norway, where Karlsefni sold his cargo of furs. Karlsefni's fame and fortune was made on the basis of his one cargo of American furs, the like of which had never before been seen in Europe. He established his home in Iceland, where ultimately he died. His widow, Gudrid, subsequently made a pilgrimage to Rome, and there gave an account direct to the Pope – still extant – of her journeys across the North Atlantic and to Vinland.[3] She returned to Iceland, and many years later died there, being remembered by the apt name Gudrid the Far-Travelled. Her son Snorri, born in Vinland, stands at the head of many Icelandic genealogies, and is the grandfather of two bishops and the ancestor of many of the Icelandic nobles of the High Middle Ages.

The sixth and final voyage to Vinland, as recorded in the sagas, was a horror story. This voyage was led by yet another relative of Leif's, this time his sister, Freydis. The voyage had two ships, one led by Freydis and crewed with 35 Greenlanders, some of them presumably veterans of Karlsefni's voyage; the other was an Icelandic ship with a crew of 30, and led by the brothers Helgi and Finnbogi. Both Greenlanders and Icelanders travelled as the nucleus of a colony with their wives and their livestock. The expedition again asserted Leif's claim to the land of Vinland through the leadership of his sister and the Greenlandic ship, yet the resources to back the expedition seem to have come from the Icelanders. The saga sets out that the two groups were antagonistic from the outset, and perhaps with inadequate resources to support them all. Ultimately under the leadership of Freydis, the Greenlanders decided upon the cold-blooded murder of the Icelanders. The saga gives no reasonable cause; today we may speculate that a dispute over ownership of Vinland might be a motive, perhaps exacerbated by shortage of food. The Icelandic men were indeed all murdered, but the Greenlanders refused to kill the women. The saga recounts that Freydis herself then murdered all the Greenlandic women. Following this bloodbath the depleted colony struggled through the winter before returning to Greenland. Freydis attempted to swear the Greenlanders to secrecy, but inevitably the story was told. The saga records Leif's horror, and states that Freydis was afterwards shunned.

These six voyages stand at the very start of the Vinland exploration, when it was effectively Icelanders who were taking part in them.

The Location of Vinland

While Helluland and Markland do seem to be relatively precise locations, Vinland is something rather different. The *Icelandic Geographical Treatise* of about 1300 – based on an earlier manuscript, now lost – sets out a geography of the North Atlantic, which includes the following brief mention:

> To the south of Greenland lies Helluland, and then Markland,
> and from there it is not far to Vinland, which some people
> think extends from Africa.

This anonymous Icelandic writer was aware of the circumference of the earth and knew that whatever Vinland might be, it could not possibly be part of Asia. The curious concept that Vinland might extend all the way to Africa indicates the size which the geographer attributed to Vinland. Vinland is not a precise location for a single place, but rather a name associated with Leif Eiriksson's land claim, which was as expansive as his ambitions. The writer of the *Geographical Treatise* is suggesting that Vinland is a continent – effectively therefore America.

The saga-writers describe what they believe was the finding of wild grapes in Vinland, and the Vikings cutting down the bushes on which the grapes grew and hanging them from the rigging of their ship for the return journey. The story sounds wrong – if grape vines were hung from the rigging of the ships the grapes would simply fall off. The sagas do not suggest that the Vikings made wine from these grapes. Probably for the Vikings in Leif's party grapes would have been valued simply as a food, as were the many berries of Greenland, but no special value above this would have attached to them. The identification of these New World berries as grapes belongs not to Leif but to the later saga-writers, whose Christian culture placed great value on communion wine (often in short supply in Iceland) and therefore on viticulture and grapes. A curious possibility is that stories of finding another berry were altered by the saga-writers. Found in profusion on the coasts of New England are gooseberry bushes, producing a berry with a superficial resemblance to a grape. Anyone who has picked gooseberries will know that the bushes have a profusion of thorns, and the concept of transporting such a prickly cargo for a day or two by tying it to the rigging and therefore out of the way of a crowded deck may at least make sense. Gooseberries, unlike grapes, hold firmly to their plant.

The supposed derivation of Vinland as 'Wine-Land' in this saga story and elsewhere has led many to believe that we should look to identify Vinland with an area where wild grapes grow. Wild grapes do indeed grow in woods in the east of America from as far north as New Brunswick, through New England, and south as far as Florida. In the north they are unusual, and in no area do they grow in the sort of profusion that would be expected if they were the source of the name. Indeed the only reason we say Vinland means 'Wine-Land' is that this is what the saga-writers tell us it means.

The traditional derivation of Vinland as 'Wine-Land' is suspect, and almost certainly wrong. Rather, *vin* is a well-established Old Norse word, and a very common place-name element. Looking just at larger settlements which follow the form of Vinland with *vin* as the first element, Norway has Vinnelys, Vinstra, and Vinje (twice); Sweden has Vingaker and Vinlinden; Denmark has Vinblaes. The meaning of *vin* is fertile land or arable land. By calling the land Vinland Leif is stressing that it is good land for farming, exactly what the Vikings were looking for.

Vinland did not, therefore, have a precise location. It was a descriptive term for fertile land which was used for a wide area of the east coast of America.

Viking Archaeology in Newfoundland

The one big Viking archaeological site in North America at L'Anse aux Meadows dates from the beginning of the period of Viking America, and is more or less contemporary with the saga stories.

L'Anse aux Meadows stands on the northern tip of the island of New-foundland. The French name for the modern community of around 70 people has been anglicised by the English-speaking residents of the area, and it is now pronounced 'Lancy Meadows'. The discovery of Viking remains was made in 1961 by husband-and-wife team Helge Ingstad and Anne Stine, explorers and archaeologists, who were cruising the east coast of America looking for confirmation of the Icelandic sagas. What they found has proved beyond any doubt that Vikings lived in North America, though their discoveries cannot be directly related to the saga stories of Vinland or to Leifs-budir, a point that has frequently been overlooked. What we have at L'Anse aux Meadows is not Viking Vinland, but Viking Markland.

The Ingstads' discovery at L'Anse aux Meadows was one that was ready to be made. The community there had long been curious about the regular-shaped mounds in their vicinity, which appeared different from Native American constructions in the area, and it is local people who directed the Ingstads to them. Immediately visible were the remains of five buildings – the number now increased by more detailed study. The first season of excavation by the Ingstads, with villagers recruited to dig trenches, confirmed that they were old, and convinced them that they were indeed Viking. The scholarly community required more proof, and as a result the site has been worked over subsequently by numerous teams of archaeologists, keen both to extract all possible information and to prove beyond any possible doubt that these buildings are indeed Viking. The Ingstads themselves excavated on the site for a further seven summers, until 1968, and work has been virtually non-stop since then. This site is accepted by all as undisputed proof that the Vikings visited. Today it is looked after by Parks Canada, and there is a reconstruction of some of the buildings adjacent to the site itself.

The Viking community at L'Anse aux Meadows was located on a low terrace a few hundred yards back from Epaves Bay, and close to a small river, the Black Duck Brook. Five houses have been found, three of which are standard Viking longhouses, the other two smaller. Additionally there is a workshop, a charcoal kiln, a forge, at least four boat sheds, and a bath-house, as well as a cluster of cooking pits. Nearby are four cairns, two in fair condition still. The site contains a natural deposit of bog iron, which appears to be the reason for the existence of this settlement. With bog iron and charcoal to power a forge, the Vikings were able to produce the iron rivets essential for the maintenance of their ships. The buildings were made of turf, using a construction technique familiar particularly from Iceland and the Faroe Islands, though rarely encountered in Greenland because of the lack of turf there.

L'Anse aux Meadows was used for about 20 years, from roughly 1000 to 1020. It therefore tells a story which is concurrent with *The Vinland Sagas*, and may take the story on for a few more years.

The site raises very many questions. First of all this is not Leifsbudir, or anywhere precisely identified in the sagas. Leifsbudir consisted of booths and later no more than two houses, and at no time had more than two ships there. Leifsbudir had a palisade for defence, which L'Anse aux Meadows does not. The northern tip of Newfoundland does not resemble the saga description of a fertile Vinland, and its winters could not be described, as the sagas do, as being exceptionally mild. Nothing about L'Anse aux Meadows fits the description of Leifsbudir.

The immediate area has land which would have provided grazing, and is one of the more fertile spots in the vicinity. A bone from a domestic pig has been identified, proving that the Vikings brought at least pigs, and presumably also sheep and perhaps other domestic animals. It is a place where much driftwood is naturally deposited, though it is doubtful whether this could have been sufficient for the activity there. The nearest woodland is around eight miles away, but this does not produce trees remarkable for their height. While their wood could have been used for the manufacture of charcoal, larger timbers would have required voyages to forests with taller trees, which are some distance away. The site is not defensive. The area may have been uninhabited when the Vikings arrived. Later it supported an Inuit population rather than any other indigenous people, a group with whom the Vikings seemed able to coexist. It offered a useful deposit of bog iron, though the geology of Newfoundland is such that this is no rarity. Rather L'Anse aux Meadows appears to have owed its existence to its location. Situated at the very tip of Newfoundland it served three sea routes. To the north a route runs up the coast of Labrador, then across the Davis Strait to Greenland. To the south-west the Strait of Belle Isle leads to the Gulf of St Lawrence, while to the south-east stretches the coast of insular Newfoundland.

The boat sheds were roofed, and each accommodated boats of up to a maximum length of around 30 feet. These are boats, not ships – they are not the size of the ocean-going *knarrs*, and were suitable only for use in coastal waters. The Vikings presumably used them for short-distance voyages around the northern tip of Newfoundland island and across the Belle Isle strait to Labrador. That provision for such ships exists suggests frequent use of these short-distance routes. Larger ships – the ocean-going *knarrs* – could have been pulled ashore, though there is no direct evidence of them. The presence of sheds for four boats suggests a fleet of boats putting into L'Anse aux Meadows, and a substantial community there.

The houses are large structures, able to accommodate in total upwards of 100 people, and perhaps on occasion as many as 200. They are supported by a collection of cooking pits, suggesting communal cooking on a large scale. The bath-house is of the type familiar today from the Finnish sauna. The water supply is from a man-made channel. The remains do not directly show the means of heating the water – probably it was in an iron cauldron hanging from a chain over an open fire – but they do contain numerous burnt stones. In Finnish style, the Vikings seem to have heated these stones in the fire, then poured water on them, creating clouds of steam. A slate seems to have been used to close the smoke hole, enabling the sauna to reach very high temperatures.

The settlement was used for no more than 20 or so years. The style of turf building is such that in the climate of Newfoundland they would have needed replacing after around 20 years, and at L'Anse aux Meadows this was not done. The abandonment of L'Anse aux Meadows was planned, which is archaeologically disappointing because it leads to rather few artefacts. Almost anything that was left by chance would have been removed over the centuries by the Inuit. The more interesting artefacts that do survive include a soapstone spindle whirl, a ring-headed bronze pin, and a needle hone, all characteristically Viking for the period, and all everyday objects. The spindle whirl demonstrates that weaving was taking place, which can probably be regarded as proof that women were present, weaving seemingly an occupation that Viking men did not take part in. The ring-headed pin would have been used to fasten clothing. Additional items include bone fragments, including whale bone, iron rivets for ships, fire-strikers of jasper, iron pyrites and flint, slag from the kiln and some unidentifiable iron fragments.

Dating has been made using carbon-14. The occupation dates of *c*. 1000 to *c*. 1020 have come to be well accepted, though radiocarbon, in fact, permits a date before 1000. Should it be possible to confirm this early date, there will be a need to re-evaluate the saga stories.

It is noteworthy that these Viking archaeological finds are very close to the date of the voyages in the sagas, but tell a story which is substantively different. While the sagas tell of just six voyages in six different years under different, named leaders and imply that these were the only voyages, the archaeological finds point to many dozens, even hundreds of voyages.

The purpose of the site is still not properly understood, even after years of intensive activity. Most plausibly it was a way-station for Viking voyagers, where it was possible to repair ships, stock up on supplies, spend time ashore and even over-winter. With accommodation for 100–200 people, many of them making just brief visits while passing through en route to somewhere else, L'Anse aux Meadows was visited by thousands of Vikings, perhaps even tens of thousands. Again the contrast with the small numbers implied by the sagas is marked.

No cemetery has been found at L'Anse aux Meadows, and in view of the work that has gone into looking for one it seems reasonable to conclude that there is not one there. Burial at sea was occasionally practised by the Vikings, but usually for disposing of the bodies of people who died while on long voyages in ships which had a full cargo. We know for example that at least one of the prospective first settlers of Eirik the Red's Greenland died on the voyage from Iceland to Greenland, and with nowhere to put the body on a ship laden with people, animals and the raw materials for starting a colony, her body was put overboard. Yet this means of disposal was sufficiently unusual for a rune-stone to be erected to her memory in Greenland, as a focus for grief.

It is possible that on occasions Vikings at L'Anse aux Meadows carried out what are termed ship burials for their dead – strictly ship cremations – yet this can only have been the case for very wealthy individuals. There are records of early Germanic kings being cremated in a ship which was set adrift and set on fire, so that it burnt to the water-line, then sank. The Old English poem *Beowulf* gives a description of this style of funeral, while stressing that it was the funeral of a king. In England at Sutton Hoo we have an interment of an East Anglian king's ashes within a ship which was subsequently buried – a curious mix of a traditional ship-cremation and a land burial. Ship burial anywhere in the Germanic world was rare. The cost of a ship was great, and its wilful destruction infrequent. When it did happen it was as much a symbolic act for a community asserting its identity as the disposal of one body, and a distant echo of this community act is found even today in the Shetland Islands. Every January in Shetland a Viking ship is set alight during Up-Helly-Aa, a festival redolent with Viking spirit by which the Shetlanders assert and celebrate their Viking heritage.

Ship burial at L'Anse aux Meadows, if it happened at all, must have been very rare. By a process of elimination the bodies of people who died at L'Anse aux Meadows must have been taken somewhere else for burial, either a putative settlement somewhere in the vicinity, or perhaps back to Greenland. L'Anse aux Meadows was not regarded as a permanent settlement, and therefore not a suitable place to bury the dead.

The reason for abandonment is similarly uncertain. In part there is an obvious motive in the decay of the turf-built buildings. Turf has a short life, calculated in the Newfoundland climate to be around 20 years, and there is no practical way to repair decaying turf buildings. Rather, they have to be rebuilt. Iceland is full of sites where successive generations have built farms adjacent to one another, and this is a frequent model. But so too is the system of relocating a settlement when its buildings need replacement. In the case of L'Anse aux Meadows, 20 years of depletion of timber in the vicinity and the resultant need to make ever-longer voyages for wood would have been a powerful spur to moving the settlement. The simplest explanation is that L'Anse aux Meadows was rebuilt some miles away, and perhaps a future archaeologist may identify such a site, or even a series of sites for successive settlements.

That L'Anse aux Meadows is not mentioned in the sagas gives us warning that they are selective, telling a limited range of stories that were of interest to Icelanders. This one location was visited by thousands of Vikings at very much the time of the Vinland voyages, yet the sagas are completely silent about it. We cannot rely on them. We certainly cannot extrapolate significance from the non-mention of something in the sagas. The sagas are stories to entertain Icelanders, and anyway only a fraction of what there once was has been preserved.

L'Anse aux Meadows is – so far – the sole Viking settlement to have been identified on the mainland of North America. Implicitly, many writers have suggested that this is because it was the only one. This thinking does not stand up to examination. The British Isles once contained thousands of Viking settlements. Many of them can be identified by their Norse names, which are still used, or in early written records, but very few Viking buildings have been identified through archaeological remains. There are two major exceptions (the Viking remains excavated in York and Dublin) and there are scattered traces of Viking buildings in the Northern and Western Isles of Scotland. Physical remains of Viking buildings in the British Isles are very rare, despite Viking presence in great numbers for three centuries, including a period when

The Gokstad Ship, a ninth-century ship in the Viking Ship Museum, Oslo. In 1893 a replica of this ship crossed the Atlantic from Bergen to Newfoundland, and sailed on to the Great Lakes.

Above. Viking Figurehead. A replica from Unst Boat Haven, Shetland.

Top right. Viking Ship's Rivet. One of the most common archaeological finds from the Viking period.

Middle right. Thingvellir. The Althing in session, as imagined by William G. Collingwood in this 1875 painting.

Right. The Icelandic Sagas. This picture, from the fourteenth-century *Flateyjarbok*, now in the Arni Magnusson Institute, Iceland, shows King Harald I Fairhair receiving the Shetlands.

Top. Green Greenland. This summer view in the vicinity of Kangerlussuaq demonstrates the appropriateness of the name Greenland.

Above. L'Anse aux Meadows. View of the reconstructed Viking buildings.

Right. The Skalholt Map. Universally acknowledged as a genuine Icelandic map showing Vinland, it is fitting that it should be commemorated on this 1967 postage stamp.

The Vinland Map.

Top. Narwhals.

Above left. Unicorn. A frequent theme of European art in the fifteenth century. This tapestry of *The Maiden and the Unicorn* is in the Musée de Cluny, Paris.

Above right. The Kensington Runestone.

Right. Viking Strap End (tenth century from East Anglia, England). This is typical of the many small metal detector finds from Europe and perhaps from America.

Left. Hans Egede (1686–1758), the missionary to Greenland.

Below. The Greenland or Whale Fishery. The eighteenth-century concept of Greenland is illustrated by this engraving, from a picture of about 1740 attributed to Thomas Baston.

Bottom. *Magna Britannia* by Petrus Bertius. This map of 1616 shows the tiny island of Rona situated off the north-west coast of Scotland.

Left. Newport Tower. Newport, Rhode Island.

Left. Sun Voyager. Jon Gunnar Arnason's sculpture on Reykjavik's Saebraut captures the spirit of adventure which took the Vikings to America.

the Vikings ruled. With a dense population, no areas that can be considered inaccessible, hundreds of years of antiquarian interest and decades of archaeological survey, Britain has been searched with a fine-tooth comb, and yet little has been found in the way of Viking sites. The reason is simple: the Vikings preferred to build from timber, and with rare exceptions timber does not last 1,000 years. L'Anse aux Meadows is situated in an area where timber of a size needed for building was not readily found, prompting building in turf, which is more durable. In addition, the climate and the sparse human settlement in the area have encouraged preservation. It cannot be argued, as some have tried to do, that because we haven't discovered Viking settlements further south they weren't there. Rather, L'Anse aux Meadows had special features which promoted preservation which would not have been present in timber-built structures further south.

The great numbers of people who passed through L'Anse aux Meadows is remarkable. Viking Greenland at its peak supported perhaps 5,000 people. At the time of the Vinland voyages and L'Anse aux Meadows the Greenland population was smaller – almost smaller than the number of people who passed through L'Anse aux Meadows. The resolution of this puzzle comes within the concept of a highly mobile Greenland population. For Greenland, travel was essential for survival. America offered the timber essential for the colony; Greenland offered farmland in an area that was without an indigenous population, and therefore safe. A reasonable hypothesis is that every community in Greenland was sending a ship to America every year for the duration of the Greenland colony. Evidence for this process is seen at L'Anse aux Meadows.

The Maine Penny

The only undisputed Viking artefact to be found south of L'Anse aux Meadows and within the borders of the USA is the so-called Maine penny. From a dig at a Native American site at Naskeag Point, Penobscot Bay, Maine, a Viking coin was found within the context of a site dated 1180–1235. The coin itself is a Norwegian silver penny, of a sort produced in great numbers and frequently encountered in digs in Europe. It dates from the reign of King Olaf Kyrre (1065–1080), but along with most silver coins was circulated for very many years afterwards, certainly including the period 1180–1235. The identification of the coin is beyond doubt, as is its location within a dated archaeological context.

The simplest explanation of this coin is that the Vikings brought it to that location. The site is by the sea, and in a place that could reasonably have been reached by the Vikings. If it had been found in a European site there would have been little question that it indicated Viking presence there, and this is indeed the most likely explanation for the presence of the Maine penny. However, a higher level of proof is demanded for American Viking finds, and an alternative explanation can indeed be suggested. It is possible that the coin was not brought there by Vikings, but was traded overland from somewhere far to the north, perhaps Labrador or Baffin Island. Finds from the site have been examined to explore the possibility that items were traded from the north, and it has been suggested that one artefact might possibly be from the Dorset Culture, and therefore from Baffin Island. This is just about possible, but the identification of this artefact – a *burin*, or flake of stone with a chisel edge – is problematic, and it is a remarkable claim that an item of scant value would have been traded from Baffin Island to Maine. The support this artefact gives to the idea of trade from Baffin Island is slight. The Viking silver penny would have had no intrinsic value to Native American people, though it may well have been a curiosity. Of course, it is possible that it was traded across many hundreds of miles and through different indigenous cultures, but this is not likely.

The finding of a penny in Maine in a well-dated archaeological context does not absolutely prove beyond all doubt that the Vikings were definitely in Maine, but this is by far the simplest explanation.

The Vinland Map

No account of the Vikings in America can avoid an assessment of the Vinland Map. This is either one of the great documents of Western civilisation, or a very clever fake. At the time of writing the pendulum has swung firmly in the direction of it being a fake, but scholarly views have changed so many times that there can be no certainty that it will not one day come to be regarded as genuine. The traditional disciplines of the humanities tend to favour the view that it is genuine, while recent scientific analysis tends to the view that it is a fake. Neither discipline can produce a conclusive result, though the twenty-first century has considerable faith in the powers of the scientists, and the respectable academic view is to assert the primacy of the scientists' opinions.

The map was discovered in 1957. It was bought by Yale University, which formally pronounced it genuine in 1965, and it remains there, though in recent years it has not been on public display, presumably reflecting the embarrassment at seemingly being duped by a forgery. The announcement that the map was genuine, made on Columbus Day 1965, offended Hispanic sensibilities to the extent that it provoked a serious riot on the streets of Yale's home town, New Haven, Connecticut. In a nutshell the announcement set out the view that the Vinland Map is a fifteenth-century world map showing part of the coast of North America, as well as Greenland and Iceland, and containing the name Vinland. Two great inlets are shown into the coast of America, one apparently Hudson Strait with the inland sea of Hudson Bay, and the other the St Lawrence River. Thus the Vinland Map, if accepted, would be a most remarkable document. If genuine, the map demonstrates European knowledge of the existence of North America and some features of its geography around 70 years before the Columbus voyage. However, over the years the most severe doubts have been expressed as to the map's authenticity.

If the map is genuine, it is assumed to have emerged from the Nazi looting of libraries and archives towards the end of the Second World War, and therefore to be a document which had lain unclassified for centuries in one of the many manuscript repositories of Europe, probably in Italy. Its owner, who introduced it to the world in 1957, was Enzo Ferrajoli, an Italian manuscript dealer and a known rogue, who later served a prison sentence in Spain for stealing manuscripts from a library there – perhaps the sort of person who may have acquired some Nazi war loot, or indeed who may have been involved in passing off a fake as a genuine document.

When the map was first presented to the scholarly world it was as an unbound document, though it was clear from binding marks that the map had once been bound within a book. Subsequently, two manuscript books appeared on the market, both believed to originate from Ferrajoli, and which are produced from the same parchment, with the same watermark, and with the same style of handwriting. Worm holes in these two books and the Vinland Map match up, demonstrating that they were once bound together. The two books are the *Tartar Relation* and the *Speculum Historiale*, neither of which bear a direct relationship to the Vinland Map or to one another (a situation very common in mediaeval binding, where two or more items were often bound together in order to economise on binding), though a world map would complement the *Tartar Relation*. Presumably Ferrajoli separated the three in order to gain a greater price than he thought possible through selling the three together. However the support that the

Tartar Relation and the *Speculum Historiale* give to the Vinland Map, and therefore to its value, is such that the decision seems to be self-defeating. It might seem that Enzo Ferrajoli did not realise quite what he had in the Vinland Map.

The handwriting of all three documents is a particular style, known to handwriting specialists as *Oberrheinisch Bastarda* – Upper Rheinland Cursive – a style used in the first half of the fifteenth century. *Oberrheinisch Bastarda* had a wide distribution in Germany and Switzerland, as well as being common in Flanders and eastern France, and in northern Italy. Some have sought to identify the handwriting specifically with documents produced for the Council of Basle in 1440, and while this attribution is plausible, it is far from proved. It is very likely that all three manuscripts were written by the same scribe. While seeking to weigh up the likelihood of the Vinland Map being a forgery it is important to note that no-one has ever been able to suggest that the *Tartar Relation* and *Speculum Historiale* are forgeries – if the Vinland Map is fake it has been produced specifically to correspond with these two genuine volumes.

The Latin of the Vinland Map passes examination. There are no faults in the mediaeval Latin. The form used for Iceland is *Isolanda*, which is the Italian word for Iceland, and which suggests an Italian scribe. Leif Eiriksson appears on the map as *leiphus erissonius*, which is an acceptable Latin formation, but seems to suggest that the scribe was unaware that the *-son* is a patronymic. Vinland appears as *Vinilanda* rather than being translated (as 'Land of Vines', *Terra Labruscarum*). There is no ready explanation for the intrusive *-i-* in *Vinilanda*. The language is consistent with a scribe who is familiar with Latin, probably an Italian, and who does not know Icelandic, therefore exactly what we would expect.

The map shows Greenland and Vinland as islands. This is, of course, accurate for Greenland, and wrong for America. The coast of Vinland is imperfectly drawn – as would be expected at the time. However Greenland is seen by some as very accurate, perhaps too accurate. That Greenland is an island was not known until the late eighteenth century, and no-one has ever suggested that the Vikings could have known this. This issue is subject to an easy solution. The mediaeval mind conceived of the land as islands floating in the ocean. The three old-world continents of Europe, Africa and Asia were seen as centred on Jerusalem, more or less where they joined, and completely surrounded by ocean. Lands off the coast of these three continents, as Britain and Iceland and the Azores and Japan, were clearly shown as islands. To the mediaeval mind, Greenland and Vinland had to be islands, and showing them as such is wholly appropriate. The Vikings had knowledge of the coast of west Greenland and part of the east Greenland coast. In effect the map shows these two coasts and draws a hypothetical line to the north – by chance sketching out something close to the real shape of Greenland. The whole of the map, with the exception of the inclusion of Vinland, is what we would reasonably expect for a world map of that date. Were the Vinland Map without Vinland it would have been accepted as a *bona fide* map of the world.

Traditional disciplines do, therefore, favour the case for the Vinland Map being genuine. Though in the 1960s the British Museum refused to give a view on the issue, numerous respected bodies at that time confidently asserted that the map was genuine – and with good reason. The parchment is contextualised with two other manuscripts, the palaeography, cartography and language all correct. The great problem is the lack of a proper provenance for the map – the underlying reason for the British Museum's caution – yet there is nothing implausible about a manuscript lying unopened and unclassified in a European archive, and coming to light through the disruption of the Second World War.

In the past 20 years numerous scientific examinations have alternately proved the Vinland Map genuine and a fake. The parchment was dated in the early 1990s by carbon-14 using an 8cm strip cut from the bottom right-hand corner of the map, providing a sample with a surface area of about $2cm^2$, with the results published in 2002 after the scholarly community had kept silent about them for nearly a decade. The result of carbon-14 dating is that the parchment dates to 1425, with just a small margin for error, which is exactly the date it should be if the map is genuine. However the test was conducted three times, with two of the results obscured by contaminants from the 1950s. What carbon-14 tells us is that we have a parchment which dates from around 1425, but which has undergone a process in the 1950s which has created considerable contamination. Indeed the weight of the 1950s contaminant is somewhat greater than the weight of the original fifteenth-century parchment, so that more than half by weight of the Vinland Map today is these contaminants.

In the long silence maintained by the academic community before releasing these results a hint can be seen of the political dimension that the Vinland Map has developed. A lobby in America wants it to be fake, as if genuine it undermines the claim that Columbus was the first European in

America, and therefore offends Hispanic sensibilities. The scientists failed to gain a simple answer from carbon-14 dating of the parchment, and this was perhaps the most unwelcome result. We have a 1420s parchment with a thick layer of 1950s contaminants, and whether this proves it genuine or a fake is simply not clear.

Dating the ink has proved even more of a problem. In theory, carbon-14 could date the ink, but there is too small a quantity of ink to enable this test to be carried out. Conventional understanding suggests the type of ink. In the early fifteenth century two sorts of black ink were commonly used: India Ink and Iron Gall. India Ink has soot as its main ingredient, producing an ink which is black when first applied and which remains black over the centuries. This is not the ink used on the Vinland Map – or indeed on the *Tartar Relation* or *Speculum Historiale*. Rather the ink appears to be Iron Gall, made from the burls on oak trees, which is black when first applied, but which yellows over the years as the ink degrades, effectively rusting to Fe_2O_3. Typically, old Iron Gall ink shows today as a light brown line with yellow edges, and may corrode the parchment even to the extent of making the parchment brittle or producing holes. There does not seem to be a process for accelerating the decay of Iron Gall ink from many centuries to a very few years, and therefore no way of artificially ageing Iron Gall ink. The Vinland Map appears to use Iron Gall ink which has aged, and therefore appears to be genuine. This was once seen as one of the primary claims to the authenticity of the document. However, spectrographic analysis of the ink has produced a surprising result: the ink of the Vinland Map is not Iron Gall ink at all, but rather anatase, TiO_2, leading to the suggestion that the Vinland Map is a forgery with an anatase-based ink used to imitate Iron Gall ink. Synthetic anatase was first produced in the 1920s, and is today used as a pigment, especially in paint. It was readily available in the 1950s. Thus the spectrographic analysis seemed to prove that the map was a forgery.

The case is not quite so simple. The high profile of the Vinland Map meant that it was one of the first mediaeval manuscripts to undergo spectrographic analysis of its ink. Subsequently many other manuscripts have been analysed, and many early fifteenth-century manuscripts which had previously been thought to use Iron Gall inks have been found to be written with inks which are based on anatase. While first synthesised in the 1920s, anatase is also a naturally occurring material, and in the light of the many manuscripts now found to use an ink made from it, anatase now has to be accepted as an early fifteenth-century ink. Yet even this is not a conclusion. Anatase is a crystalline material. When produced synthetically the crystals are of a relatively even formation; when produced naturally the crystal shape is variable, but tends to be less even. A transmission electron micrograph can distinguish the shape of the crystals in the anatase of the Vinland Map, and report the result that they are relatively even, though not quite as even as most synthetic anatase. Indeed, it is possible for such even crystal structure to be found in natural anatase. The balance of probability therefore is that the anatase on the map is synthetic, but there remains a significant possibility that it is natural anatase.

If the Vinland Map is forged, it is a superb forgery. The starting point for the forgery would be to identify a manuscript of the right period with a large, blank piece of parchment bound within it. This is perhaps possible, but is not easy, as parchment was expensive and the mediaeval binders were not in the habit of including blank sheets. Additionally, a forger would need to source his parchment within a volume to which a map could plausibly be added. The actual work of forgery requires an ability to copy convincingly the handwriting of the early fifteenth century, and to produce convincing Latin for the period. It also requires a detailed knowledge of the world map of the early fifteenth century. Enzo Ferrajoli did not have the skills needed to forge it himself. Plausibly he employed a forger; plausibly he came across a forgery which he passed off as a real map, perhaps even ignorant of its real status. Very few individuals had the skills needed to make such a forgery. The skills are so rare that we might even hope to identify a possible forger. A thesis by Kirsten Seaver suggests that the forger may be Josef Fischer (1858–1944), a German Jesuit priest who had an interest in maps of this period, an interest in the Viking world, good Latin, and perhaps access to an appropriate manuscript. If the Vinland Map comes to be accepted as a forgery then Fischer is certainly the most likely suspect. By a process of complex reasoning (which I find incomprehensible), Seaver argues that Fischer may have produced the map to frustrate Hitler. It seems to me that the effect would have been the opposite. Germany in the 1930s saw the biggest-ever promotion of academic studies of the Germanic languages, literatures, cultures and histories, with a view to glorifying the achievements of the Germanic peoples, and the story of Viking – and therefore Germanic – presence in America before Columbus was of considerable interest to the Third Reich. In the 1930s – before the discovery of L'Anse aux Meadows and most of the Greenland archaeological sites – the Vikings in America lacked proof. The Vinland Map would have offered that proof, and Fischer had the skills to fake it. The weakness with this argument is, of course, one of date, for a Vinland Map faked for this reason would have been expected to be presented to the world in the 1930s.

The doubts expressed about the Vinland Map make it hard to accept as genuine. Yet when the evidence against it is considered there is only one truly telling argument, and that is in the composition of the ink. That it should be anatase is surprising; that the anatase shows a regular crystalline structure most often encountered in synthetic anatase is problematic. Nevertheless, natural anatase is now accepted as an ink used in the early fifteenth century, and the possibility that an ink was made using a natural anatase with a particularly regular crystalline structure does exist. The presence of contaminant from the 1950s on the manuscript presumably attests to interventions made by Ferrajoli, who had no concept of preserving the integrity of the artefact, as can be seen by his decision to divide it and sell it in separate lots. Quite what he might have done to the manuscript in the 1950s to introduce so much contaminant seems not to have been adequately explored. Whatever it was, it was unfortunate, but does not in itself prove the map to be a fake. The jury remains out on the Vinland Map, and while an observer of the court case will predict a guilty verdict, it is within the bounds of possibility that it will one day come to be accepted as genuine.

5
Viking Exploration of the High Arctic

On an August day in 1978 I was excavating an ancient house ruin
on a small island on the central east coast of Ellesmere Island in
the Canadian High Arctic. The collapsed sod house had been
built more than 700 years ago by Thule culture Eskimos, ancestors of all present-day Inuit in Canada and Greenland.

I was removing floor debris near a stone-lined meat pit when
my trowel struck a hard object. Carefully I brushed away the dirt
and lifted the find up to have a closer look. I could hardly believe
my eyes – in my hand I held a lump of rusted, interwoven iron
rings – pieces of mediaeval chain mail! Later in the day I was
about to reach the bottom of the meat pit when the trowel once
again struck iron – a Viking ship rivet in a thirteenth-century
house ruin in the High Arctic.

THIS is archaeologist Peter Schledermann's account of his sensational Viking
discovery.[1]

No-one in their wildest dreams could have expected to find the Vikings
on Ellesmere Island. This is the world's northernmost island. It is not just
in the Arctic, but rather in the High Arctic, in a region which experiences nearly six months of polar night and the full severity of Arctic winter
storms. From Ellesmere it is a mere 500-mile walk across the sea-ice to the
North Pole. No land on earth is closer to the Pole than is Ellesmere Island.
It seems incredible that the Vikings were here. Yet archaeological remains
prove just that.

Ellesmere Island

Ellesmere Island lies just 15 miles from north-west Greenland across the
Smith Sound. On a map it is coloured red as part of Canada, and Canada

indeed asserts sovereignty over it. Yet the right of Canada – or anywhere else – to claim ownership of this remote island is dubious. Uninhabited in the mid twentieth century and today with just a tiny, introduced population, it could be argued that it belongs to no-one. Indeed, the United States does not recognise Canada's claim to this and many other Arctic islands. Between Ellesmere Island and Greenland lies Hans Island, a sliver of land disputed by Canada and Denmark. Each year both these countries send a naval patrol boat to Hans Island, and raise their national flag. Recently the crews from the two nations have taken to leaving a cache of alcohol for their rivals to collect on their next visit. It is the very politest of border disputes, but nonetheless it is a dispute, in a land so remote and deserted that it seems beyond ownership.

Ellesmere Island is truly the end of the world. Once it was the bridge used by many of the peoples who populated Greenland on their journey from the central Canadian Arctic, but now it is simply the northernmost of the Canadian islands, the ultimate reach of supply boats and light aircraft, the northern point of the American continent. It is the historic gateway to Greenland for mankind and for animals, with a solid ice sheet across Smith Sound for most of the year, which in colder summers remains unbroken through the whole year. The island is enormous – the world's tenth largest island, almost as big as Britain, and with an area of over 75,000 square miles. Today Canada administers it through the province of Nunavut, and has designated much of the island a Canadian National Park. There is even a Canadian Mounted Police base there.

This vast island is almost uninhabited. The 2001 census records a population of 168 living in the three settlements of Alert, Eureka and Grise Fiord. Of these the first two are military and scientific bases, with no truly permanent inhabitants. Alert is the northernmost year-round human habitation in the world; Eureka, the second most northerly. Alert was built as part of the Cold War early warning system – the name echoes its function in alerting North America to incoming Soviet missiles flying over the Pole – and is still a Canadian Forces Station (CFS). Eureka, too, is a military base, with a weather station and an observatory alongside. Grise Fiord is different, being a civilian settlement of around 100 people, mainly Inuit, supplied by a once-yearly supply boat which visits in late August, and by light aircraft that fly in from Resolute, a flight of about 90 minutes. Grise Fiord is also controversial. The people living there today were resettled from locations further south by the Canadian government as a way of asserting its rule over Ellesmere Island.[2] There was no economic or cultural reason to resettle people so far north, and while the settlement has continued, and rejoices in the designation 'town', there is very little employment and seemingly little reason other than Canada's land claim for it to be there.

The lack of people on Ellesmere Island in recent years may be contrasted with a surprisingly extensive history of settlement. For thousands of years Stone Age peoples lived in Ellesmere Island. The Vikings were there. Archaeology, both of the settlements of the Arctic peoples and of the Vikings, has been exceptionally productive, and in view of the little field work that has so far been done, there is every reason to expect that much more is waiting to be discovered. Despite this legacy of millennia of settlement, history records 1616 as the year of the supposed discovery of Ellesmere Island, when William Baffin sighted the coast as part of his exploration of what we today call after him Baffin Bay. Only in 1852 did the island receive its name, in honour of Francis Egerton, the 1st Earl of Ellesmere, a patron of Sir Edward Inglefield's expedition that charted part of its coast. Thus the world's most northerly island is named after an English lord's estates in the English county of Cheshire.

Much of the island is glacier covered, though in contrast to the single ice cap of Greenland, Ellesmere Island has many smaller and distinct glaciers. Along its north coast is the Ward Hunt Ice Shelf, in parts as much as 80m thick, which abuts the frozen Arctic Ocean, providing a continuous ice bridge to the pole. It is from Ellesmere Island that many polar expeditions have set out, and from Ellesmere Island that Robert Peary made the journey that took the first man to the Pole.[3] To future generations Ellesmere Island may well be seen as one of the pivotal places in the advance of climate change, for in the summer of 2002 the Ward Hunt ice-shelf experienced a massive and unprecedented break-up in what may come to be regarded as an irreversible step on the road towards global warming.

Ellesmere Island has a remarkable local climate. The name for climates of its type is 'polar desert'. It receives on average less than 6cm of precipitation per year, which is even less than the Sahara Desert. As a consequence, the land is without a cover of snow even in midwinter. What little snow falls is blown by the wind, leaving virtually all of the unglaciated land free of snow. Because it is free from snow, Ellesmere Island may be regarded as a polar oasis. Thus, for example, in the vicinity of Eureka the summer sun remains above the horizon for 147 consecutive days, with around 70 days frost-free – the temperature comfortably above freezing for all 24 hours of the day – and there are almost as many days again which have some hours of above freezing temperatures. At Grise Bay on the south of the island late August temperatures are typically between 10°C and 15°C, and with the intensity of the polar sun it is perfectly possible to get sunburn.

In these conditions Arctic plants grow extremely well, particularly Arctic poppy, mountain aven and campion, along with sedges, lichens and moss. Without snow on the ground animals can graze year round. Musk oxen and Peary caribou are the larger grazers, once numerous, though both have suffered in the twentieth century from over-hunting. Musk oxen are now very rare, reduced to an estimated 60 animals, at long last with protection, and their population now considered stable at this low level. At the start of the twentieth century the musk oxen numbered many thousands. The Peary caribou is a dwarf form of the familiar caribou found throughout the American Arctic (and under the name reindeer in the Asian and European Arctic). Peary, after whom the animal is named, was also responsible for the start of its decline through over-hunting. There are now just a few hundred Peary caribou, with their numbers still declining. Fox, ermine, lemming and polar bears are found on Ellesmere Island. Birds are represented by around 30 nesting species, which on this most northerly of islands are all inevitably at the northernmost extreme of their range. Here can be found the gyrfalcon, the great northern diver – also known as the loon, in which guise it appears on the Canadian $1 bill – the snowy owl, the jaeger, and several species of goose and duck. The interior of Ellesmere contains remarkable Lake Hazen, one of the world's largest fresh-water lakes, surprisingly with ice-free areas for most of the year.

In the sea immediately to the south of Ellesmere Island is the North Water polynya,[4] an example of an Arctic phenomenon where warmer water from hundreds of miles away wells up, keeping an area of sea ice-free even in winter. The North Water polynya, or polynias – it may variously be regarded as one phenomenon or a series of related phenomena – is an area roughly the size of Switzerland, and has an enormous impact on the ecology of Ellesmere Island. This is one of the world's most bountiful seas, teeming with life. Among the larger mammals are polar bears, seals, walrus, beluga and narwhal; fish abound, and the expanse of open water modifies the climate of the region. This amazing feature of the far north makes the area not only habitable for man, both today's Thule Inuit and the Vikings, but also desirable in terms of the resources it offers.

On the Greenland shore facing Ellesmere Island is the Thule or Qaanaaq district of north-west Greenland, which is populated. The airport built by the USA during the Second World War was given the name Thule, echoing the name the Roman geographer Pytheas of Marseilles gave to the furthest point north in the fourth century BC. It is off-limits to visitors, and exists in a world of direct supply of everything it needs by cargo plane from the United States. Around 130 miles north is the town of Qaanaaq, the main community of the Thule Inuit, with five villages in the vicinity. These are all modern communities in terms of the infrastructure of transportation links (mainly scheduled helicopter), shops, schools and clinics, but unlike Ellesmere's Grise Fiord they are the successor to much older communities. The Thule Inuit have been occupying these lands for centuries. There are traditional occupations for the people who live there, giving them a reason to live where they do. The contrast with until recently uninhabited Ellesmere Island is striking.

Ellesmere Vikings

Ellesmere Island offered much to the Vikings. First of all, the land offered a mild climate for such a high latitude, with the ice-free sea moderating the air temperature even in the most severe winters. The Vikings would have found it an attractive spot for summer camps, while over-wintering and even settlement were possible. The seas were navigable. Baffin Bay is ice-free for the summer months, the North Water polynya ice-free year round, and the coasts of Ellesmere and Devon islands ice-free for much of the year. The land provided ample food for summer, and some food for winter. Peary caribou and musk oxen have been mainstays of the diet of later explorers as they presumably were to the Vikings; seal, narwhal and perhaps beluga and polar bear supplemented fish and seabirds. The North Water offered a bonanza.

Probably the main reason for the Vikings venturing this far north was the whales, particularly the narwhal. The whales of the area are numerous today both in terms of the number of animals and the range of species, yet in Viking times they were even more common. Great whales in these waters are today represented by the Greenland whale, the sei whale, and the humpback whale; white whales by the narwhal and the beluga whale; and toothed whales by the orca, the white-beaked dolphin, and the harbour porpoise. In Viking times the grey whale may also have been found in Ellesmere waters; it was certainly in the North Atlantic, but today the Atlantic population has been destroyed by whaling; a small population survives today in the North Pacific. The blue whale is still found in the North Atlantic though reduced to just a few hundred animals worldwide; in Viking times it was far more common in the North Atlantic and presumably ventured into Baffin Bay.

The great whales were all too big to be hunted. The blue whale is famous as the largest animal on the planet, though the Greenland whale – also called the bowhead – is very little smaller, and sei and humpback whales still enormous. Accidental strandings doubtless provided an occasional bounty, as they have done over the centuries to northern populations in Iceland, the Faroe Islands and Scotland, but the Vikings could not hunt them. The toothed whales presented special hunting problems, in that the carcass of a slaughtered toothed whale sinks, and as a consequence of its great weight cannot usually be hauled into a ship. This problem was faced by whalers of the nineteenth and twentieth centuries who learned to ignore them, concentrating instead on the great whales, which they called 'right' whales – the right whales to hunt because they do not sink.

For the Vikings two whales were particularly sought. The beluga whale, a glorious white whale, grows to around 16 feet in length, making it one of the smaller whales. It is a whale of shallow waters, eating mainly fish, which it finds close to shore and in river estuaries. Belugas are generally unconcerned at the approach of a small boat, which can come within touching distance of a beluga resting on the surface. For the Vikings it was an easy whale to hunt simply by approaching in a boat and spearing it. Its dead body floated and could be recovered. No particular skill was needed to slaughter a beluga, and the weapon was a simple spear, not a harpoon, and therefore readily to hand. While belugas can be found all along the west coast of Greenland, they are prolific in the north.

Despite the beluga's value, the real reward for Viking hunters was the narwhal. This whale is a little smaller than the beluga – growing to about 14 feet – and has a complementary distribution. Both whales are fish eaters, but while the beluga feeds in coastal waters, the narwhal usually remains in deeper waters. It was harder to hunt than the beluga because its range was not as easily accessible. However the narwhal was considered worth the effort because it has a feature unique among whales – a horn.

Narwhal horn is a specially developed tooth. Usually found only in males, a single incisor tooth in the upper jaw – usually the left one – erupts into growth as a tusk often up to 9 feet in length, and spiraled.

The tusk is ivory, and may be carved with the facility of elephant or any other ivory. Its great length represents a significant quantity of material, far more than can be harvested, for example, from a walrus. In terms of its ivory value the narwhal was much prized. Yet hunting the narwhal posed the Vikings enormous difficulties. As a deep-water whale it was encountered only well out to sea in the Davis Strait and Baffin Bay, and then only as occasional sightings. It was difficult to get close enough to kill the whale, then difficult to tow a massive cargo perhaps hundreds of miles to shore. While butchery at sea may have been possible, Viking ships were not designed for such work, and the operation would have been difficult – certainly impractical and perhaps impossible.

The one place where the narwhal could be hunted close to shore was in the North Water polynya off Ellesmere Island. Here, and uniquely here, the narwhal come close to the shore, and gather in great numbers, feasting on the bounty of this northern oasis. Here the narwhal appear to play, the males skimming the surface and fencing with their tusks. The sight is spectacular.

To the Vikings the narwhal ivory represented the most valuable item they could trade back to Europe. The spectacular spiral tusks were sold in Europe not as whale teeth, but as unicorn horns.

The unicorn is familiar to us all today from countless images, and perhaps also from stories. Few mythical beasts have entered so fully on the western consciousness, and none has the entirely positive connotations of the unicorn. Today the unicorn is represented as a creature in the form of a white horse but with the addition of a single white horn growing from its head. This is the image for example which is the heraldic beast of Scotland, and which today in Britain supports the Royal Arms.

The mediaeval world was more varied in its portrayal of the unicorn. While the horse shape is a standard feature, frequently it is adorned with the beard of a billy goat, the tail of a lion and the cloven hooves of a bull. The unicorn symbolised redemption and rebirth, and was even taken, along with the lamb, as a metaphor for Christ. The single horn was given a name – the alicorn – and attributed with healing properties, particularly the ability to neutralise poison.

The ultimate source of the unicorn is in Greek natural history, which presents the animal as actually existing, in contrast to the many fabulous beasts of Greek myth. So Ctesias in his *Indica*[5] describes the unicorn as an Indian wild ass which is fleet of foot, and has on his head a single horn a cubit and a half long (less than 3 feet), coloured white, red and black. Drinking vessels made from this horn were a preventative against poisoning. Aristotle appears to have been copying Ctesias when he describes a unicorn

simply as an 'Indian ass' (in *Historia anim.* ii.1 and *De part. anim.* iii.2).
Pliny the Elder provides a later Latin account of the unicorn, which clearly
draws on sources other than just Ctesias and Aristotle. To Pliny (*Natural
History* viii:30 and xl:106) the unicorn is an Indian ox – not an ass – and is 'a
very ferocious beast, similar in the rest of its body to a horse, with the head
of a deer, the feet of an elephant, the tail of a boar, a deep, bellowing voice,
and a single black horn, two cubits in length, standing out in the middle of
its forehead' which 'cannot be taken alive'. This is the text upon which later
views of the unicorn were ultimately based.

Pliny's remarkable animal might have become no more than a curiosity for
classicists had the animal not been taken over by the fathers of the Church as
a symbol for Christ. Tertullian, writing in AD 200, makes the earliest recorded
use of this allegory, and he is followed by Ambrose, Jerome and Basil. To the
Church Fathers, the unicorn comes to symbolise salvation and rebirth to
everlasting life, and mankind's quest for these is allegorised as the hunt for
the unicorn. To the early mediaeval world the unicorn could not be captured
by a man, but will lay his head in the lap of an honourable maiden, often considered an allegory for the Virgin Mary. Once captured by the maiden, the
unicorn can be killed by the hunters, but phoenix-like will live again.

The image presented by the Church Fathers had popular appeal within literature and art. The best preserved visual presentation is the series
of seven early renaissance Brussels tapestries now exhibited in New York's
Cloisters museum.[6] These tapestries present the stylised view of the unicorn
hunt. The final panel shows the unicorn chained to a tree, bloodied, but
very much alive, perhaps an allegory of Christ on the cross bringing everlasting life, perhaps simply an exuberant working of what was by 1500 a familiar theme. Other unicorn tapestries exist, notably the *Dame á l'alicorne*
in Paris's Cluny Museum – about the same time as those in the Cloisters
and of a similar provenance – suggesting that unicorn tapestries were a commonplace of the period. Today the unicorn is a part of our culture, an animal readily recognised by all.

When the Vikings traded narwhal horns to Europe there was ready acceptance that these were unicorn horns. Their size and spiral pattern is impressive, and it is easy to see how an age that believed in unicorns would
make the link. Europe had no comprehension of sea creatures with horns,
and readily assumed that the single horns were from land animals. Perhaps
the Viking traders did little to educate their buyers. In Denmark, unicorn
horns provided by Viking traders were used to make the royal throne, while

the Scottish court and aristocracy acquired many of the horns as curios. In both Denmark and Scotland, cups were fashioned from 'unicorn' horn and were claimed to ward off poison.

In Britain, such was the fame of the unicorn that it influenced even the translators of the Bible. Readers of the King James Bible will find a string of references to this animal: Job xxxix. 9–12; Psalms xxii. 21, xxix. 6; Numbers xxiii. 22, xxiv. 8; Deuteronomy xxxiii. 17; Psalm xcii. 11, and even a reference to the 'horns' of a unicorn. Yet every one is a mistranslation. The Hebrew word is *re'em*, which poses translational problems, but which certainly doesn't mean *unicorn*. A better translation would be *bull* or *ox*, or even *auroch*. The argument that the Hebrew word *re'em* is related to Assyrian *rimu*, meaning a *wild bull* or *mountain bull*, may well be persuasive. Yet the translators of the 1611 Authorised Version of the Bible were so convinced that the unicorn existed that they allowed it to be a translation of a Hebrew word they did not understand. The narwhal horns circulating in England provided the proof they required.

Thus the King James Bible presents a view of the unicorn as a powerful and untameable beast, as in Job xxxix: 9–12:

> Will the unicorn be willing to serve thee, or abide by thy crib? Canst thou bind the unicorn with band in the furrow? or will he harrow the valleys after thee? Wilt thou trust him, because his strength is great? Or wilt thou leave thy labour to him? Wilt thou believe him, that he will bring home thy seed, and gather it into thy barn?

Today European museums and stately homes are full of unicorn horns brought to Europe in the Middle Ages. The seas off Ellesmere Island are the only place they could have come from, providing an enduring witness to the trade the Vikings carried out from the world's northernmost island to the cultural centres of Europe. A base on Coburg Island gave ready access both to the North Water polynya and the smaller Lady Ann Strait polynya. The coasts of Coburg Island are ice-free June to October, while the polynias usually maintain open water through the winter. Its climate is moderated by the proximity of the polynias, ranging from a summer maximum of around 4°C down to a February low of -28°C – cold, but survivable. In contrast with Ellesmere Island, Coburg Island is not a desert, again reflecting the influence of the polynias.

Another island off the coast of Ellesmere is Washington Irving Island.[7] In 1875 Sir George Nares, commander of an expedition attempting to reach the Pole, visited the island and discovered two cairns there, clearly ancient. The supposition that they are Viking has been generally accepted, largely because there is no Inuit tradition of building such cairns, and it is hard to see who, other than the Vikings, could have built them. There is, however, no way of proving the age of a cairn. On nearby Norman Lockyer Island the same expedition encountered a stone-built eider duck shelter. This is described by Edward L. Moss, the ship's doctor, in his account of the voyage, *Shores of the Polar Sea*:[8]

> It consisted of four stones piled together like a miniature 'Druid's altar', so as to form a chamber large enough to shelter a nest. Generations of eider-duck had been hatched in it in security since the last wild hunter left the shore. When we found it, it held a deep nest of eider down with three eggs, fresh but cold, probably belonging to a duck we had killed before landing.

Eider duck shelters are found throughout Scandinavia, and have not changed in construction for 1,000 years or more. While it is possible to collect eider down from a natural nest, it is not practical. Far easier to encourage the ducks by providing suitable nest sites, and having a structure which keeps the eider down from blowing away.

Otto Sverdrup also found eider duck houses in several locations on the shores of Jones Sound, particularly on St Helena. In *New Land* (1899) he describes them:

> . . . well sheltered under the sides of the mountain were long rows of eider-duck's nests. The sites of several tents told us, too, that some time or other the Eskimo must have been here. As far as I could understand, they had even built nests for the ducks of the same construction that is the vogue to this day in Nordland [the Nordland section of Norway]. Certainly I have never heard that the Eskimo were in the habit of protecting the birds in this fashion.

Sverdrup was writing for an age which believed the Vikings had not travelled much further north than the Western Settlement, and assumed that these structures had to be Inuit. He correctly notes that the structure and form are distinctly Scandinavian.

The Vikings were drawn to Ellesmere Island, to the North Water and associated polynias. They certainly had a presence there, and while the implicit assumption of writers is that the settlement must have been summer only, we really do not have the evidence to know for sure whether Ellesmere Island was purely a summer settlement, or whether there was year-round occupation – whether Ellesmere Island was in effect a new settlement, self-sufficient and independent of Greenland's Eastern and Western settlements. Nor do we have evidence to suggest what ultimately happened to Ellesmere Island.

There is room, however, for cautious speculation. Realistically, over-wintering in Ellesmere Island must have occurred. With hundreds of years of exploitation of this region it is inevitable that sooner or later a ship would decide that an early onset of winter made the voyage south perilous, and that it was safer to stay. We have seen evidence for over-wintering at Upernarvik at 73° north on Greenland where the world's northernmost runic inscription was found, and while at these latitudes the jump to 76° north for the southern tip of Ellesmere Island represents a significant increase in the length of unrelieved winter night, it does not necessarily represent a comparable fall-off in temperature. Today the winter temperatures of Greenland's Upernavik and Ellesmere Island's Grise Fiord are remarkably similar. The Vikings, by over-wintering at Upernavik, demonstrated their ability to over-winter on Ellesmere Island. Over-wintering would have offered the advantage of a longer season in which to harvest ivory, and would have made economic sense.

Ellesmere Island provides a year-round food supply. While a diet consisting of meat, seabirds and fish and almost entirely without grain, fruit or vegetables seems strange to the Western world, it has for centuries been the diet of the Inuit, and even in the twentieth century a diet not so far removed from this was followed by the inhabitants of Scotland's remotest island, St Kilda. The vitamins that we associate with fruit and vegetables can be obtained from other sources, particularly the liver of seal and the flesh and oil of the fulmar. There is no reason why Ellesmere Island could not have fed the Vikings, as it has for millennia fed the Inuit and other northern peoples.

The primary purpose for Viking presence in Ellesmere Island was the narwhal, which was of value as a trading commodity. Being in Ellesmere meant being a trader, and therefore travelling. The Ellesmere Vikings were used to making long sea journeys to trade. Amongst the shortest journeys they made was the thousand miles or so to the Greenland settlements. Despite the distance, contact with the Greenland settlements must have been regular, presumably every season, whether we see Ellesmere Island as a summer settlement of Greenlanders, or as an independent settlement trading to Greenland. It was their only route to the rest of the world. And crucially Greenland was the only place where ships could be repaired and rebuilt. Greenland had addressed its own wood shortage by import, from Europe and from America, and had the ability to supply the needs of the Ellesmere Island Vikings. Timber supplies kept Ellesmere Island linked to Greenland.

Of course, the destruction of the Greenland settlements would have been catastrophic for Vikings on Ellesmere. As the Western Settlement was destroyed in the summer we may be sure that there were Vikings at Ellesmere Island at this season. Speculation becomes strained, yet there are two sources which might give some insight into the ultimate fate of Ellesmere Vikings.

The first source is Inuit stories. These are full of references to Europeans who once lived in this area of the Arctic. Knut Rasmussen's accounts of Inuit stories, particularly the Thule Inuit, asserts specifically that the Vikings were in the vicinity of Smith Sound, the strait which separates Ellesmere Island and the Thule Inuits' Greenland home. The Thule Inuit, living closest to Ellesmere Island and visiting annually for hunting, include in their stories abundant references to Europeans. While the possibility exists that these stories might have been told for approaching 500 years, this is out of keeping with the conventions of Inuit storytelling. It would be truly remarkable if an Inuit cultural memory extended back over so long a time span, as there is nothing else in Inuit stories to suggest that there is a folk memory of history over this length of time. Rather, the stories suggest that the Ellesmere Vikings survived the destruction of the Greenland colonies.

European records give strong corroboration to the concept of survival of the Ellesmere Vikings. By 1500 at the very latest, the Greenland colony had been extinguished. Yet in 1721 Denmark sent a Norwegian missionary, Hans Egede, to Greenland with the stated intention of preaching the gospel to the Norsemen they were convinced were there. The story of Viking settlement in Greenland was, of course, known to the Danes, but so too was the story of the destruction of Greenland. There are many accounts of the destruction in Danish, for example from a 1632 description of Greenland by Peder Claussen. There is an odd dichotomy between, on the one hand, knowledge of the extinction of the Greenland colony and, on the other, a view that there were still Vikings there, and in need of a Christian missionary.

Denmark had for long asserted her claim over Greenland. Thus in 1648 when King Frederik III ascended the joint throne of Denmark and Norway the royal arms were revised. The new arms included a polar bear (in blue), a stockfish (i.e. a dried cod), and a sheep, representing respectively Greenland, Iceland and the Faroe Islands. Around the same time the Danes proposed the view that a northern land ran from the north-east coast of Greenland across the far north of the Atlantic, and touched the coast of Russia around the Kara peninsula. Such a land does not exist, though the Danes were aware of the boundary of the Arctic Ocean sea ice which is found in roughly this position. The whole of this fictitious northern land they called Greenland, and when in 1596 William Barents discovered Spitsbergen, Denmark asserted sovereignty over that land on the grounds that it was part of Greenland. In such an action we see Denmark ambitious to assert her claim to the whole North Atlantic.

So what had changed by 1721? The Sunday school story of the worthy missionary is that Hans Egede himself conceived a wish to travel to Greenland and preach there, yet the facts scarcely back this up. The decision to send a missionary to Greenland was an intensely political one made at the Danish Court. The mission was fraught with danger for Denmark. Should the descendants of the Norse not be found there, Denmark would in effect have weakened her own claim to Greenland. The man chosen subsequently demonstrated many admirable qualities, yet the motivation for his selection seems to have as much to do with his accent and place of birth as his missionary zeal. Hans Egede was from Sengen in the north of Norway, and spoke a language close to that of Old Norse, and therefore close to the speech of Iceland and that presumed for the Greenland colonies. His background in a northern farming community gave grounds for believing he could farm in Greenland. He was an admirable choice as missionary, and by all accounts enthusiastically embraced the challenge. Politically the decision to transport Egede to Greenland made sense only if Denmark was sure that there really were Norse there. Financially Denmark was committing three ships to the mission, settling just over 40 people, and making a commitment to supply them for many years. Whatever missionary zeal may have existed in Denmark, it is clear that this project was driven by political ambition, supported by a firm belief that the Norse still lived there.

In the early eighteenth century, European sailings to Greenland were sporadic, but they were occurring. Most sailings were to south-western Greenland only. Voyages were sponsored by commercial interests, seeking quick profits – though few profits seem to have been made. The cost of equipping a ship for the lengthy and dangerous voyage to Greenland could not be recouped by the scant cargos they brought back. The Inuit they encountered had little to trade of any description and nothing in bulk, and trade was further frustrated by the lack of a common language. We have only fragmentary records of the few official voyages to Greenland which took place from the sixteenth to eighteenth centuries, and almost no record of the voyages of failed traders, many of them little better than pirates.

Yet something one of these voyages discovered seems to have brought about a change of view in Denmark. From a belief in the mid seventeenth century that the Greenland colony had completely died out by at the latest 1500, Denmark switched abruptly to a belief that Norse people still lived there. Egede's voyage was conceived as a voyage to re-establish contact with these people.

A hypothesis may be advanced. As yet there is not the evidence to test it, but it may be hoped that archaeological surveys of Ellesmere Island will turn up materials that can do just this. It may be suggested that by the early fifteenth-century Viking presence had become well-established on Ellesmere Island. The settlement was dependent on trade with Greenland and Europe for timber and for luxury goods, and was characterised by summer camps and smaller over-wintering groups, but had generated a basic self-sufficiency in food. The destruction of the Viking settlement in Greenland cut a vital trade route for the Ellesmere Vikings. Supply routes now become at the minimum 2,000 miles, and all directions in their different ways problematic. Iceland, the nearest surviving Viking land, required a crossing of the Denmark Strait, particularly perilous for Viking ships. If any Ellesmere Vikings made the voyage to Iceland they would have found that Iceland had no direct need for the northern produce they wished to trade, and a poor supply of the timber the Ellesmere Vikings required. Alternatively, voyages to the eastern seaboard of America, perhaps in the vicinity of L'Anse aux Meadows, offered the prospect of timber, but not of manufactured goods. Direct trade from Ellesmere Island to Europe adds another thousand miles each way to the established, but already well-extended, trade routes from Greenland to Europe.

Perhaps the obvious solution was evacuation. It is perfectly possible that one or more shiploads of Ellesmere Vikings settled in Iceland or Norway or somewhere else. European records are just not complete enough or detailed enough for there to be much chance of finding a reference to refugees landing on a lightly settled European coast. Yet perhaps too there was disbelief amongst the Ellesmere Islands that the events in Greenland would result in an end of Norse presence, and a conviction that the Vikings would soon be back in their old settlements, farming good land.

The hypothesis is that a group of Vikings in effect became marooned on Ellesmere Island, and as their last ship sailed or fell to bits they became utterly dependent on the arrival of a ship that never came.

There is evidence for this assertion.

1) In 1540, more than 40 years after the end of the Greenland settlements, a Hamburg sailor known to history as John 'Greenlander' made a voyage to Iceland during which he was blown off course, finding himself instead in Greenland. He described settlements comparable to those he later saw in Iceland – and therefore Norse rather than Inuit – but abandoned. Yet he found one recently dead body of a European, dressed in leather and cloth and with a knife. A possibility is that this body might have been a Viking from Ellesmere.

2) Europe was convinced that somewhere in Greenland there were still Vikings living. In 1605 and 1606 King Christian IV sent two expeditions to Greenland with the intent of finding the Norse Greenlanders. Expeditions were expensive, and were not mounted without a belief in their likely success.

3) In 1623 in Iceland a report was made of pieces of a ship of Greenlandic design washing ashore.

4) In the Thule Inuit stories recorded by Knud Rasmussen there is frequent assertion of European peoples living in Ellesmere until the late eighteenth or just into the early nineteenth century. However, Sir John Ross's 1818 voyage to Thule and the Smith Sound found no trace of Norse people. Plausibly, the mini ice age of the mid eighteenth century was the end of the Ellesmere Vikings.

5) The missionary Hans Egede was not sent to the known location of the Viking Greenland settlements, but to a point well north of the Western Settlement. This puzzling decision seems to have received little comment from historians. Denmark knew the location of the Greenland settlements, yet sent their missionary somewhere else. When Hans Egede landed in 1721 in the vicinity of present day Sisimiut he found no Norse

people. He searched for them for many years, travelling extensively from Cape Farewell to around 66° north. He found plenty of Viking ruins – all south of Sisimiut – but no sign of the Norse. Yet the hypothesis set out here suggests that they were indeed in the region, but many hundred miles further north than Sisimiut.

Archaeology tells us that the Vikings were in Ellesmere Island. The narwhal horns found throughout Europe come from this location, and provide a purpose for Vikings being so far north. This much is secure. Speculation concerns what happened to these northernmost Vikings, though a case of sorts can be made for their survival, perhaps to the eighteenth century. Hopefully one day archaeology will provide evidence.

6

Viking Hudson Bay

THE north-centre of the North American continent is a vast area running from the Canadian High Arctic through Hudson Bay, and south to the Great Lakes and Great Plains of North America. Within this enormous area is to be found some of the globe's worst weather. Winters are particularly cold. Yet there is also enormous climatic variation, and during the summer season many locations have surprisingly warm weather. This is the third direction in which the Vikings penetrated. Today we are familiar with communication routes through Canada and the USA which run predominantly east–west, linking Atlantic with Pacific. However, the natural route into the heart of the continent made by the sea is from the Arctic through Hudson Bay. This was the route used by many nineteenth-century migrants to the American Midwest, and it was the route accessible to the Vikings.

Popular views of this part of the globe emphasise the winter cold. The misfortunes of so many nineteenth-century expeditions to the area encouraged the stories, which are an aspect of the climate, but by no means the whole story. British popular opinion on the Arctic was first captivated and then shocked by the story of the Franklin Expedition, and American views in many respects followed those of Britain.[1] For the Franklin Expedition should not have failed. Setting out in 1848 the expedition aimed to glorify the British Empire by discovering a passage by sea around the north of America to the Pacific and the Far East. It was considered the best-equipped expedition of its age, and with two specially strengthened ships travelling together, success was confidently predicted. The ships, the *Erebus* and the *Terror*, crossed the Atlantic, put in briefly on the west coast of Greenland, and then vanished into the labyrinth of the Northwest Passage. Only after a wait of three years did search parties set out to seek the fate of the expedition, and found a harrowing tale of ships trapped for two successive winters in the ice, and finally a grim, corpse-strewn march south as the survivors made a last effort to escape. All died.

The Franklin Expedition

So much of what we know about the area is associated with expeditions that were sent to discover the fate of Franklin that some description of that catastrophe is useful. The tale of the Franklin Expedition has been unearthed slowly over the centuries, and a consensus view has emerged as to what went wrong. A crucial flaw is now believed to lie in the then-new technology of tin cans, and it may well be that this one technological fault alone destroyed the expedition. At that time tin cans were considered to be the solution for storage of food for many months, but the technology was fatally flawed in that the cans were closed with a solder of lead and tin. We now know that the lead seeped into the food, poisoning all who ate it. Lead poison weakens, though it is unlikely in itself to have killed within just a few years. Rather, it appears that the sailors on the Franklin Expedition, as a result of lead poisoning, became lethargic and prone to illness, particularly tuberculosis. The crew soon became incapable of the work of running their ships. Furthermore, lead poisoning causes violent temper along with an inability to make reasoned decisions. Thus the Franklin Expedition was doomed by physical lethargy and mental instability.

Yet even without this unique problem there were fundamental weaknesses in the planning of the expedition. Early European expeditions to the Arctic had little success in living off the land. While modern guns are effective in killing seal, bear, musk oxen, caribou and other Arctic wildlife, the weapons of the early nineteenth century lacked the accuracy to make a kill from the closest distance to which the animals could usually be approached. Early European hunters with guns went hungry. Trapping would have been more successful, but this seems rarely to have been practised. Along with hunger they faced cold. The clothing of the European expeditions was inappropriate for the Arctic winter, as if those in Britain responsible for equipping the expedition were unable to comprehend the winter cold of the High Arctic. Furs were not worn; while wool can in theory be adequate if worn in a sufficient number of layers, the men were not so equipped. Rather, they had naval uniforms which had been designed more for the parade ground than for practicality. Even their boots were of thin leather; for their hands, many had only fingerless woollen mittens.

With their ships marooned the officers decided on an overland march south in the hope of reaching civilisation. The final march of those of the Franklin Expedition who sought to walk out of the Arctic is a chilling tale of mistakes and desperation. Afflicted by weakened health through lead poisoning and facing hunger and cold, the officers added breathtaking stupidity. The men were required to drag over the rough ice life-boats which they had mounted on skis, and filled with provisions, most of which they didn't need: formal dining crockery and cutlery and many cooking pots, a meal gong, button polish and curtain rods. The work of pulling these crude sledges of excessive weight would have been exhausting – it was not a practical undertaking, as should have been apparent from the first yards of transportation. One by one the men died. Ultimately the expedition sank to cannibalism, confirmed by recent examination of knife marks on recovered human bones.

The death of the Franklin crew was witnessed by the native Inuit, who for many years afterwards told tales of men who died as they walked. There is evidence that the Inuit made an effort to help the crew, but faced with many dozen sick and starving men were unable to prevent their deaths. Inuit stories record their amazement that these men were dying, surrounded by the bounty of the Arctic summer. The Franklin Expedition, the best-equipped expedition of its age and the glory of the British Empire, perished in a land where the Stone Age Inuit found abundant food and shelter.

Britain reacted to the fate of the Franklin Expedition by stressing the dangers of the High Arctic. Perhaps this was easier than facing up to the catalogue of mistakes that had caused the disaster.

The reality is that Franklin and his men were not equipped for the conditions of the Arctic – in contrast to the Vikings, centuries earlier. For example, Eirik the Red and his band had lived from the land and sea when they over-wintered on Breithafjordur, and many of the early Greenland settlers would have had comparable experiences. They knew how to find food. The Vikings used furs as well as woollen garments, and they trapped animals for food. They had a familiarity with the lands of the north and how to live there. Greenland was to them an attractive land; Hudson Bay was survivable.

Evidence of Viking penetration of the Central Arctic, Hudson Bay, the Great Lakes, and even further south is patchy and problematic. We do not have indisputable archaeological remains of the sort found in Newfoundland or Ellesmere Island, nor do we have a tale of exploration of the region from the sagas. However, evidence for Viking presence does exist. It comes from the following sources:

1) Our awareness of where the Vikings had the technological ability to travel to.

2) Inuit stories

3) Archaeological find which are not disputed

4) Archaeological finds which are disputed

5) Genetic traces

Taking these sources together something can be said about the Viking reach in this area.

Viking Potential

So far it has been difficult to set bounds on the abilities of the Vikings to travel. Their ships were seaworthy across the North Atlantic, including the difficult seas of the Denmark Strait, a challenge to shipping even today. In Europe the same ship design took the Vikings through the great rivers of Russia, to the Caspian and Black seas, and on to the Mediterranean. Most dramatically, the Ellesmere Island finds show the Vikings sailing the High Arctic right up to the edge of the multi-year ice. The ice edge was familiar to the Vikings not just from the vicinity of Ellesmere Island but from the whole of the North Atlantic, where the edge of the Arctic ice runs from Greenland to Spitsbergen. The North Atlantic ice edge even entered into Viking religious belief, where the ever-frozen ice-ocean is seen as one of the two principal elements of creation – the other being the heat of the south. Viking voyages took place along the edge of the ice, with Spitsbergen known to be visited by Icelanders in 1194 and quite possibly earlier – a land that was supposedly discovered by William Barents in 1596. To the north-east of the Atlantic the Vikings travelled as far as the White Sea, and in the Arctic Ocean east to the pack ice. The Vikings went as far as it is physically possible to go in a boat before the invention of ice-breakers. In the Mediterranean, the Middle East and Russia the boundaries of Viking expansion were political rather than geographical. Settled land presented a challenge. Yet even here the Vikings penetrated as merchants and mercenaries, with significant presence in cities including Rome, Athens, Constantinople, Jerusalem, Baghdad and Tehran.

The Vikings' Arctic boundary was never political, but rather the geographical one of the edge of the multi-year ice. In Ellesmere Island they were right up against this boundary, just as they were in Spitsbergen and the White Sea, proving that they could go every mile that is theoretically possible. There is no reason to think that the Vikings would not have had the physical ability to sail any waters of the Arctic which are open during the summer months. They even had one great advantage over the ships of the nineteenth and early twentieth centuries – their ships were smaller. Paradoxically a small ship is much safer in these waters. It is more manoeuvrable and therefore has a much better chance of escaping encroaching pack ice and avoiding becoming iced in. It is also possible to pull a small ship up onto a beach to escape storms. The violence of Arctic storms in waterways full of rocks and ice has frequently wrecked large ships which must remain at sea in the absence of a harbour, and this one expedient of beaching a ship is a vital advantage that the Vikings had over nineteenth- and earlier twentieth-century explorers with their much larger ships.

There are two major routes west from Greenland: the northern route of the Parry Channel, and the southern route of the Hudson Strait.

The Parry Channel appears on a map as a straight east–west channel situated at around 74° north. It is not as far north as Ellesmere Island, and the Ellesmere Vikings must have passed its entrance. The channel as a single geographical feature exists more in the minds of map-makers than in reality. It is a sequence of channels and areas of open sea ranging from ten to fifty or more miles in width, bounded not by continuous shore but by numerous islands. To nineteenth-century mariners it was a maze in which many simply got lost. With their rudimentary navigation it must have been even more challenging to the Vikings. Today its western end is virtually blocked by multi-year ice, though a ship might just navigate past the ice in late summer. While the climate in the early Viking Age was a little milder than today, this channel would still have been only barely open for just a few weeks in late summer, and presumably only in some years. In theory the Vikings could have made this journey, and there is even some ethnographic evidence which suggests we should give the possibility serious attention. Nevertheless, penetration of anything more than the entrance of Parry Channel would be surprising. Before the Ellesmere Island finds, the idea that the Vikings might have been here at all would have seemed incredible; today we must modify this view.

The other route east from Greenland is the Hudson Strait, with its mouth across the Davis Strait and directly opposite the Eastern Settlement on Greenland. With its entrance at 61° north, this is much less extreme than the Parry Channel, though still with all the perils of Arctic waters, and it ices over every winter. The mouth of Hudson Strait was in the backyard of the Vikings in the Eastern Settlement, and in the centuries of their occupation there, it is reasonable to expect that exploration, both planned and accidental, would have taken place. A journey in the region of 1,000 miles – roughly the distance from the Eastern Settlement to L'Anse aux Meadows or the Western Settlement to Ellesmere Island – reaches to Hudson Bay. We know that within a very few years of settlement in Greenland the Vikings had reached Vinland. It is not a tenable proposition to presume that in the nearly 500 years of their settlement in Greenland they did not penetrate the Hudson Strait. Indeed, the balance of probability is that Hudson Bay was discovered around the same time as Vinland.

The name 'Hudson Bay' is misleading. With a breadth of 500 miles and a maximum length of 800 miles, anywhere else in the world this stretch of water would be called a sea. In winter Hudson Bay freezes almost in its entirety, and ice may be found on the east coast year-round. Yet it is in the middle of a continent and has the continental climatic extremes, so while the winters are cold, much of Hudson Bay has a relatively warm summer. A summer sailing season would have been sufficient to take the Vikings from Greenland to Hudson Bay and back again. This was well within their capability without reaching any physical barrier.

Technically they could have travelled further. The ice that millennia ago scoured the central region of the North American continent has left a vast area of mostly level land – the Hudson Bay Lowlands – characterised by acidic, waterlogged soils, of the sort called in the Cree language *muskeg* and in English *peat bog*. The rivers which flow into Hudson Bay are mostly navigable, or have modest falls and rapids which could have been managed through portaging of ships. The technology which enabled Viking ships to travel the rivers of Russia was adequate for the rivers of the Hudson Bay catchment. From the point of view of the technical capabilities of their ships, the Vikings could have made Hudson Bay the departure point for numerous journeys deep into the interior of North America. There was, in theory, nothing to have stopped them.

Elsewhere in the world, Vikings demonstrated that they would travel as far as their ships could take them. It is worth investigating what evidence there is of Viking travel to Hudson Bay and into the American heartland.

Inuit Stories

A plausible source of information about Viking penetration into the Canadian High Arctic should be the stories told by the Inuit. It is the Inuit who gave early explorers stories of Europeans in Ellesmere Island, and reasonable that they would remember Europeans elsewhere in the Arctic. Yet there is a problem. While the stories of Europeans in Ellesmere Island represent events perhaps no more than a generation or two before the storyteller, any Inuit stories of Europeans in the Hudson Strait or Hudson Bay area would be looking back many centuries.

Inuit stories from many centuries ago may be remembered by the Inuit, but within a cultural framework so different from that with which the Western world is familiar that interpretation is problematic. There has been a tendency for commentators either to see clear evidence of the Vikings in the Inuit stories, or to dismiss everything that these stories say.

Part of the problem is that the Inuit people do not have a mythology in the way that this is understood in most cultures. They do not separate myth and history in the way that western culture does. One modern Inuit writer, Rachel Attituq Qitsualik,[2] expresses this concisely: 'The Inuit cosmos is ruled by no one. There are no divine mother and father figures. There are no wind gods and solar creators. There are no eternal punishments in the hereafter, as there are no punishments for children or adults in the here and now.'

There is nothing comparable to the complex stories of gods and men found in Western mythologies. Nor do the Inuit have the concept of traditional stories containing within them some recollection of real events. Expressed in Western terms, there are no gods of Mount Olympus and no siege of Troy. Yet there is a religious imperative, expressed through animism, the belief that all living things have souls, and all life is therefore precious. As the reality of life in the Arctic is that living things must be killed for food and clothing, there is an Inuit cultural problem of reconciling their own existence with belief in a vengeful spirit world where every animal has a soul. Knud Rasmussen reported his Inuit guide as replying to a question on Inuit beliefs with the comment 'We don't believe. We fear.' Inuit stories predominantly describe rituals and taboos by which a ferocious spirit world is pacified, and these stories mix perceptions of the natural and supernatural world to an extent that it is not clear whether something is a man or an animal or a spirit or a monster – or even a Viking!

The manner of story-telling in Inuit society has been that women, typically grandmothers, relay the stories to the children. As the stories are very similar throughout the Inuit area, it is reasonable to assume that they are centuries or millennia old. They address themes which are enduring characteristics of the

Inuit lifestyle. Stories told throughout the Inuit world include the abused orphan who takes revenge; the woman who prospers following separation from a husband who mistreats her; the man, rejected by a woman, who takes a bird as a wife; children raised by animals; the wise, old man who encounters evil spirits and escapes by outsmarting them. While a few characters have names – Kiviuq and Sedna are the most frequently encountered – there is no suggestion that they were ever real people, rather they are archetypes created to embody the taboos expressed. The stories reflect a lifestyle which is as old as the Inuit people, and as the interest is in the unchangeable realities of the spirit world there is little interest in creating new stories or modifying old ones to reflect real events. The framework is not promising for finding references to the Vikings. Indeed, what little is found may be all the more significant because of its unlikely location.

What is found in Inuit stories from the Canadian High Arctic (but seemingly not further west) are stories of giants – Tunit. These are described as real, just as animals in Inuit stories are real – and in contrast with spirits, which are clearly identified as such. The giant Tunit are physically strong, sometimes peaceful and sometimes aggressive, and there is interaction between them and the Inuit. The Tunit seem to be a non-Inuit people with whom the Inuit came into contact, and it does seem that the stories describe real encounters.

The Inuit certainly encountered indigenous people in North America, particularly around the tree-line, where Inuit settlement and culture were supplanted by peoples inhabiting a different environment. None of these people can reasonably be called giants. It has been suggested that the Inuit stories refer to people belonging to the Dorset Culture, which they would have encountered to the north of Baffin Bay, and that the Dorset Culture people are the Tunit of the Inuit stories. Indeed the equation of Tunit with Dorset Culture, and even with the last surviving Dorset Culture tribe, the Sadlermiut, has been repeated so often that it has gained respectability. Yet the identification is imperfect.

A plausible interpretation of Tunit is that the name applied simply to non-Inuit peoples who were taller than the Inuit. Stories told by the Inuit refer not just to the people of the Dorset Culture, whom they certainly encountered, but also to other non-Inuit people, possibly including the Vikings. Standing an average of four inches taller than the Inuit and with a heavier build, the Vikings do fit the description of the stories in a way that the Dorset Culture do not. Accounts of the last surviving Tunit tribe stress their peaceableness, and seem hard to equate with the aggression often associated by the Inuit with the Tunit. Given that the archaeological finds now indicate that the Vikings were present in the Canadian High Arctic, the possibility that some Tunit were Vikings must be seriously considered.

High Arctic Viking Archaeology

Within the immensity of the Canadian High Arctic, very little territory has even been adequately surveyed, and only a tiny number of archaeological excavations have been carried out. That Viking remains have been found at all is truly remarkable. The relative frequency of such finds suggests a widespread Viking presence, and in some numbers.

The most common Viking find in North America is iron ship rivets. These are distinctive to Viking ships, and finding one on a shore demonstrates that at some time a Viking ship was pulled up on the beach. Metal detectors are beginning to locate these rivets, though bearing in mind the thousands of miles of coastline, and the inaccessibility of most northern areas, it may be presumed that only a tiny fraction of the rivets have been found, and that a much fuller picture will in time emerge.

One Viking rivet has been found on Axel Heiberg Island.[3] That the Vikings reached this island is staggering – though what they were doing there is far from clear. Axel Heiberg is west of Ellesmere Island, but lacks the polynias and open water that make the Ellesmere Island climate attractive. Discovery is usually attributed to Otto Sverdrup and his Fram expedition of 1898–1902, and it is Sverdrup that named the island after one of his sponsors, a brewer in Oslo. Though in the top 30 islands in the world in terms of size, it remained virtually unexplored until the 1950s, and today is a corner of the world that has been largely forgotten. One of the world's great wildernesses, Axel Heiberg lacks any form of formal protection as a National Park, though perhaps has the best possible protection through its inaccessibility. Today it has no permanent population; there is a tiny scientific base at Expedition Fiord. There is some scant archaeological evidence of Inuit settlement on the east coast, presumably summer camps that were made by hunters from Ellesmere Island. In terms of resources the island has little that would have been of interest to the Vikings. Its climate is a little more extreme than that of Ellesmere Island. While Peary caribou and musk oxen are found there the island lacks the former prolific animal populations of Ellesmere Island. A curious feature of Axel Heiberg Island is the many square miles of mummified wood, believed to be the remains of a 45-million-year-old forest. The wood is mummified – not fossilised – and will therefore burn. Conceivably this mummified wood was seen as a resource, though firewood that burns but poorly seems a disappointing cargo for a long voyage.

There is open water to Axel Heiberg for just a few weeks in some summers. The Vikings came, perhaps exploring, perhaps even lost. At least one Viking ship was dragged onto an Axel Heiberg beach and deposited a rivet there.

The Axel Heiberg Island find is remarkable for its location. By contrast, the High Arctic can offer finds which are surprising in themselves. On Baffin Island at an excavation of a Dorset Culture site a three-metre length of cord has been found, spun from the fur of the Arctic hare, and dating from around 1200. This cord is not compatible with Dorset or any other American culture – where spinning and yarn manufacture were virtually unknown – but it is directly comparable to textile fragments found in Viking Greenland. It is widely accepted that this is evidence of Viking presence on Baffin Island: a European yarn-making technique utilising a local resource to produce a Viking Arctic product.

Hudson Bay and Great Plains Viking Archaeology

Archaeology of the Canadian High Arctic has been hampered by the remoteness of the location. Many areas were visited only by the Inuit until well into the second half of the twentieth century, and there has not yet been an adequate survey of archaeological structures which are above ground, let alone any significant archaeological work which requires digging. Further south in Newfoundland, L'Anse aux Meadows was clearly visible above ground and in the vicinity of a village, yet had attracted little attention until the Ingstadts visited. High Arctic archaeology for the Vikings at this moment is little more than a list of promising sites which need excavating. Save for Ellesmere's Coburg Island, almost nothing has been excavated.

The region is full of intriguing sites. Typically, these are the foundations of stone-built buildings which cannot be attributed to the Inuit, and which carbon-14 dating of associated remains dates to the Viking period. It is a long step from saying these buildings are not Inuit to asserting that they are Viking, yet at the moment a Viking provenance is the most credible idea that has been advanced. The alternatives are not at all plausible. That the Inuit developed a culture innovation of making these stone buildings and then forgot that culture seems most unlikely. That they belong to a Native American people that we have otherwise not recorded is also an implausible solution. Farley Mowat's assertion that they are built by the Irish I find likewise implausible,[4] yet at least it suggests a European provenance. The Vikings do seem the only possible builders, and similarities with stone buildings from Viking Orkney and Shetland are strong, yet until proper archaeological investigation is carried out this idea must be considered unproven.

The vicinity of Ungava Bay also offers a number of stone crosses. These are in the form of an upright, a balanced horizontal stone, then a smaller upright on top. As with the stone building foundations, these cannot reasonably be attributed to the Inuit – and the Inuit believe them to be a relic of a different people. We do know that the sailors of Frobisher's voyages to Baffin Island set up stone crosses, but Ungava Bay is some distance from Baffin Island. The cross builders seem to have selected a horizontal stone for each cross which is thicker at one end than the other, which might suggest that they are not Christian crosses, but rather representations of Thor's hammer. This is an intriguing possibility, but so far without proof.

The greatest cluster of disputed archaeological finds is in the state of Minnesota. If there is any possibility of them being accepted as Viking, then a plausible means of entry for the Vikings must be suggested.

In fact, there is a clear route, as we can see from much more recent exploration of the area. On the south-west shore of Hudson Bay at the settlement of York Factory the Hudson Bay Company set up its main trading post.[5] The location was determined by trade routes. The estuary of the Nelson River provided a major entry into the American interior. At first the Hudson Bay Company relied on Native Americans bringing furs to York Factory for trade; later Hudson Bay Company traders moved up the Nelson River. Transport was by boat. The Nelson River does have rapids, and porterage of boats is needed, but the distances are such that this is possible. There is no reason why the Vikings, who navigated the great rivers of Russia, could not have navigated the Nelson River. At its head is Lake Winnipeg.

No consideration of the Vikings in North America can avoid commenting on the Kensington Runestone, which appears to be a runic inscription found in the US state of Minnesota. Very many eminent scholars have staked their reputations on its authenticity; as many have insisted that it is a fake. Scholarly respectability was given to the artefact in 1949 when Dr M. W. Stirling of the Smithsonian Institute proclaimed the Kensington Runestone as 'probably the most important archaeological object yet found in North America'. If it is genuine he and countless other scholars are correct in their assessment of the impact of the find. This one artefact would act as incontrovertible proof that the Vikings reached deep into the American heartland in what is now the state of Minnesota. The Kensington Runestone alone would rewrite history.

The stone was discovered in 1898 by a farmer, Olaf Ohman, and his son, as they removed the root of an old aspen tree on their farm outside the village of Kensington in Douglas County, Minnesota. They found a stone covered in clearly cut runes – and as a Swede Ohman recognised them as runes. After a few weeks Ohman realised that his find was important and brought it to the attention of a local museum, which in turn called in specialists from the Smithsonian. Within months specialists had concluded that it was indeed genuine.

The stone itself is a chunk of rock called Minnesota graywrack, a type of slate, and as its name suggests this is local to Kensington and vicinity. An outcrop of this rock is found in the immediate vicinity of the place where the Runestone was unearthed. It has a face roughly 30 inches by 16 inches, and is just over 5 inches thick. Without any doubt at all it had been buried for some years prior to its discovery, as the cuts of the inscription show weathering of a type which in slate is caused only by exposure to soil. The very shortest period of burial which is believed able to create this weathering is 20 years, which gives a latest possible date for the carving of the runes of 1878. On it is carved a long runic inscription, which is intact. Most of the runes are on the face, but a few – the end of the inscription – are on the side. There are very few difficulties in reading the runes, which are exceptionally clear. Similarly, translation is relatively straightforward, although there has been some scholarly revision over the years. The original reads:

> 8 göter ok 22 norrmen paa opthagelse farth fro winlanth of west Wi hathe läger weth 2 skylar en thags norder fro theno sten wi war ok fiske en thag äptir wi kom hem fan X man rothe af bloth og ded AVM frälse af illum

> har X mans we hawet at se äptir wore skip 14 thag rise from theno odh Ar wars Herra 1362

I offer the following as an idiomatic translation:

> *We are eight Goths and twenty-two Norwegians on a journey of exploration to the west of Vinland. We set traps by two shelters one day's march north of this stone. One day some of us went out fishing. When we returned to camp we found ten men red with blood, dead. May the Blessed Virgin Mary save us from evil!*

> *We left ten men by the sea looking after the ships fourteen days' journey from this property. The year 1362.*

One name needs clarification – Goths. The term Goths usually means a Germanic people of late antiquity and the early Middle Ages, one of the groups of barbarians that destroyed the Roman Empire. However in Scandinavia in the late Middle Ages, Goths had another meaning, simply an inhabitant of Gotland, part of modern Sweden. Some translators of the Kensington Runestone translate not as Goth but as Swede, which is correct in as much as the Gotlanders were a type of Swede – but the runes actually read Goth.

The problems with this inscription are numerous. Many have concluded that it is a fake, and with good reason.

First of all it is too perfect. It is the longest runestone inscription known from anywhere, it is conveniently dated, it gives precise information about the composition of the expedition, it mentions Vinland and, above all, it tells in brief an exciting story. An item of this nature would be precisely what an archaeologist would love to find, and there seems in retrospect to be little doubt that the experts who first examined it were so excited by it that they wanted it to be genuine. At the end of the nineteenth century, America was fascinated by the publication of a translation of *The Vinland Sagas*, and there was a popular cultural context in which evidence of Viking presence in America was wanted. With its reference to Mary the inscription found favour with clerics of the Roman Catholic Church in America as it suggests that pre-Columban exploration was Roman Catholic in character. This was exploited as a counter-blast to the pivotal role conventionally assigned by American Protestants to the non-conformist, Protestant Pilgrim Fathers. In short not just the experts but almost the whole of America wanted the Kensington Runestone to be genuine, and the critics of today argue that this is why the stone was not examined with enough scepticism.

There is plenty of cause for scepticism. The scenario it implies is implausible. Fourteen days' journey north from Kensington by small boat down the Red River might take the supposed band of Goths and Norwegians to Lake Winnipeg, a vast expanse of water which could reasonably be called sea, and where the ships mentioned may have been moored. The distance from Lake Winnipeg to Kensington is substantial for a small party of explorers, and there is no obvious reason why they should have travelled so far inland, and particularly why they should leave the main artery of the Red River to follow a route through a series of minor streams and lakes to Kensington. Presumably we can infer that it was the Native Americans who slaughtered ten of the party, and the survivors now had to make the fourteen-day journey through hostile territory to regain their ships. For us this might make an exciting story; yet the supposed Vikings must have been full of dread at the prospect, and it seems strange that instead of making a start on this dash to safety one of them should spend time carving a long inscription. No specific work seems to have been carried out on just how long it would have taken to carve the Kensington Runestone, but the time would be several hours, perhaps a day's work. If the stone is genuine we have to assume that there was enough time for one of the band to find a suitable piece of stone, roughly shape it, carve the inscription – which is just over 200 runes in length – and set it up. There is no obvious motive for this. A message for other members of the party could have been much shorter, and would not have needed to spell out that the party consisted of eight Goths and twenty-two Norwegians.[6]

The critics have found fault with the language of the Runestone. They have argued that some of the runes are not genuine, or were not used in 1362. They have argued that the dating style by which the year is expressed is not appropriate for an inscription from 1362, and that two words used in the inscription are not recorded in Middle Swedish. For Erik Wahlgren writing in 1968, the Kensington Runestone is the prime example of what he calls 'Buckram Vikings', the false supposed relics of Vikings in North America.

Answers could be advanced to all these objections, and the energetic work of Richard Nielsen throughout the 1990s has indeed provided rebuttals. That the Runestone is remarkable does not necessarily mean it is a forgery. That the story it tells seems implausible might in fact be our lack of understanding of the world of Viking America; perhaps if we knew the context we would have no problems with it. The language issues are far from clear – some rune specialists have asserted that the rune forms are genuine, and use mediaeval forms not understood in 1898 but discovered since. The vocabulary may well be correct for Middle Swedish, for we know so little about this language that we are in no position to say that the Runestone does not present genuine forms. Thus any one objection to the Runestone could be resolved, but cumulatively the objections do seem to suggest that the Runestone is probably a forgery.

Those scholars who see the Runestone as a forgery conclude that Ohman created the inscription as a joke, using a mix of his native Swedish and some Old Norse he had picked up from a book, and that what we are seeing is a crude prank which may be readily dismissed. It is noted that very many Swedes do know runes, as they are part of Swedish popular culture, and there are even cases of immigrant Swedes in the vicinity of Kensington in the late nineteenth century scratching a few runes on a lintel of a new home as a good luck charm. To the critics the matter is resolved. Ohman is the forger.

Yet the Runestone cannot be so easily dismissed. It is in its language that the inscription has its greatest strength. Ohman spoke the Swedish of the nineteenth century, which is substantially different from the Swedish of the fourteenth century – just as the English language of the nineteenth century differs markedly from the fourteenth-century language of Geoffrey Chaucer. It is possible for English readers today to familiarise themselves with the language of Chaucer to the extent that his work can be read without too many difficulties, but it is another matter entirely to write convincingly in Chaucer's language. Should someone wish to do this, grammars and textbooks for Chaucer's Middle English do exist, and there is a scholarly community that has expertise in Chaucer's language. It could be done, though it would be exceptionally hard to write good, Chaucerian English. There are so many areas of vocabulary and grammar where a mistake could be made, and which would inevitably be spotted when the text produced was scrutinised by the academic community. For Middle Swedish the problems are much greater. Even today reference books for Middle Swedish are limited, while in Ohman's day there was nothing at all available. In theory Ohman had access to work on the grammar and vocabulary of Middle Swedish's parent language, Old Norse, though the books were for the Old West Norse dialect, while the ancestor of Middle Swedish is Old East Norse. A particular problem is in the area of word-order. The ordering of words in Old Norse and Middle Swedish was significantly different to that in modern Swedish. Word-order studies did not exist in 1898, and there is no possible reference book for a forger. Indeed it is only in very recent years that scholars, myself included, have looked in detail at the word-order of Old Norse, while no-one appears to have done any significant work specifically on Middle Swedish. Yet the word-order exhibited by the Kensington Runestone conforms with the best information available today on word-order in Middle Swedish. In short the linguistic achievement needed to produce as a forgery the text of the Runestone is prodigious. It is just possible that the author was a linguist of genius who used his intuition as a native speaker of Swedish, his extensive reading in Old Norse and the Scandinavian languages and, additionally, had a lot of luck. The result might be an inscription of the linguistic sophistication of the Kensington Runestone – yet it seems implausible that this could really have happened.

In effect we have two possible views on the Kensington Runestone, both of them stretching credulity. Most commentators have seemed reluctant to set them out with the boldness that is required. For either the Runestone is one of the greatest forgeries ever, or it rewrites history.

The first view is that the Kensington Runestone is a fake. However, if this is so it is a linguistic *tour de force* produced with enormous skill by a linguist of genius. It was certainly not written by Ohman. He was not particularly well educated, did not have access to the reference books available, was not trained in philology, had not learned Old Norse, and had no access to the scholarly community in European universities where some work on Old Norse was being conducted. Ohman didn't write this text. Perhaps someone else wrote it – yet even assuming the forger to be an academic, a scholar of Old Norse and Swedish philology, perhaps a professor at Copenhagen, Oxford or Cambridge, it is very hard to believe that anyone in the late nineteenth century had the linguistic knowledge to produce this text. Additionally, there are problems with the concept of burying the inscription for at least 20 years before Ohman found it – which means that the forgery was created even earlier, when knowledge of the language was even less developed. The idea that the Runestone is a forgery is in its way every bit as problematic as the idea that the Runestone is genuine.

Though I am a philologist specialising in Old English and Old Norse I could not produce from scratch a forgery with language approaching the quality of the Runestone, and there are but a handful of people today who could attempt such work. Scholarship has advanced since the late nineteenth century and today's academics have far better information to guide them, yet it would still be a difficult task. Were I to make the attempt I would seek the one sure way of minimising errors. I would wish to copy a genuine text as far as possible, and make as few changes to it as possible. Perhaps in this methodology is a possible solution. Rather than claiming almost impossible linguistic skills for Ohman, or whoever else the forger might be, it seems possible that an argument could be constructed on the lines that the Runestone is a modern copy – with minor changes – of a runic text found somewhere else. For this we need to suppose a genuine fourteenth- or fifteenth-century model which was copied by the forger, and adapted to make reference to Vinland. The scenario would be that Ohman had access to the text of a real Swedish runestone that was a memorial to a completely different expedition, for example perhaps a Swedish runestone recording an expedition from Sweden to the east, and that he made some small changes in substituting the place name 'Vinland', and changing the directions. With this hypothesis we have a mechanism for explaining the high quality of the language – it is copied from an original. The great problem with this idea is that no such original is known. Had it existed it would itself have been one of the longest Swedish runestone inscriptions, and we would expect to know about it. Perhaps we should consider that Ohman could have put together two or three shorter inscriptions, which might explain the juxtapositions of the Kensington Runestone text – though in this case none of these originals have survived. In order to make the idea of a copy work we have to suppose one or more originals which have since been destroyed, without having been previously noted by antiquarians, and therefore leaving no trace. This again is implausible. Runic inscriptions were studied throughout the nineteenth century, and it is unlikely that a major inscription would not have been commented on. Additionally their solid construction – basically a slab of rock – discourages wanton destruction. Notwithstanding this, something along these lines has to be assumed if we are to argue that the Kensington Runestone is a forgery. As a scenario we have Ohman becoming acquainted with the text of one or more Swedish runestones, subsequently lost without trace, and taking much time and care in producing his fake Runestone, which was a copy with small modifications of this original. Then he buried it for some years in order to weather it – at least 20 – dug it up, and presented it as real. The prank was premeditated and took very many years to implement. As he made no money from the Runestone his motive seems not to be profit. Indeed the only motive that has ever been advanced is that it was a prank to discredit the academic community – though why Ohman should be interested in such a thing has not been set out.

Perhaps a re-examination is needed of the alternative possibility that the Runestone is genuine. Amazingly, European archives provide a perfect context for the Runestone. In 1354 Paul Knutson was authorised by the Swedish King Magnus Eiriksson to make a missionary voyage from Sweden to Greenland because the Greenlanders had renounced Christianity and returned to paganism. Behind this proselytising zeal there was also a commercial motive, for because the Greenlanders had renounced Christianity they had also stopped paying their tithes. The voyage took place, with a mixed Swedish and Norwegian crew, and including a priest to help in the process of reintroducing Christianity to the Greenlanders. The expedition took ten years, returning in 1364. There is no contemporary extant account of the voyage, though several sources mention that an account did exist, now lost, written by Jacobus Cnoven. A letter dated 1577 from cartographer Gerardus Mercator to John Dee – Queen Elizabeth I's most prominent man of learning – gives a précis of this account, specifying that the voyage went to Greenland and lands beyond, returning with just eight men alive.

Within the story of the Knutson voyage a context could be found for the Kensington Runestone. A ten-year voyage of exploration to Greenland and lands west could conceivably have followed an established Viking route to Kensington. Furthermore the Kensington Runestone, therefore, has a different function from runestones in Sweden. There the most common function of a runestone is to commemorate a dead person when there is no body. Typically a runestone might say that someone died on a Viking trip, and usually gives the name of the person who set up the stone. The Kensington Runestone does not do this. The ten dead are not named, or otherwise identified (perhaps they could have been identified as a named person's followers or crew of a specific ship). The rune writer does not name himself. The reference to eight Goths and twenty-two Norwegians at first sight seems almost pointless. The geography is strange. West from Vinland implies that the Vikings have travelled west from the Atlantic seaboard, though no-one could conceive of this journey taking just 14 days overland (and Ohman would have been aware of pre-railway-age pioneers who had made the journey, and known it was much longer). The geography only makes sense if a vast area of what is now the eastern United States was termed Vinland and an equally vast area – today's Midwest – was termed the land west of Vinland. This suggests substantial Viking exploration of the interior of North America. Possibly the Runestone is part commemorative of the ten dead, part a land claim. By setting up a dated monument the Vikings are establishing their presence – though it would be reasonable to expect a named person to be mentioned. Perhaps we are seeing a Runestone used without the pagan mysticism that would accompany their use in Sweden, and that in this new guise we have a much longer and more prosaic stone, utilising a slightly different set of runes to those found in Swedish runestones of the same period and a slightly different vocabulary. The year 1362 is late for a runestone. Norwegians and Swedes did still use runes, but they also used the Latin alphabet. The great strength of the runic alphabet is that it is made of straight lines only, and is much easier to carve into stone than the curves of the Latin alphabet. Perhaps a context for the Kensington Runestone is to be found not in runic inscriptions, but in Latin inscriptions of the period. This would contextualise the length, the dating convention and the use of precise detail. Realistically, we just don't know.

If the Runestone is genuine, it rewrites history. And the implications of this rewriting are too great. The most recent linguistic assessment of the Kensington Runestone (2004) comes from Sweden's University of Uppsala. A joint statement has been prepared which bears the names of both Richard Nielsen, the foremost advocate of the view that the Runestone is genuine, and Henrik Williams, Professor of Scandinavian Studies at Uppsala, a philologist and sceptic. The statement notes that a consideration of the language presents problems both for identification with the fourteenth century and with the nineteenth century. After several paragraphs of scholarly hedging the statement issues its final and definitive conclusion: the Runestone 'requires further study'. This should perhaps be the last word on the subject. Yet there is more.

In December 1998 the Runestone underwent a physical examination by a geologist. Save for a cursory examination in 1910 this was the first real geological examination. The process proved protracted. Scott Wolter, a forensic geologist who had established a reputation as a professional witness, was commissioned to carry out the examination. He chose to compare the stone with the effects of weathering on incised surfaces of old gravestones made of the same stone. A cut surface on this type of slate contains some pyrite which can be seen under a microscope, and which degrades through time. The cuts in the Kensington Runestone show no pyrite at all – though a newly made scratch on the Runestone shows the expected pyrite. The question is, how quickly could the pyrite degrade to nothing? Exposure to the air is not sufficient to cause the degradation, so the process has not happened since 1898. Rather, it is a process caused specifically by contact with soil. Wolter's conclusion is that the stone must have been buried for a minimum of 200 years to cause the degradation observed. There is no way of determining a maximum period of burial. Wolter draws attention to ice scars on the back of the stone which are many thousands of years old, but remain sharp like the carved runes. If Wolter's findings are accepted, then he has effectively proved the Runestone to be genuine. The area around Kensington Minnesota was first settled by Europeans in 1858; a runestone in local stone carved, according to Wolter's dating, prior to 1698 cannot be a forgery. At the time of writing the University of Uppsala is repeating Wolter's test. Consideration is being given to the idea that the test itself is at fault.

Had this stone been unearthed in Sweden with a comparable inscription it would have been accepted as genuine. The language is simply too good for there to be any likelihood for it to be a forgery. Its location in America means a higher standard of proof is needed. In the light of an apparently sound geological test stating that it is genuine, I feel unable to discount this artefact. Yet I am reluctant to accept it as genuine either.

Leaving aside the Kensington Runestone, there are plenty of Viking finds associated with Minnesota. All must be treated with great caution. Anyone who cares to search for 'Viking' in the art and antiquities section of eBay will find on any day a few small Viking artefacts for sale. Typically these are small metal objects – strap ends, brooches, pins, lead weights – many found in eastern England. Usually they are metal detector finds, sometimes being sold by the finder, sometimes by a coin or antiques dealer. The provenance might be given as a county, sometimes as a village. If the items are genuine, and most are, no-one ever doubts the claimed provenance, though most have been collected outside the archaeological context of a professional dig, and often without a witness to the finding. We know the Vikings were in England, and small Viking finds from England are common; there is no difficulty believing that the belt buckle which the finder says is from Norfolk really is from Norfolk. Over the years, Minnesota has produced its own haul of small, 'Viking' artefacts. They have been found by individuals outside an archaeological context, and because they are said to have been found in America rather than Europe they are all considered to be fraudulent. The assumption is that the individual has acquired a genuine Viking item from Europe, and claimed to have found it in Minnesota, and perhaps this scenario is an explanation for many of the finds reported. However, it would only take one genuine, contextualised find to satisfy the scholarly community of the Viking presence in Minnesota.

At Cormorant Lake, Becker County, Minnesota, three rocks have been found with a man-made, triangular hole through them. During the Viking

Age such rocks were fashioned to take a wooden spar and form an anchor. Were such rocks found in a known Viking context, they would be accepted as Viking anchor-stones. As with all stone objects there are considerable difficulties in dating, and we are without an objective date for these curious stones. In the absence of such a date it has been asserted that they were made more recently, for an unknown purpose.

Until such time as a Viking object is found in Minnesota in the course of an archaeological dig it would seem that no evidence of Viking presence there will be accepted by the scholarly community. The standard of proof presently required is very high indeed – perhaps rightly so – and while items claimed to be from Minnesota are being shown to be genuine, it is asserted that they cannot satisfy proof of provenance.

Vikings on Victoria Island – the Blond Eskimos

There is slender evidence that the Vikings reached Victoria Island in the Canadian High Arctic. Victoria Island is another enormous island, the world's ninth largest island and only slightly smaller than Great Britain. That even today few people are aware of its existence, even in Canada, is testimony to its remoteness. The population was numbered at 1,309 by the 2001 census, almost all living in the two widely separated settlements of Cambridge Bay and Ulukhaktok. There is little clarity on population levels at earlier times, but it is likely that the population was once higher, and that there were several or even many other settlements.

The island was known to late nineteenth-century explorers, who named it after Queen Victoria, and at that time whalers engaged in some trade with the native Inuit. However, the first lengthy visit by a European to the island is as late as the winter of 1905–06 when a Dane, Christian Klengenberg, made an extended trading visit. Klengenberg made extraordinary reports about the Inuit he encountered on Victoria Island, stating that many of them had blue or grey eyes, fair hair and fair skin. While his stories were published in the Canadian press, little general notice was taken of them. For the first proper description of the people of Victoria Island we are indebted to Vilhjalmur Stefansson, who visited over the years 1908 to 1912.

Stefansson was the pre-eminent Arctic explorer of his generation. It is largely thanks to his copious writings on the Arctic that the nineteenth-century picture of the inhospitable Arctic was challenged, with his concept of 'the friendly Arctic' providing a useful balance. In every area of Arctic studies his observations are accurate, and his work a corner-stone for all subsequent studies. Stefansson's visit to Victoria Island was as part of the Canadian Arctic Expedition, a large-scale project which was well-resourced and well-supported. His observations, agreed by his colleagues and meticulously written up, deserve to be taken seriously. Indeed, in his work on Victoria Island he is frequently credited with providing the best study of any Inuit group before frequent contact with people from outside the area changed their lifestyle and culture.

Stefansson did indeed observe Inuit who had features not usually associated with them. While the majority of the Victoria Island Inuit had characteristic Inuit features, including brown eyes and black hair, a very few people did display precisely the features that Klengenberg had described: blue or grey eyes, fair hair and fair skin. These features are simply not characteristic of the Inuit or any indigenous North American people. Effectively, they are specific characteristics of European ethnicity.

Stefansson identified three possible reasons for the ethnic characteristics he observed, and even a century later his three possibilities do seem to be the only ones. He suggested:

1) It may be that in antiquity a European people moved through Siberia and across the Bering Strait into the Canadian High Arctic, and that an echo of this European ethnicity was observable on Victoria Island.

Stefansson gives little credence to this theory, and today we are able to discount it. In a century of study of the indigenous peoples of North America, no evidence has been found to suggest a European migration across the Bering Strait. This cannot be the answer.

2) It may be that European whalers visiting Victoria Island had left behind their genetic signature, and that the Inuit showing European features were testament to such recent contact.

There is ample evidence of such contact elsewhere in the lands inhabited by the Inuit. Greenland in particular has had four centuries as a Danish kingdom, and has had a resident Danish administrative and trading population throughout. Many Greenlanders today do exhibit European features. Clearly it is possible that the whalers who were in the vicinity of Victoria Island were responsible for the 'blond Eskimos'. However, Stefansson gives two powerful counter-arguments. First, the Inuit who displayed European features did not believe they were descended from whalers. Elsewhere in the Arctic, Inuit groups made no secret of descent from Europeans, and there is no reason to distrust the beliefs of the Victoria Island Inuit on this point. Second, Stefansson compared the position of the Inuit in the eastern Canadian Arctic, where whaler contact had been far more extensive and for a far longer period. In these areas Inuit with European features were occasionally found. However, such individuals were (according to Stefansson) far less frequently encountered than on Victoria Island.

3) Stefansson's third possibility was that in the Victoria Island Inuit he was seeing the product of a mix of Inuit and Viking blood.

The idea received a lot of newspaper attention, with headlines proclaiming that 'Blond Eskimos' had been found in the Arctic. Indeed, the media exaggerations and the subsequent academic unease with the subject did little to help solve the questions raised by the physical appearance of a few Victoria Island Inuit. Nevertheless, Viking origins is a plausible explanation for the ethnic features noted.

The story for a time became little more than a footnote in Arctic research. However the new understanding of DNA appears to offer a way forward, and a project has recently been conducted by two Icelandic geneticists, Agnar Helgason and Gisli Palsson. They sought to compare the DNA of about 100 Victoria Island Inuit with that of Icelanders. Published in 2003, their result was that they could not find any trace of Icelandic (or indeed European) DNA in their sample.

Their result indicates that neither the Vikings nor European whalers nor any other European group are part of the gene stock of their sample. They can offer no explanation for the ethnic features observed first by Klengenberg, then by Stefansson and his whole team. Nor did they themselves see any evidence of such ethnicity. Indeed the implication of their work might be to suggest that Stefansson could not have observed Inuit with European ethnicity as he reported. Yet with a source as reliable as Stefansson, this seems unlikely.

A solution seems to lie in the depopulation and movements of the Inuit throughout the Canadian Arctic. In a nutshell, the Inuit of Cambridge Bay today, the people studied by the Icelandic team, are simply not the same people as those observed a century ago by Stefansson. The DNA tests need to be carried out on Inuit living in the other modern settlement on Victoria Island, or DNA needs to be sought within analysis of human remains from archaeological sites.

At the moment we don't have the evidence to know whether the Vikings did visit Victoria Island. Stefansson's account raises the possibility. Perhaps Victoria Island was the extreme distance reached by the Vikings. Further west, south and north the ice presents a barrier that was surely beyond the capabilities of a Viking ship, yet Victoria Island, given favourable conditions, is technically just reachable in a summer of voyaging from Greenland.

High Arctic Vikings

Viking traces in the Canadian High Arctic and Hudson Bay are in areas where we would once never have expected to find them. This is one of the last corners of the earth to have been explored in modern times, and in the nineteenth century was perceived as a near-impenetrable wilderness. It would have been remarkable had a single Viking ship made a voyage into the Canadian High Arctic. Yet these voyages were of such a number that they have left archaeological traces which we have found even in the immensity of the Canadian High Arctic. No one seems to have attempted to extrapolate from the number of Viking archaeological finds an estimate of the number of Viking ships that voyaged in the Canadian High Arctic. The supposition must be that numbers were substantial. The Vikings had the ships and skills to sail these far northern waters, and they travelled as far as their technology would permit.

The Inuit may remember them – though it would seem that they had little interest in the Vikings. There may or may not be Viking genetic traces in some Inuit populations – with the increasing frequency of DNA testing, time will tell.

Most problematic are the disputed Viking archaeological finds, particularly the Kensington Runestone. Of course it has to be a fake – anything else would be just too big an upset to received history. Though we cannot suggest how it may have been forged or why, scholarly caution must regard it as a fake, and it is hard to imagine the acceptable test or evidence that could prove it genuine. Nevertheless, Viking archaeological remains could exist in the vicinity of rivers which drain ultimately into Hudson Bay – the sort of location in which Kensington is found. There should be Viking remains along the passages into Hudson Bay and on its shores, particularly the south-west. There should be evidence of Vikings along the rivers that drain into Hudson Bay, including those that provide access to the great plains of North America. The people whom we know voyaged to such extreme destinations as Ellesmere Island and Axel Heiberg Island and perhaps Victoria Island plausibly made journeys to the Great Plains, which were more attractive in terms of climate and resources. Sooner or later such archaeological remains must surely be found, and which will satisfy the most stringent tests of authenticity to which they will be subjected.

A generation ago, the idea of Viking presence in the centre of the North American continent was gaining both academic and public support. The Minneapolis-based American Football team, the Minnesota Vikings, took its name in 1960 reflecting in part the Scandinavian heritage of many of the nineteenth-century settlers in the region, in part the scholarly acceptance that finds including the Kensington Runestone were then enjoying. Today the pendulum has swung towards greater scholarly caution, to the extent that it is possible to wonder just what evidence the scholarly community would need to consider Viking presence in the region proved.

Some of the evidence of the possible Viking penetration of the Canadian High Arctic, Hudson Bay and the American Great Plains will surely be shown to be false. But already we have sound evidence in even less hospitable High Arctic regions, and if the Vikings could sail such difficult waters, they certainly had the ships to reach Hudson Bay and the rivers that drain into it. Surely time will show that the Minnesota Vikings are well-named, and the world will come to accept that the Vikings penetrated as far as present-day Minnesota.

7
Vikings and Inuit

GREENLAND was the lynch-pin of the trans-Atlantic route, and the peaceful interaction of Viking and Inuit within Greenland crucial to keeping open the passage from Europe to America. Curiously, Viking interaction with the Inuit is a topic which has received little attention, with almost all that has been written on the subject devoted to the questionable theory that the Inuit were responsible for the extinction of the Greenland colony. While the evidence remains sparse, enough now exists to establish a broad picture of the two peoples who lived side-by-side in Greenland for around four centuries.

Since 1977 the term 'Inuit' has been used in place of 'Eskimo', a term now deemed offensive. Eskimo is a Native American Micmac tribe name meaning 'raw-meat eaters'. Inuit, as used today, designates one ethnic, linguistic and cultural group. Ethnically the Inuit people are of Asian origin and cognate with the Mongolians; linguistically they speak one of three closely related Inuit languages; culturally they have a highly developed and specialised culture which enables survival in the High Arctic. The dog team and dog sled, the kayak and umiak boats, the toggled harpoon and the igloo are all unique developments of Inuit culture.

A fair measure of confusion has been brought to the field by the tendency to label many non-Inuit groups who lived in Greenland and the Canadian High Arctic before the Inuit as 'Inuit'. Popular books on Greenland abound with assertions that the Inuit have occupied the country for millennia, yet this is simply not the case, for while Greenland has a long history of occupation, the early peoples were not Inuit.

Pre-Viking Peoples of Greenland
There is a pressing need for a consolidated study of the prehistory of all the Arctic peoples of northern America and Greenland, along with work on the

prehistory and history of the Inuit. The many misconceptions relating to the peoples of the Arctic and Greenland need to be addressed. At present, while there is work on the history and archaeology of the prehistoric peoples of Greenland, the work which is most reliable tends to be restricted to one group or archaeological site, while the remainder is for the most part overly broad in its scope.

The west coast of Greenland was without people at the time of the Vikings' arrival. Probably there was a small settlement of a pre-Inuit people on the mid east coast – and possibly there were people on the northern coast. The part of Greenland that the Vikings occupied and the surrounding regions were empty, and had been for some hundreds of years. Yet while the land was without people at the time of the Vikings' arrival, it had once been populated. The story of these early peoples in Greenland gives clues to the ways in which their successors stood to flourish or decline, and suggests how the Inuit and Vikings would have interacted.

The earliest people of Greenland are known from scanty archaeological remains, and are called simply the 'Independence I Culture' after the area – Independence Fjord – in which the first recorded archaeological remains have been found. The very earliest remains of people of the Independence I culture date from around 3000 BC. Five millennia before our time and four millennia before the Vikings arrived, man had reached Greenland. Independence I Culture people entered Greenland from the opposite direction to the Vikings. In the far north-west, Greenland comes close to the Canadian Arctic islands, and the winter ice of Smith Sound provides a bridge from Ellesmere Island, at its closest just 12 miles from Greenland. This is the route that the people of Independence I Culture took, and from their landfall at Greenland's north-west corner they spread along the north coast. The inland ice meets the sea in north-west Greenland, presenting an effective barrier to southward expansion on the west coast to this people, who are believed to have been without boats; the poor hunting resources of the north-east coast appear to have been similarly effective in preventing southward development of Independence I Culture down the east coast. The first human settlement in Greenland was therefore in the extreme north, and at latitudes as far north and further north than those inhabited by anyone today or in historic times. Indeed, with the exception of the Nord scientific station (which is no-one's permanent home), no-one in Greenland now lives as far north as the territory occupied by these first settlers of Greenland. Their population is estimated at about 500 people, stable for a millennium and a half; they were Stone Age hunters. They were not Inuit in terms of either ethnicity or culture. Independence I and all other pre-Viking cultures did not make igloos, keep huskies or sail in kayaks, and had no connection whatsoever with the modern Inuit culture. Their ethnicity may have been related to the Plains Indians of North America.

Around BC 1800 another culture is found in Greenland, the Saqqaq culture. People belonging to this culture are found inhabiting land south of that occupied by Independence I on both east and west coasts, suggesting that these new migrants had boats. Indeed, it has been suggested that their migration into Greenland was by boat across Baffin Bay and the Davis Strait from Baffin Island rather than across the Smith Sound ice bridge from Ellesmere Island, though this route remains little more than speculation. Independence I and Saqqaq peoples coexisted, occupying different parts of Greenland. Their culture was separate, and they appear to have lived within different ecological environments.

Around BC 1400 a third migration into Greenland occurred, using the Smith Sound ice bridge. Again these are a non-Inuit people, with a completely different culture to the Inuit, and like Independence I without boats, dogs or igloos. They occupy the land previously held by Independence I, and as the early evidence of this culture was found on the shore of Independence Fjord overlying the remains of Independence I they are called Independence II Culture. Like Independence I, they are a Stone Age hunting community, though they must have possessed a strategic advantage which enabled them to swamp a population that had been present for many centuries. While initially established on the north coast, towards the end of its period Independence II moved south on both east and west coasts, indicating that they had learned the use of boats, perhaps from contact with Saqqaq Culture peoples.

The final chapter in pre-Viking settlement of Greenland is the Dorset Culture. A climatic disturbance around BC 500 disrupted hunting patterns and weakened both Saqqaq and Independence II Cultures. Shortly after BC 500 the more advanced Dorset Culture replaced both Saqqaq and Independence II Cultures. The Dorset Culture take-over of Greenland may be a new migration into Greenland from around BC 500 – a view conventionally held – or it may be the expansion of a culture which had already gained a toe-hold in Greenland. Recent excavations at Qeqertasussuk (in the Disko Bay area) have unearthed remains (as yet unconfirmed) of Dorset Culture from as early as BC 2000. Assuming these results are confirmed, they suggest a migration of the Dorset Culture into one or more localities, including Disko Bay, prior to BC 2000, and the subsequent spread of this culture throughout Greenland following BC 500, when climatic disturbances caused difficulties for Saqqaq and Independence II Cultures. Dorset Culture appears heavily influenced by both Saqqaq and Independence II Cultures, which is consistent with coexistence of the cultures in Greenland in the period BC 2000–500. The Dorset Culture, like those that went before it, was a Stone Age culture of hunters, but modified through some use of iron, made possible through collection of iron meteorites from the ice cap. In the early centuries of the first millennium AD climatic changes in the form of a gradual warming led to a slow decline of the Dorset Culture, especially in the south. As Stone Age hunters they flourished better where seal and walrus were more common, and as the climate warmed the seal and walrus numbers declined, and with them the Dorset Culture. Well before the Vikings arrived, the Dorset Culture had relinquished occupation of south and west Greenland. At the very latest they survived in the north and east of Greenland to AD 1200, though even here they may have vanished by AD 1000. There are no accounts in the sagas or archaeological evidence for interaction between the Vikings and the Dorset Culture; rather, there is just one brief encounter on the east coast, the visit to the Scoresbysund area by Thorgils Orrabeinfostre where he reports an encounter with 'witches'.

The early cultures show a surprising pattern of settlement expansion in Greenland in that it was north-to-south.[1] The earliest settlements are all in the north, with a gradual spread down the east and west coasts. Only the last wave of the early settlers reached as far as the south of Greenland, and this was the first area they deserted as the climate warmed. Hunters flourished on the resources of the High Arctic, but found areas further south to be marginal for survival. For such communities the boundary between ice and open sea, with the rich fish and seal life this margin supported, was essential for survival, and the northern and eastern areas were therefore more attractive. The climatic disturbance that led to the extinction of the Dorset Culture was not a cooling but rather a warming, which disrupted their food supply. By contrast the Vikings, as farmers, were equipped to occupy the south-west Greenland area that was no longer able to support hunter-gatherers. The different niches inhabited by the pre-Viking hunter-gatherers and the Viking farmers are illustrated from the very beginning.

The distribution patterns of three of the early cultures – Saqqaq, late Independence II and Dorset – indicates that they had boats, though what they were made from is not known. Presumably the boats were used in the fjords of Greenland and along the sea ice-edge, even crossing Baffin Bay by hugging an ice-edge. There is no evidence that early peoples from Greenland made voyages further east, for example to Iceland, and presumably their boats were not capable of such a crossing. Yet they must have known of the existence of Iceland, for the ice-capped mountain of Snaefelsness can be seen from Greenland. The Denmark Strait served as an absolute barrier. The special achievement of the Vikings is that they were the first people to have ships capable of crossing this barrier, the most challenging gap between the North Atlantic stepping-stones.

When the Vikings arrived in Greenland the very last of the Dorset Culture there was on the point of extinction. The few members of that people briefly encountered on Greenland's east coast represented a tribe that vanished within a few years. Throughout the High Arctic the Dorset Culture was in decline. On Baffin Island it may have survived for a little longer – at Cape Dorset, for example, the archetypal site from which the Dorset Culture takes its name, and where the people were most securely established. Yet even on Baffin Island the Dorset Culture was in fast decline. Presumably the Vikings must have encountered them here, though there is no record. Possibly the presence of a people on Baffin Island may be the reason why there seems to have been no Viking settlement there.

The very last survival of Dorset Culture was on three islands in the north of Hudson Bay: Southampton, Coats and Walrus islands. Here a people, called by the Inuit the Sivullirmiut, meaning 'first inhabitants', existed until into the twentieth century, and some description of the people and their lifestyle has been preserved. As their own name for themselves has not been noted, the Inuit name Sivullirmiut is the only one available.

The Sivullirmiut were clearly not Inuit. They lacked the artefacts central to Inuit culture: dogs and dogsleds, kayaks, igloos and toggled harpoons. The earliest description is from Captain George Francis Lyon,[2] a whaler who visited the area in 1824 and noted that they spoke a 'strange dialect' – presumably meaning that his Inuit interpreter could not translate. He describes the people in the following terms: '. . . mild manners, quiet speech, and as grateful for kindness, as they were anxious to return it'.

Contact with Westerners led to Western diseases, and by 1896 it was noted that the population had declined to around 70 people. A 1902 visit by a whaling ship, the *Active*, resulted in an outbreak of disease, probably typhoid or typhus, with the result that the whole community died with great speed, so that before the *Active* sailed at the end of the winter this people was extinct.

Lyon gives us a description of a crude boat used by the Sivullirmiut, which was made from three inflated seal-skins tied together with seal intestine and rowed with a paddle of whalebone. This is completely different from the finely crafted kayak and umiaq of the Inuit. Reports note distinctive hairstyles. Men wore their hair gathered into a ball on their forehead. Women twisted their hair into two heavy 'clubs' hanging from each temple. Both men and women were tattooed. They wore mittens made from bird skins, and trousers from polar bear hide – this last fashion found also in some Inuit groups. Material culture, mainly from excavations, show a prevalence for tiny stone blades.

In the Sivullirmiut we have a survival into the twentieth century of a Stone Age culture. It is, of course, possible that there was intermarriage between the Inuit and the Dorset Culture, and in this way the present-day Inuit may claim the Dorset Culture as their kin. Yet it should be stressed that the Dorset Culture are a completely different ethnic and cultural group, and the modern trend in Greenland and Canada to label the Dorset Culture as 'Inuit Culture' or even just 'Inuit' is simply wrong.

After all these cultures in Greenland it is a coincidence that the Vikings arrived at just the time when Greenland was uninhabited – at least in the areas where the Vikings settled. Save for the last remnant in Greenland of the Dorset Culture people on the east coast, the Vikings had the whole of an enormous land to themselves. Had their migration been a few hundred years earlier or later they would have found the land occupied, just as they did on the American mainland. Had timings been different it is unlikely that the Greenland colony would have been established because it was not then an empty land, and hence unlikely that the Viking American adventure would have happened.

The Inuit Arrival

The empty land of the High Arctic and Greenland proved attractive to another group, the Inuit. Their expansion in the region corresponds with the Viking Age.

The present-day distribution of the Inuit is vast. In the west they are found in Siberia on the Chukov Peninsula facing the Bering Strait. Across the Bering Strait in Alaska the Inuit have settled most of the coast including the Aleutian

Islands. Their distribution includes the coast of the Barren Lands of northern Canada, many islands of the Canadian Arctic archipelago, the northeast and west shores of Hudson Bay, and the Labrador coast. In Greenland today Inuit are found on the west coast from Thule to Cape Farewell, and on the central east coast. This is a truly remarkable spread through the Arctic. In so many areas the Inuit are unique. They alone in historic times have maintained wholly self-supporting settlements in the far north, as far north as Thule at 78° north. They alone have settled the High Arctic both summer and winter. By contrast in Siberia, the Chukchi and Samoyed people visit the High Arctic in the summer, but migrate south into the shelter of the forests for the winter – the Inuit are the only habitual year-round inhabitants of the far north.

The Inuit expansion is a recent one.[3] Archaeology confirms this. While writers hesitate to consider the question of Inuit origins to be completely solved the consensus is that the Inuit have spread from Siberia. Ethnically they are an Asian people related to the Mongolians, whom they most closely resemble. The date of their expansion out of Asia is still a matter of conjecture, with dates proposed ranging from around 6,000 years ago to around 1,500 years ago. The issue seems capable of a solution in language terms. Linguistically a divergence much more than 1,500 years ago is simply not possible. From Siberia to east Greenland they have one language, which is mutually comprehensible, though divided into dialects. The isolation of Inuit communities would be expected to promote the development of linguistic variation and therefore the rapid development of different languages. That this has not occurred suggests that the expansion of the Inuit is recent – scarcely more than 1,500 years old. Indeed, the proposed dates of up to 6,000 years ago seem to be part of an effort to see pre-Inuit peoples of Greenland, Baffin Island and elsewhere in the Arctic Archipelago as Inuit.

Approximate key dates in Inuit migration have been established by archaeological evidence. Migration into the coast of the Barren Lands around the MacKenzie Delta can be dated to around the year 1000. A century later, around 1100, there is an expansion west and north-west to Victoria Island and to the Thule region of Greenland. Migrations south occurred to Baffin Island and the Melville Peninsula around 1200, to south-west Greenland perhaps around 1350, to Labrador and much of Hudson Bay around 1500, and to the Chesterfield Inlet region as late as 1800. Much of the Inuit expansion therefore took place at precisely the times that the Vikings were exploring these same territories. Interaction of the two groups was inevitable, and it may even be that each group in effect facilitated the expansion of the other.

Where the Vikings and Inuit met depends on the speed of their expansion. Everything that is known about Viking expansion shows it to be remarkable for its rapidity, so for example the Vinland voyages were undertaken by the son of the first colonist of Greenland. My own view is that with no factor to limit their expansion, the Vikings would have explored very quickly. We know that the Vikings reached Ellesmere Island and perhaps Victoria Island, though not when; we know that the Inuit reached these same islands around 1100, passing through Ellesmere for Thule in Greenland. A meeting of Viking and Inuit early in the twelfth century seems the best fit for the evidence available.

The Inuit expansion was rapid. From the Barren Lands around the Mackenzie delta to Thule is in excess of 1,500 miles by any plausible route, yet was accomplished in a generation or two. While the decline of the Dorset Culture may have facilitated the expansion, it is not in itself sufficient to explain it. A hypothesis may be advanced that the factor which explains the Inuit expansion comes from contact with the Vikings – and plausibly this factor is metal-working.

Inuit culture in the West is a Stone Age culture. Only in the High Arctic of the Canadian Archipelago and in Greenland is metal used, which suggests a discovery of metal working around 1100, and carried east following the direction of Inuit migration. The Inuit in the east use both copper and iron, in effect jumping in a generation or two from the Stone Age not to its natural successor, the Bronze Age, but direct to the Iron Age. Metal-working may be a skill learned through contact with the Vikings.

Inuit Metal-Working

Metallurgy – the smelting of ores to extract metal – is unknown in Native American cultures anywhere north of present-day Mexico. Even south of Mexico, where the cultures of Central and Southern America did develop metallurgy, it was used predominantly for working gold and silver into ornament. The production and working of bronze and iron, central to the cultures that followed the Stone Age, is found nowhere in North America. The nearest approach to conventional metal-working was in locations where copper occurs naturally in its pure form, for example in the Upper Midwest, where there was some use of the metal to produce ornaments. The metal was worked through hammering, which creates brittleness, making the metal unsuitable for functional uses as tools. Closer to the Inuit area, the Eyak people of Alaska had access to copper, which can be found as pure nuggets in river silt, and used these nuggets as decorative beads. Even the Dorset Culture in Greenland is known to have made some rudimentary use of meteorite iron. But all these processes are without smelting, and are using metal as a malleable stone rather than truly working the metal.

Within this American context of no true metallurgy, the Inuit's use of metal is all the more surprising. On Victoria Island the Inuit group is known today as the Copper Inuit,[4] accurately reflecting their use of copper. Pure copper can be found in the Coppermine River and in the vicinity of Coronation Gulf, which are areas accessible to the Inuit, though requiring journeys of considerable length. For Inuit in the vicinity of the present-day settlement of Holman this is a trip of more than 100 miles in each direction, and that the Inuit have undertaken the journey on a yearly basis until recent times emphasises the value they place on copper. The copper is used for spear-heads, knives of all descriptions, and for a variety of inventive functions. For example copper is used as a staple to fasten together the pieces of a broken pot. Copper that was simply hammered to make the implements would be brittle. The Copper Inuit have mastered annealing, a process of slow heating which hardens the metal. Annealing is not smelting, and is not true metallurgy, but it is a significant step further along the road of metalworking than is exhibited by other Native North American peoples.

Further to the east, copper does not occur naturally. In Greenland the Inuit, particularly the Polar Inuit of Thule, discovered a source of iron in meteorites. Most meteorites are composed almost entirely of iron, and in theory could be used anywhere in the world as a source of workable metal. However, in most parts of the world they are not easy to find. By contrast in Greenland the central ice cap produces conditions which do make them easy to find. The ice cap is completely without terrestrial rocks or debris on its surface. Winds blow away what little snow falls, leaving anything that falls on the ice clearly visible. A black meteorite on the ice sheet is readily found. The Polar Inuit made use of meteorites to produce much the same range of metal tools as the Copper Inuit. The process was one of chipping away excess metal, and hammering to produce the required shape and blade. This is laborious, but it does result in serviceable tools.

In addition to naturally occurring copper and meteoric iron the Inuit had access to salvaged metal. The nineteenth and early twentieth centuries offer numerous examples of European and American shipwrecks that were stripped by the Inuit, with the iron nails and metal fitments particularly valued. The Viking Age would have provided some scrap metal.

The thesis has not elsewhere been considered that the Inuit learned to value metal and to work it through contact with the Vikings. Alone among the indigenous peoples of North America the eastern Inuit developed metal-working skills sufficiently advanced to produce functional tools. This advance occurred at the time of contact between the Vikings and the Inuit, and is associated with a sudden, rapid expansion of the Inuit east from Victoria Island. That the Vikings taught the Inuit to work metal is plausible.

Inuit and Viking in Greenland

One remarkable feature of Inuit culture in Greenland is their use of iron from one specific, massive meteorite.[5]

In 1818 John Ross made the discovery that the Thule Inuit of Greenland were using iron for knife blades, harpoon points and engraving tools. He seemed to be seeing a Stone Age people who had advanced direct to the use of iron without the usual intervening stage of copper-working – a people that had by-passed the Bronze Age as they moved direct from stone use to iron use. He enquired as to the source of the iron, but received no answer, perhaps because the Inuit wished to safeguard their supply. It was not until 1894 that Robert Peary discovered the source, in the form of a nickel-iron meteorite.

Named the Cape York meteorite as it was found on an island just off this cape, this is one of the largest meteorites to have hit the earth. It is believed to have fallen around 10,000 years ago, well before any human settlement of Greenland. The meteorite broke up as it fell, resulting in a scatter of large rocks as well as smaller pieces. The biggest fragment was called by the Inuit *Ahnighito* – 'the tent' – and is around 11 feet long, with a weight of 31 tons. Other fragments, called by names such as 'the woman' and 'the dog', would on their own be large meteorites. Their composition is nickel-iron, and they have been a source of metal for the Thule Inuit since the Viking Age. The primary technique used was to break off fragments of the meteorite – aided by its pitted and irregular shape – and hammer these into a tool. The task was aided somewhat by heating the metal fragment by putting it in a flame from a whale-blubber or seal-oil lamp, though little heat could have been achieved compared with that of a forge. The technique is fundamentally cold-hammering. The resulting tools lack the hardness and durability of commercially produced iron, but they were better than anything else then available to the Inuit.

The jump from Stone Age culture to one which made use of found metal to produce iron tools was assisted by cultural interaction. The Inuit saw the Vikings using iron tools, acquired these tools, and came to value them. They learned to scavenge for scrap metal in abandoned Viking settlements, and to hammer metal they found into tools they could use. The technique was then extended to using the naturally occurring scrap metal of the Cape York meteorite. The tools which John Ross saw the Inuit using were evidence of cultural interaction with the Vikings enabling a new technology to develop.

Sadly the Inuit lost their meteorite. Robert Peary managed to transport most of the pieces to ships through the expedient of constructing a short length of railway, the only one ever built in Greenland.[6] He sold the meteorite for $40,000 to the American Museum of Natural History in New York, where the Cape York meteorite can be seen today. Imported iron tools, available to the Inuit from the time of Peary's visits, were indeed superior in quality to those made from the meteorite, though available only at a cost, and it is hard to see that the Inuit did other than lose by its removal. There must have been a cultural impact too, as the meteorite had an accretion of stories around it.

8
Memories of Vikings in America

BETWEEN the end of the Greenland colony in the early fifteenth century, and with it the breakdown of the North Atlantic stepping-stone route, and Columbus's 'discovery' of the New World in 1492 is around two generations of apparent interruption of European awareness of North America.

History has repeated the myth of the Columban discovery of North America, and helped to diminish awareness of the many contacts across the North Atlantic prior to 1492. Yet in the years before Columbus, Europe did not forget the existence of the New World.

Iceland

For the people of Iceland, knowledge of Vinland was never lost. The sagas continued to be read. A survival from the sixteenth century is an Icelandic map which clearly shows Vinland. The well-verified Skalholt Map, named after the place where it was drawn, is dated *c.* 1590 and shows, in the manner of a sketch map, the North Atlantic. It is, of course, a century after the Columban voyages, yet on the American continent are four Viking names: Helluland, Markland, Skraeling Land and the Promontory of Vinland. In contrast to the Vinland Map, this map is universally acknowledged to be genuine. Although a century after Columbus and at a time when reasonably accurate maps of the east coast of North America were being produced, this map takes no notice of these maps whatsoever. Rather it is a map which draws entirely on Icelandic sources, and presents America within an Icelandic tradition. Between the first Vinland voyages around AD 1000 and this map of around 1590 stretch some 600 years of continuous knowledge of Vinland. On the basis of Icelandic sources, the Skalholt cartographer knew the continent was there.

Recently scholars in Iceland have begun to assert that Columbus actually visited Iceland some years before 1492, and that he over-wintered in

Olafsvik on the Snaefelsness peninsula, as set out in parish registers from Olafsvik.[1] Olafsvik is the closest harbour to Greenland, and the point of departure for many Icelandic boats voyaging to Greenland. Eirik the Red's first voyage to Greenland departed from nearby Breithafjordur, and the manuscript of *The Vinland Sagas* was preserved on Flatey, an island in the vicinity. Behind Olafsvik is the glacier-covered peak of Snaefell. In certain weather conditions it is possible to glimpse the ice of Greenland from this mountain; a ship which sails west from Olafsvik can, in conditions of good visibility, see Greenland before Iceland is lost to view. If the Columbus who visited Olafsvik is accepted as the same man who made the 1492 voyage, then a clear link between the Viking mariners and Columbus has been established.

Iceland's knowledge of Vinland was never really lost. As the centuries passed Iceland became more and more remote. While the Danish and Norwegian languages developed, Icelandic remained exceptionally conservative, thereby becoming progressively less and less comprehensible to the outsider. With over-population came poverty, and a great waning of scholarship in Iceland. Before the Second World War, Iceland was almost unknown to the outsider, while in the decades following independence it was geographically isolated. Even today Iceland boasts a well-stocked Mediaeval Studies library at Reykholt which is without a proper catalogue and virtually without scholars, though it is readily open to academics who wish to work there. Icelandic sources have simply been overlooked. That Columbus visited Iceland before 1492 and stayed in the very fishing village from which boats to Greenland and America set out seems to be established by Icelandic records – yet this information has not generally found its way into popular accounts of Columbus.

Denmark

Denmark's memory of the New World is tied up with the market for narwhal horn in Europe. Even today narwhal horn has a surprisingly high value. In 1994 the London auction house Christies sold an old narwhal horn for just under half a million pounds – the seller had acquired it among a job lot of old walking sticks he had purchased from Hereford Cathedral. Up to the beginning of the seventeenth century unicorn horn prices were astronomic. There is a 1553 valuation of one belonging to the king of France at £20,000; in today's money the equivalent is many millions. Queen Elizabeth I of England was presented with one by Martin Frobisher; around

1580 it was valued at £100,000. Recorded prices include £24 an ounce (in 1609) and 128 florins an ounce (in 1612) – roughly comparable prices. The cost of narwhal horn per ounce was about 20 times that of gold, far higher than the prices ever attained for elephant ivory. Thomas Decker, writing in 1609, makes the expansive comment that a unicorn horn was worth 'half a city'.

The value of unicorn horn was a function both of its scarcity and the high demand for it. The word used to describe its properties was *alexipharmic*, a word in the dictionary but perhaps not in most people's vocabularies. Alexipharmic means that it acts as an antidote to poison in food and water, and as a cure-all for maladies, particularly stomach complaints. Its use was predominantly medicinal, and for this purpose it was powdered and ingested. That so few unicorn horns have survived from the Middle Ages is simply because the nobility ate them! There is a similarity with the Chinese practice of ingesting powdered jade because it was believed to give long or even everlasting life, and jade, like unicorn horn, was accorded value because of these perceived medical benefits. An important difference is that jade is a poison; 'unicorn' horn (at least in small quantities) is harmless.

Unicorn horn was a major source of wealth for Denmark throughout the High Middle Ages and into the Renaissance. Symbolically this was recognised by the throne of the kings of Denmark, which was constructed of unicorn horn and gold. In practical terms the Danes safeguarded their wealth by restricting the supply, assisted by their *de jure* monopoly of trade with Greenland. Their supply continued even after the end of the Greenland colony, indicating continuing voyages from Denmark to Baffin Bay. It is curious to speculate how much the kings of Denmark and their advisors might have known about the true origin of the horn they were selling as unicorn horn.

In narwhal horn the Greenland settlements had access to a commodity that was of phenomenal value. The restrictions placed on trade by the Danish monopoly were undoubtedly onerous, but the value of the commodity was such that wealth must have flowed back to Greenland. That Greenland broke the monopoly by trading with other countries was inevitable when the Danish price was not the market price, and it would seem that at least some trade with Scotland did take place.

What emerges is a motivation in Denmark for keeping quiet about Greenland. The trade was of immense value, a very major source of Denmark's wealth, and was therefore worth the effort to protect it. The trade routes to Greenland were not made public, nor was information about the lands beyond Greenland, either north and east into the Canadian Arctic or south to Vinland. Greenland, Canada and America were trade secrets – and even Iceland, as a key stepping stone of the North Atlantic. This mercantile motive for secrecy backed by the power of king and court goes a long way to explain why there is so little written about Greenland and the lands to the west in the High Middle Ages.

Scotland

The Vikings of Greenland had every incentive to circumvent the Danish monopoly on their trade. If the price the Danish offered through their monopoly was not high enough it was inevitable that merchants would look elsewhere, and as there was no effective policing of the North Atlantic, the monopoly could be breached. The easiest alternative destination was Scotland, and there is evidence that a trade took place.

Unicorn horn is the most obvious item for trade from Greenland. By weight it is by far its most valuable export. It is presumably significant that around the time when trade with Greenland would have occurred the unicorn makes its appearance as a symbol for Scotland. The unicorn is not frequently encountered as a heraldic beast, and does not seem to exist at all in the earliest heraldry of Europe. Its first appearance in Scotland is at the end of the fourteenth century, when it is used as the official seal of Robert III (r. 1390–1406). It is during the reign of his son, James I (r. 1406–37) that the unicorn is first used as a supporter to the royal arms of Scotland, replacing the dragon. Subsequently the unicorn becomes a symbol of Scotland, for example as the decoration on the unicorn and demi-unicorn gold coins, valued at eighteen and nine shillings respectively. When James VI of Scotland inherited the throne of England in 1603 he created arms for his new United Kingdom which symbolised England by a lion and Scotland by a unicorn. Heraldry tells us that from at least the reign of King Robert III, unicorns mattered in Scotland.

Trade between Greenland and Scotland is magnificently exemplified by the Lewis Chessmen, now acclaimed as one of the greatest treasures of the United Kingdom.[2] The Lewis Chessmen were found in 1831 at Uig, Isle of Lewis, one of Scotland's Western Isles. Following a storm they were dis-covered by Calum nan Sprot among the debris of a piece of sea-meadow – called machair in the Western Isles – that had fallen onto the beach. He saw the faces of these tiny figures, thought they were goblins and fled in terror. The Presbyterian minister for Uig, Alexander MacLeod, exorcised the site, retrieved the chessmen, and sold them to the British Museum. Subsequently other chessmen were found, up to a total of around 120. Of these, 81 are now in the British Museum and 11 in the National Museum of Scotland. The hoard consists of 8 kings, 8 queens, 16 bishops, 15 knights, 12 rooks, and 19 pawns, as well as some other gaming pieces. The kings, queens, bishops, knights and rooks are presented as human figures, finely carved.

The carving shows exceptional detail and a sensitivity that makes them truly works of art, such that they are now popularly regarded as one of the very top artistic treasures of Britain. The date for the chessmen has been set as 1150–1200, predominantly on the basis of the clothing styles of the pieces – a date closer to 1150 is usually favoured, though conservative fashions wherever they were made might suggest a later date. There are pieces from at least four chess sets. The plausible assumption is that the chess sets were part of a merchant's stock; why they were concealed is a matter for conjecture.

In the Viking world the ancient game of chess developed in a distinctive form called *taefel*. Dating back to Germanic prehistory, certainly at least as far as the first century AD, it was an unusual variant of chess in that the two sides were of unequal numbers. The king and his associates were the smaller group, situated in the centre of the board, while the larger group was the attacking army. The object of the game was for the king to reach safety at the edge of the board, and for the attacking army to prevent him doing so. The Vikings were passionate about *taefel*, with almost everyone playing it, and they considered proficiency in the game to be a required skill of a noble – indeed it was considered that *taefel* embodied the heroic ideal. When Leif Eiriksson over-wintered in Vinland it is a virtual certainty that he and his men whiled away the winter evenings playing *taefel*. The game that we know as chess reached the Viking world around the early twelfth century, where it blended with *taefel*, the same pieces often being used for both games. The Lewis Chessmen are pieces from the game of chess, but heavily influenced by the Viking styles of *taefel* pieces. Thus for example the rooks are depicted as berserkers, the maniacal warriors of the Viking period, biting their own shields.

The Chessmen are almost all made from walrus ivory, with the remainder being carved from whale tooth. The walrus ivory must be from Greenland. The walrus has a distribution which is circumpolar, living predominantly at the edge of the ice pack and moving north in summer and south in winter as the ice-edge moves. In Europe walrus are found only in Spitsbergen and along the edge of the Arctic Ocean ice. In these areas they were unmolested by man in Viking times as the area was too remote. Populations accessible to hunters are found in Greenland, both north-east and north-west coasts, and in the Arctic archipelago. The walrus ivory of the Lewis Chessmen was either harvested in Greenland or transported via the Greenland colonies. In artistic style the chessmen cannot be precisely attributed to any area; indeed, they are artistically unique. Both Trondheim and Dublin are among the places suggested for their production, though without any real evidence for either. The scenario most writers envisage is that the ivory was exported from Greenland to either Norway or Ireland, carved there, then somehow found its way to a west-facing beach on Lewis – a location that in European terms is on the way to nowhere. A far simpler explanation is that the walrus ivory was taken from a Baffin Bay hunting ground to the Greenland settlements, carved there, then brought to Scotland as a luxury good for trade. Uig on Lewis is more or less the closest Scottish landfall to Greenland, and precisely where a ship from Greenland might reasonably have landed. The simplest explanation for the unique style of the Lewis Chessmen and the location of the find is that they are a product of Viking Greenland. Quite how this thesis might be tested is unclear. Perhaps they should be regarded not just as a treasure of Britain, but also as a treasure of Greenland.

A hint as to the existence of trade between the British Isles and Scotland is provided by early maps. One such is by Petrus Bertius, the *Descriptio Britanniae Magnae* of 1616. This postcard-sized map draws on a long tradition of mapping the British Isles, and like most of these early maps shows the island of Rona. Rona is an island which today has been left off almost all maps of the British Isles. It is a speck of land with an area a little over half a square mile, part of it a cliff-bound hill rising 355 feet, part a plateau of rock at sea level. The whole island is rock-bound, and has no anchorage. It is not on maps because of its extreme remoteness, for at 44 miles NNE of the Isle of Lewis and a little more NNW of Cape Wrath, it is the extreme north-western point of Britain, and is simply off the page for most maps. Of the few that mark it, some call it North Rona to distinguish it from another Rona in the Inner Hebrides. The island is virtually unknown. Although even more remote than St Kilda, evacuated in 1930, or Foula, currently Britian's most remote inhabited island, there has been little recent interest in the island, largely because of its inaccessibility. At least until the 1950s an annual boat visited from Lewis to harvest seabirds, but with the decline in popularity of the Highland goose and other seabirds on British tables the harvest has ceased. Rona has a Norse name – Ron Ay, or Seal Island – and is believed to have been inhabited continuously from the eighth century until 1885, when its last two inhabitants died on the island.

The surprise is that this scrap of land should play such a prominent part on early maps. A solution is available within the context of the sea routes to Greenland. Sailors leaving the Viking settlements on the west coast of Greenland travelled south along the coast until Cape Farewell, Greenland's southernmost point, was rounded, then due east across the north Atlantic. Cape Farewell is at 59° north, precisely the latitude of Rona. The high hill of Rona makes the island visible from a distance – at least in good weather – in theory even from as much as 50 miles away in the pollution-free atmosphere of the Middle Ages. If Rona was missed a ship might well be in trouble. If the ship passed to the north of Rona it might make a landfall on Orkney, the Fair Isle or Shetland; if it missed to the south the landfall might be Scotland's north coast around Cape Wrath, or the west coast of Lewis – specifically Uig, where the Chessmen were found.

Rona is no place to land a ship; rather it is a direction indicator. A ship from Greenland on the due east heading we know was used and turning due south at Rona drops neatly between Cape Wrath – a key Viking direction headland – and the Butt of Lewis, into the more sheltered waters of the Minch, and can find a harbour there, perhaps at Dunvegan.

The Vatican

The greatest archive of European history is held by the Vatican. Completely separate from the Vatican Library which routinely admits scholars, the collection has the official title of 'L'Archivio Segreto Vaticano' – The Secret Archives of the Vatican.[3] It is an immense collection, the most important single mediaeval and renaissance archive anywhere in the world. There are at least 50 miles of shelving of materials covering all periods of European written history, and for most periods the Vatican's collection is believed to be the largest.

Restrictions on access to archives do exist in most national collections. The motivation is the preservation of the privacy of individuals, maintenance of commercial secrets, and restrictions on the publication of the deliberations of governments. Generally there is a maximum duration of 100 years on restrictions to access, and frequently the duration of restriction is 30, 50 or 70 years. At the moment there is a global trend to avoid secrecy, and fewer and fewer archives are unavailable. Thus for example in the United Kingdom the Freedom of Information Act grants considerable access rights to individuals and to groups.

The Vatican by contrast restricts access to all records. It is certainly possible to apply for access, and access is even sometimes granted. Yet the process is byzantine. The decision on access is made in theory by the Pope himself, in practice by the Prefect of the Archive, a priest who oversees the archive. The Prefect takes into account criteria which include the academic credentials of the applicant and their reason for visiting the archive. If there is already a scholar who has been granted access who is deemed to be working in a similar area then the application is likely to be refused. If the research is considered inappropriate, or the indication of what the scholar wants to see is not precise enough, then the application will probably be refused. Almost all applicants are refused. Almost all successful applicants are Roman Catholic priests. In 1999 a total of 1,444 scholars gained access to the Archives, the largest number in one year ever. This is comparable to the number of people visiting a small-town archive office in Europe or North America – somewhere with records primarily of local interest only.

As far as I am aware no request for access in order to investigate Vatican records of Vinland and Greenland has ever been approved. In a Kafkaesque move it is not even possible to access the highly imperfect index – for the index is available only to those who have been granted access, and draconian measures are in place to stop copying.

A scholar who actually gains access to the Secret Archives is faced with innumerable practical problems. In the words of Maria Luisa Ambrosini, the leading writer on the Secret Archives, 'The difficulties of research are so great that sometimes a student, having enthusiastically gone through the complicated procedure of getting permission to work in the Archives, disappears after a few days' work and never shows up again.' In the restrictions presently in place for access to the Vatican Secret Archive we have a system which suggests that the Vatican believes it has something to hide, and a level of secrecy that in the legal systems of European nation states would tend to be illegal.

Without access being granted for scholars it is hard to be sure just what the Vatican did and did not know about America before Columbus. Yet they knew something! Take for example the monument to Pope Innocent VIII, which was erected first in the old St Peter's Basilica, then moved to the new, with the following inscription added, where it remains today. The inscription reads as follows:

D.O.M.
INNOCENTIO VIII CYBO PONT MAX
ITALICAE PACIS PERPETVO CVSTODI
NOVI ORBIS SVO AEVO INVENTI GLORIA
REGI HISPANIARVM CATHOLICI NOMINE IMPOSITO
CRVCIS SACRO SSANCTAE
REPERTO TITVLO
LANCAE QVAE CHRISTI HAVSIT LATVS
A BAIAZETE TVRCARVM IMPER TYRANNOI DONO MISSA
AETERNVM INSIGNI
MONVMENTVM VETERE BASILICA HVC TRANSLATVM
ALBERICVS CYBO MALASPINA
PRINCEPS MASSAE
FERENTILLI DVX MARCHIO CARRARIAE ETC
PRONEPOS
ORNATIVS AVGUSTIVSQ POSVIT ANNO DOM MDCXXI

> *To God, the Best and Greatest, and to Innocent VIII Cybo, Pope, perpetual guardian of the Italic peace, distinguished for the glory of the New World discovered in his time, for having imposed the name Catholic on the King of Spain, for having recovered the most Holy Cross and the spear that pierced the side of Christ sent as a gift by Bajazet tyrant of the Turks, this eternal monument was moved here from the old basilica by Alberico Cybo Malaspina, prince of Massa, duke of Ferentillo, marquis of Carrara etcetera, his great nephew, who, with great decorum and magnificence, placed it here AD 1621.*

The Holy Cross and the spear that pierced the side of Christ are relics recovered by Innocent VIII, while the title of Catholic Kings was indeed granted by him to the rulers of the newly united Kingdom of Spain. Most curious is the reference to the New World as 'discovered in his time'. Innocent VIII died nine days before Columbus set out on his first voyage. This monument with its new inscription was set up in the most prestigious spot possible, the

Basilica of St Peters in Rome. A mistake is scarcely possible as an explanation. Even were Innocent VIII to have been alive when Columbus made his voyage it is difficult to see how the popes could have claimed any credit for it – the voyage was funded by the Spanish monarchs. Rather the claim seems implicit that the popes sponsored voyages to discover the new world prior to 1492. Columbus's voyage was not a discovery, but rather a piece of propaganda by which the newly unified Spain could lay claim to the New World.

England

The key link between Viking exploration and later British exploration is the voyage made by Nicholas of Lynne, who took part in an expedition 1360–64, and made a report of this voyage to the King of England, Edward III. The report should be seen within the context of the expansionist ambitions of Edward III (*r.* 1327–1377), one of the longest reigning English monarchs, whose policy set the direction for England for centuries to come. Edward III saw himself as king not just of England, but also of France, and his assertion of this claim precipitated the Hundred Years War in which England initially consolidated its claim to much of what is now France. His wars against Scotland sought to extend English power to the north. Something of the spirit of English nationalism can be set out in his plans to revive King Arthur's 'Round Table' – an idea proposed in 1344 but not directly acted upon – and his subsequent creation in 1348 of the Order of the Garter as a chivalrous military order in part inspired by the stories of King Arthur. The report given by Nicholas of Lynne would have been seen as a description of lands over which England could seek to extend its influence and perhaps its rule. It is a foretaste of the colonial age, and the expansionist spirit that would create the British Empire.

The voyage which Nicholas of Lynne joined was not an English venture, but rather a military expedition carried out on the orders of King Haakon of Norway on which an Englishman was present. Possibly he – or Edward III – paid for the privilege; possibly the Norwegians required an expert in the use of the astrolabe, a skill which no Norwegian may have possessed. The expedition had orders to travel to Greenland, then to the lands west from there. That it took place is beyond doubt, and we know that multiple accounts of it once existed, though no complete account has survived. We are, therefore, left to piece together the story from fragmented sources.

The simplest confirmation of the visit to Greenland is the existence of two Inuit kayaks which the expedition took as souvenirs, and which were for many years kept in Oslo. So Archbishop Claus Magnus writes: 'In the year 1505 I personally saw two skinboats above the western entrance within the cathedral dedicated to the sainted Halward . . . It is stated that King Haakon captured them when he with his battle fleet passed the coast of Greenland.'[4]

After Greenland the expedition travelled to Labrador, and as far as 54° south, which is the latitude of Hamilton Inlet. The expedition then travelled north along the Labrador coast, west through Hudson Strait and into Hudson Bay.

Very little is recorded about Nicholas of Lynne. Richard Hakluyt (*c.* 1552–1616), Professor of Geography at Oxford, states that he took part in a voyage to lands near the North Pole around 1360. By the North Pole he meant the north magnetic pole, so the reference is to what is now the Canadian High Arctic. He is described as 'a priest with an astrolabe' and 'an English minorite from Oxford', that is, a priest in the Minorite order of St Francis. As the astrolabe was used to make maps, we can infer that Nicholas of Lynne was working as a map-maker for Edward III. His 1364 report to the king was described as an account of lands from 54° north towards the Pole. Called the *Inventio Fortuna*, this document is now lost. So too is the account that was given by the expedition to King Haakon of Norway. An account deriving from Nicholas was written down by a Dutch explorer known to later English writers as James Cnoyen of Boise-le-Duc. Again this account, written in 'Belgica Lingua' (presumably the Flemish language) is lost, but it was read by Gerardus Mercator (1512–94), the cartographer who gave us the Mercator projection. Mercator made notes which he passed to John Dee (1527–1608), mathematician and man of letters.

What information has survived is from John Dee's notes, and relayed through the rather long list of intermediaries as set out above. The account we have is abbreviated, fragmentary, and many steps removed from the original source. John Dee's notes read as follows:

> As Mercator mentioneth out of a probable author, there was a frier of Oxford who himselfe went verye farre north aboue 200 years ago . . . He reporteth that the southwest parte of that lande is a fruitful and holesome soil. The northeast parte is inhabited with a people called pygmei, whiche are not at the uttermose above four foote high . . . there is never in these parts

so much wind as might be sufficient to drive a cornmill . . . it
is divided into four partes or Ilandes by foure greate guttes, indrafts, or channels, running violently and delivering themselves
into a monstrous receptacle and swallowing sincke, with such
a violent force and currant, that a Shippe beying entred never
so little within one of those foure indrafts, cannot be holden
backe by the force of any great winde, but runneth in headlong
by that deep swallowing into the bowels of the earth . . .

The story as it has come down to us is a curious one, though resolves reasonably well into a coherent description. An astrolabe was a mediaeval instrument for determining the altitude of the sun, or any other celestial body.
Using this information, along with the time of day and the date, it was possible to calculate latitude. Thus the astrolabe was an early sextant, though
rather harder to use, and in the absence of tables to look up a reading and
get the latitude, it required a fair competence in mathematics to use. The
astrolabe seems to have been invented by the Arabs around the eighth
century AD, and knowledge of it was brought back to Europe through the
crusades. In the late fourteenth century the use of the astrolabe was something of an English speciality. Geoffrey Chaucer, remembered today for the
Canterbury Tales and other literary works, was known in his own age as the
author of *A Treatise on the Astrolabe*, written around 1391 and the oldest
description in English of any complex scientific instrument. Chaucer com-
piles his work for the latitude of Oxford, which is the city associated with
Nicholas of Lynne. Presumably the Norwegian expedition required an expert in the use of the astrolabe, and employed an English expert.

A strange comment in the description is that an area of the north: 'there
is never in these parts so much wind as might be sufficient to drive a cornmill . . .' While this seems implausible there is in fact a place which fits this
description. Uniquely, Hudson Bay is 'singularly free from storm or fog'
(*New International Encyclopedia*), while meteorological records confirm
the virtual absence of high winds on Hudson Bay, and often the absence
of any significant wind. The description plausibly refers to Hudson Bay,
and cannot reasonably refer to anywhere else in Europe or North America.
The four channels of the description can be understood as the entrance to
Hudson Bay, where Hudson Strait is obstructed by three islands, Salisbury,
Nottingham and Mill islands, forming four channels as it passes them. The
reference to strong currents is correct for this location. Within Hudson

Bay, the south-west suggests the area around the estuary of the Churchill River. This is a forested land which could reasonably be described as fruitful and wholesome. The north-east of the same land mass is the Chesterfield Inlet region. Today the indigenous people are Inuit; however, the Inuit have arrived subsequent to the fourteenth century. In the time of Nicholas of Lynne the people living there were members of a pre-Dorset Culture, known by the tools they have left as the Arctic Small Tool Tradition. I cannot find a reference to their height as no cemetery appears to have been excavated, and therefore cannot comment on the appropriateness of the description 'pygmies'. The African people today sometimes known as pygmies were, of course, unknown to the mediaeval world. Rather the mediaeval term 'pygmy' relates to descriptions by Pliny and Aristotle of an apparently mythical people of short stature. The tradition from Nicholas of Lynne is simply that a people of short stature lived in this area.

In John Dee's account of the voyage of Nicholas of Lynne we have a plausible description of Hudson Bay and the lands around it. We also have an indication of the interest John Dee had in the Arctic lands.

John Dee

British exploration of the Americas is inspired by John Dee (1527–1608), surely the strangest figure of the Elizabethan age, as well as its greatest scholar.[5] Shakespeare modelled Prospero in *The Tempest* upon him, and the character of Prospero encapsulates his many achievements: scientist, historian, alchemist, magician, a curious mix of renaissance scholarship and mediaeval gnosticism. It was Dee who provided the English explorer Martin Frobisher with the Viking sailing directions for America, and Dee who asserted Britain's claim to America on the basis of what he believed to be the discovery and settlement of America by Celts and Vikings. Furthermore, it was Dee who provided the intellectual and legal foundation for the idea of a British Empire, along with the concept of Britain's God-given right to govern an empire. Without Dee, Queen Elizabeth I would not have commissioned the English voyages to America, and perhaps Britain would not have embraced imperial expansion.

Educated at Cambridge and immersed in his studies throughout his long life, John Dee is the outstanding mathematician of his age, responsible for reintroducing the sixteenth century to the work of Euclid. He provided Martin Frobisher with navigational instruments and tables which he had himself designed, as well as a synthesis of the best descriptions available of sailing routes to North America. This much is tangible achievement of the sort that the twenty-first century understands and approves. Yet it scarcely touches the surface of Dee's world. Dee saw himself not as a scientist but as an alchemist – a mediaeval designation with a long pedigree, even used much later by Isaac Newton – and saw the scientific and humanistic work he did as based upon his spiritual understanding. Queen Mary I imprisoned him for witchcraft; subsequently her sister, Queen Elizabeth I, made him her personal astronomer and her friend. Protected by Elizabeth and funded by her, Dee collected a personal library of over 4,000 volumes, most of which had been scattered during the dissolution of the monasteries – and most of which were subsequently destroyed by a mob who attacked his library. It is clear that Dee had many remarkable works in his collection. For example his writing shows that he was familiar with the *Book of Enoch*, an apocryphal book of the Bible which was thought lost until rediscovered in 1773. He pursued studies which were occult and cabbalistic, claiming divine inspiration for his work, and is associated with the Gnostic Rosicrucian movement, of which he may have been the founder. The twenty-first century is sufficiently ill-at-ease with these ideas to feel a need to treat Dee with caution, and there has perhaps been a tendency to minimise his body of work, yet his undoubted achievements in mathematics alone are sufficient to earn his place as a great thinker.

John Dee used the account of Nicholas of Lynne to support an English claim to the North Atlantic lands the Vikings had discovered. In his role as the alchemist and antiquarian attached to the court of Queen Elizabeth I he was encouraged to develop an academic framework for British interests in the area. His view is that Britain had a legal right to these lands, as is neatly set out in a very long chapter heading to the last chapter of his *Volume of Great and Rich Discoveries*: 'That all these Northern Iles and Septentrional Parts are lawfully appropriated to the Crown of this Brytish Impire: and the terrible adventure and great loss of the Brytish people and other of King Arthur his subjects perishing about the first discovery thereof. And the placing of Colonies in the same Iles and Regions by the same King Arthur. And an entire and general Description of all the part of the world within 12 degrees of the North Pole and somewhat more.'

The supposed justification is that King Arthur ruled not only the whole of the British Isles and much of continental Europe but also the people who discovered Iceland, Greenland and lands to the west. This strange idea was not completely a creation of John Dee. In Geoffrey of Monmouth's *History of Britain*, which enjoyed much popularity in the Elizabethan age, we read of King Arthur that 'After an entire conquest of Ireland, he made a voyage with his fleet to Iceland, which he also subdued.' However John Dee extends the story by reference to an otherwise unknown, lost manuscript, which he calls both *Gestae Arthur* and *Principio Gestorum Arturi*. This apparently dates Arthur's conquest of the north to 530. While there can be no credence in these stories, what can be seen is that John Dee is presenting the English state as the successor to all the peoples of the British Isles – including the Vikings – and therefore the rightful owner of the lands visited and settled by the Vikings.

It is in the British exploration of North America that a tangible link with the Viking tradition may be sought. The clearest evidence for this link comes from the information on Viking routes that was given to Martin Frobisher for his 1576 voyage to Greenland, but earlier voyages bear witness to knowledge in England of the Viking achievement.

English Exploration in the Footsteps of the Vikings

The lands reported by Christopher Columbus on his return from his first voyage of 1492 would not have been considered a new discovery by the mariners of England. Fishing on the Grand Banks just a few hundred miles off the coast of North America had become commonplace, with most of the ships setting out from Bristol. Storm-driven ships inevitably sighted land to the east. What the Spanish proclamation of their discoveries did was convince England of the need formally to stake a claim to these new lands. In 1496 King Henry VII was persuaded to authorise a westward voyage of discovery, and he did not choose an Englishman to lead it, but the adventurer John Cabot. Genoese by birth, Venetian by adoption, and a resident at times of both Spain and Portugal, Cabot was a truly international figure. He had travelled widely in the eastern Mediterranean, and said he had visited Mecca. Cabot's was a name which lent international credibility to the voyage. That said, the expedition which Cabot led out of Bristol in 1497 was a thoroughly English affair. It was funded by England, and Cabot's ship, the *Matthew*, was crewed by Englishmen and flew the English flag. Crucially, it followed in the footsteps not of Columbus, but of the countless Bristol fishermen who had sailed to the Grand Banks. In the course of a voyage from Bristol to America and back to Bristol that lasted for less than three months – a shorter round-trip than some one-way voyages in the following centuries – Cabot made a successful reconnaissance of Nova Scotia and Newfoundland, and reported to Henry VII the existence of these lands. It was scarcely a new discovery, rather a formal confirmation to the king and to the world of the existence of lands the Bristol merchants already knew existed, and a proclamation of English interest.

English exploration of John Cabot's discoveries made a slow start. Cabot was instructed to make a second expedition, this time with five ships, departing in 1499. Of the five, two turned back and three vanished, presumed wrecked and sunk. Cabot himself was in one of the missing ships. This disaster brought about a pause in formal exploration, though fishing on the Grand Banks continued. At that time there was not a sufficient motive for exploration, certainly not for exploration that resulted in this sort of loss of lives and ships. The coast of North America was without resources that England wanted, and the expense of voyages was too great for them to be undertaken purely in a spirit of adventure. Rather the demand was for a sea route to the riches of India, China and the Far East. Within England hopes were directed on the belief in a Northwest Passage – the idea that there was a sea route around the north of America through which ships could reach an unknown ocean and subsequently China and India.

England became fixated on the idea of a Northwest Passage. John Cabot's son Sebastian grew up in Bristol, and in 1508 was commissioned by Henry VII to undertake a voyage in the wake of his father. Sebastian Cabot explored to the north of Labrador, and is now usually credited with discovering Hudson Strait. While the voyage was a success as an exploration, it brought no tangible benefits, and English interest waned. Indeed, it is only at the end of the century that funding was again made available for voyages to America, sponsored by Queen Elizabeth I. The drive was again to the north, putting into action the British claims made by John Dee. This phase commenced with Martin Frobisher's voyages to Baffin Island (1576–78), and the three successful voyages of John Davis (1585, 1586 and 1587) charting the Davis Strait. Under the Stuarts, exploration continued: Hudson (1610), Button (1612), Bylot and Baffin (1612, 1613 and 1616), Foxe (1631) and James (1631–32), all motivated by an absolute conviction that a Northwest Passage existed, though there was no overt evidence to back up this belief. The eighteenth, nineteenth and twentieth centuries saw expeditions almost without number setting off from England in search of the Passage. Today we know it does exist, although as a maze of ice-choked channels which can be navigated only in late summer and which have never offered a commercial trade route.

Recent scholarship has given scant consideration to this remarkable English belief in the existence of a Northwest Passage. By the early sixteenth century, exploration of the New World had discovered a coast running for thousands of miles, a whole continent standing between Europe and Asia. What little knowledge was available, supplemented with guesses, suggested that Greenland arched across the whole of the North Atlantic and joined Russia, and that Greenland was itself joined to the New World. An alternative view, not consistent with the first, was the belief in a northern ocean of open water, through which it would logically be possible to sail to get to Asia. Depending on which view was held, either there was no Northwest Passage to Asia, or Asia was to be reached through a broad northern ocean. Neither concept can be equated with the idea of a Northwest Passage. Yet for 400 years first England and then the United Kingdom sent out numerous expeditions to explore and penetrate this supposed Northwest Passage. There was absolute conviction that such a passage existed, and that it would provide a short-cut to Asia.

The mediaeval world had a concept of the very map of the world reflecting the order of God's creation. Jerusalem takes its place in the centre; the land mass of the world forms a great circle, with Asia comprising half the circle and Europe and Africa each a quarter of the circle. The whole is surrounded by the ocean. In seeking an explanation for the English insistence on the existence of a Northwest Passage it may be that an extrapolation of this concept of cosmic order was extended to the New World. With the discovery of a passage through the south of America – the Strait of Magellan – there was an assumption based on cosmic order that there must be a matching strait to the north of America, the Northwest Passage. Yet this sort of reasoning does not stand up to scrutiny. While the mediaeval world certainly drew maps of the world as a Jerusalem-centred circle, they were aware that the world was a sphere and that this was not literally how the world looked. Their maps were not intended to be an accurate representation, but rather a way of conceptualising their understanding of the universe. The English belief in a Northwest Passage cannot be seen as a relic of mediaeval thought, as mediaeval thought does not need to imagine a passage to the north of America. Nor is the idea tenable of a mirrored creation, in which a strait in the south has a comparable strait in the north. Magellan discovered the strait that bears his name in 1520; the first English voyage looking for a Northwest Passage took place in 1508.

Why the English should have been so certain of the existence of a Northwest Passage is therefore a puzzle. Certainly it would have been convenient, but an open ocean would have been even more convenient. An explanation is that they knew it existed, and knew because England had information about Viking voyages. Some support for this idea can be found in the later Frobisher voyage of 1576, and the sailing directions with which Frobisher was furnished.

The Pilgrim Fathers

Were even the Pilgrim Fathers travelling in the footsteps of the Vikings?

The story as told is that of a first settlement in America by 102 Puritans, many of whom had endured persecution in their English home village of Scrooby in Nottinghamshire.[6] They fled first to Holland, where they lived for 11 years – without managing to learn Dutch – and, dissatisfied with the religion there, they sought a solution, and found it in the form of a grant from the Virginia Company giving them permission to settle on the Hudson River, in the vicinity of today's New York City. For transport they hired the *Mayflower*, and after their last English landfall of Plymouth set out across the Atlantic. After a rough and very slow Atlantic crossing of over two months, they landed many miles from their intended destination at a place on the coast of America they called Plymouth, New England.

The Pilgrim Fathers were the most unlikely colonists. Their occupations were those of the city dwellers they had become in the Netherlands: tailors, merchants, a printer, a shop-keeper, a hatter and so on. They had not brought livestock with them, had little seed for crops, and few materials for building their settlement. The *Mayflower* remained berthed in the bay over the winter, with little interaction between the crew aboard and the Pilgrims on land. The crew had rations and were prepared for the winter, and seem to have had few problems. When spring came the *Mayflower* and her crew left for England. Of the 102 Pilgrims on land, 48 had died in that first winter, most of them of consumption. Just 54 remained, half of them children.

The survival of these remaining Pilgrims is explained by the help they were then given by the local Native American tribe. The story relates that they first met a Native American called Samoset, who explained that he was himself a stranger in the region, but that he had a friend called Tisquantum who was a native there, belonging to the Wampanoag tribe. The Native Americans helped the Pilgrims plant corn and find food. And, of course, at the end of the year Native Americans and Pilgrims sat down together to the first Thanksgiving meal.

This story has received an unthinking and uncritical reception. First of all, most Native American peoples were hunter-gatherers who did not practice agriculture. It is strange indeed for supposed non-farmers to be showing the Pilgrim Fathers, who came from an agricultural village, how to farm. Then the Wampanoag tribe spoke the Algonquin language. This is as different as a language can be from English or any European languages that the Pilgrim Fathers might have known. Can we really believe in a speaking knowledge of this language from a group of poorly educated English who had largely failed to learn Dutch despite 11 years' residence in Holland? People who had never before encountered the Wampanoag tribe or the linguistic complexity of any agglutinative language? Indeed, even after years of friendship the Pilgrims were still struggling with the name Tisquantum, calling him instead Squanto.

The puzzle is solved by the account which the Pilgrim Fathers themselves have left us: both Samoset and Tisquantum spoke English. Furthermore they note that Tisquantum's English was fluent, Samoset's less good, and that Tisquantum spoke Spanish also. Both the Pilgrim Fathers and the Native Americans they encountered knew that there had been significant prior contact between Europe, particularly England, and New England. The Pilgrim Fathers are particularly remembered because they are the group that formally sought permission to set up a colony – from the Virginia Company – and therefore made a voyage that had a paper trail. Many Europeans had been to North America before them, and many had settled there.

In the Pilgrim Fathers we have a settlement building on the legacy of earlier European encounters with America, and supported by the remarkable resource of two Native American tribesmen who both spoke English and knew how to farm. The Pilgrim Fathers are part of a long tradition of European exploration of the continent, a tradition which ultimately goes back to the Vikings.

9
Legacy of the Vikings in America

DOES it matter that the Vikings were in America? Does it really make any difference whether the European discoverer of America was a Hispanic Christopher Columbus or a Norse Leif Eiriksson? Whether Europeans have known about America for 1,000 years or for just half that time surely makes no difference to Europe or America in the twenty-first century.

But rather, yes, it does matter. The Vikings have left an enduring legacy on both sides of the Atlantic. Without the Vikings' discovery and settlement of North America the world would be a different place. It is important, too, to understand the centuries-long European amnesia on the topic, and the failure even today for the story to be given the attention it deserves. These are things which are relevant today.

There are several ways in which the Vikings in America have stamped their mark on the world.

Genetics and the Case of the Narragansett Indians

A particularly enduring legacy would seem to be in the genetic make-up of indigenous peoples of North America. The idea is simple – if the Vikings were in America for a significant length of time there would have been intermarriage between Vikings and Native Americans, and we should be able to find Viking genes in Native American indigenous populations. There should be Viking blood in the New World.

The prospect is both exciting and tantalising. There is enormous media and public interest in DNA projects, yet results are often elusive. When looking at the 'Blond Eskimo' of the Victoria Island the evidence is actually from early twentieth-century anthropological observations rather than from a recent DNA study. The early twentieth-century ethnographers found a characteristic deserving comment; the early twenty-first century work has failed to support the ethnographers, but hasn't disproved them either.

Today much work on human ethnicity is linked in one way or another with the Human Genome Project, a mass of fundamental research whose impact is just beginning to be felt. It may be hoped that in time, studies developing from this project will demonstrate the place of the Vikings in America. Its achievement has been to sequence the three-billion human DNA sub-units. This is a tremendously exciting project, but one which has being conducted for reasons other than to assist in the study of history, archaeology and human migration, with the result that there are real issues in trying to apply its insights in these disciplines. Nevertheless, its impact is to transform these disciplines, and in the future an assessment of the extent of the Viking impact on America will come from studies related to the Human Genome Project.

When looking at the genetic profile of Native American indigenous populations it is possible to identify genetic signatures characteristic of each group, and it is also possible to see represented in an indigenous population genes from other ethnic groups. What it is not possible to do from a study based on people alive today is to determine whether a European or Norse genetic signature comes from the post-Columban settlements, or from an earlier Viking settlement. In order to examine the issue of Viking genes in pre-Columban populations we would need to examine pre-Columban human tissue – and in this there are problems. First of all, there is little human tissue suitable for analysis which has survived from over 500 years ago. Then there are religious and ethical reservations in carrying out such tests on human remains, an issue often particularly sensitive within the context of Native American beliefs.

However, one area of research has opened up, and has yielded unexpected results. This is the case of the Narragansett Indians.[1]

Genetics can help this study in understanding ethnic variation in human resistance to disease. Tuberculosis – TB – is a case in point. TB is very common indeed in human populations today, with around one person in three worldwide carrying the infection, though most display no symptoms, and are not at risk themselves of developing the disease. Because TB is present in human populations everywhere it is crucial that all individuals gain resistance to it, and this usually happens through mild exposure while in good health. Resistance can be broken down through malnutrition, frequent contact with the bacteria through overcrowding, and through close contact with sufferers. Tuberculosis is therefore associated with poverty, and with the overcrowding of urban slums. In the late nineteenth century the

161

cities of Europe and North America, with their overcrowding and poverty, were perfect breeding grounds for TB, and in these locations it flourished. From around 1830 there is a marked upturn in the frequency of TB, and while this peaked around 1900 and showed some signs of decline in the early twentieth century, it was not until the introduction of antibiotic treatments in the 1950s that TB showed a substantial decline. Today in the developed world, a combination of effective antibiotic treatment and the impact of immunisation programmes have greatly reduced the frequency of TB. In the developing world, by contrast, it remains a major cause of death.

The reduction of the number of instances of TB in the developed world in the half century 1900–50 cannot be explained through medical interventions alone. Improvements in living conditions in cities had an impact too, along with welfare schemes which ameliorated the worst overcrowding, and some public perception of the means of transmission. The crucial factor was the growing genetic resistance to tuberculosis. Even if today the cities of Europe were as poor and overcrowded as a century ago, and without the medical advances, there would still be a reduction in the incidence of TB because of genetic changes within the population reducing susceptibility.

The genetic increase in resistance within a population can be understood by looking at the incidence of TB over several generations. Different individuals exhibit varying levels of susceptibility or resistance to TB. It is possible for a family living in overcrowded conditions to be affected so that some contract TB and die from it, while others who have been in close contact with the infection remain free of the disease. This variation in susceptibility is believed to be an inherited trait, though – as for many such traits – the gene responsible has not yet been identified. Its existence can be postulated by the clear impact it has on human populations.

In the cities of nineteenth-century Europe the genes for susceptibility or resistance played a crucial role. Genetic resistance was crucial to avoid TB. Those who had genes making them susceptible contracted TB, usually either as children or as young adults, and in most cases died from it. In general those who were susceptible to TB died before they were old enough to marry and pass on their genes to their children. Even in as short a time as the period 1830–1950, perhaps four generations, a marked increase in the genetic resistance to TB of European and North American urban populations took place.

The towns and cities of mediaeval Europe in no way compare in size with those of the nineteenth century, but they did have populations living in poverty in great overcrowding. Viking Dublin was as bad as any; the cities of Constantinople, Jerusalem and Rome, visited by many far-faring Vikings, exhibited the same problems. In these cities, as in the cities of classical Europe, TB found a ready breeding ground. Additionally, rural overcrowding occurred during the winter months when a small group of people would be for the most part confined within a small farmstead. As a consequence, within populations a genetic resistance to TB developed, with the result that all of the population has some resistance, though the level of resistance varies, leaving some more susceptible than others. The Vikings who crossed the North Atlantic on the stepping-stone route carried with them a high level of genetic resistance.

By contrast the indigenous people of the Americas had a far lower level of resistance to TB.[2] On the eve of the Viking arrival in North America the Vikings had an Old World heritage of as much as 5,000 years of close-proximity living, and a high level of genetic resistance. By contrast the Native Americans had no cities, no communities with European-style close proximity. Genes giving substantial resistance to TB had not developed, though TB existed as a disease. Rather, it was contained by geographical isolation of one Native American group from the next, and by the lack of cities as a breeding ground. This lack of high-density populations was both the reason why TB did not spread so as to wipe out whole peoples, and the reason why genetic resistance to TB did not exist.

A Native American living before contact with Europeans and contracting TB had a low level of genetic immunity to it, and therefore died from it very quickly. A European of the same period contracting TB had a higher level of genetic immunity to it, and was likely to survive for some time – though the result in the days before antibiotic treatment was usually death. Bones of Europeans from antiquity through to the twentieth century frequently show distinctive lesions which have been caused by TB, and show that the body has attempted to fight the infection before the sufferer had died, either from TB or from something else. Bones of pre-settlement Native Americans never show this feature, indicating that either they had not contracted TB, or if they had that they died quickly. There is just one North American exception.

Pre-settlement remains of Narragansett Indians show bone lesions caused by the body attempting to fight a TB infection. Their bones demonstrate that they had genetic resistance to TB.

This is a startling finding which needs an explanation. It is, in theory, possible that they developed these genes independently, yet as they had no cities or comparable high-density populations, which seem to be the necessary environment for such a development, this seems most unlikely. Alternatively these genes must be of European origin, suggesting intermarriage with Europeans, of whom the Vikings are the prime candidates.

The Narragansett tribe are located in Rhode Island, around the town named after them. Around 1600 their estimated population was in the region of 10,000 individuals; today a revived Narragansett tribe has just over 2,000 members, most of mixed genetic heritage. Some of the worst examples of slaughter at the hands of the Europeans alongside disease and displacement from traditional lands saw a sharp fall in Narragansett numbers through the seventeenth century, and by the end of the nineteenth century the tribe had lost its language and culture.

The genetic evidence comes from cemetery RI 1000 where 59 skeletons have been excavated, dating from around 1660. While the date is well after Columbus, there was no European settlement there at this early date – certainly nothing of a scale that could explain the dramatic results. There is of course no DNA, for bones do not preserve DNA; what has been found are lesions on bones which have been caused by tuberculosis. In this cemetery, 17 of 59 skeletons show tuberculosis lesions, which is an unparalleled result among Native American peoples. One of the skeletons with lesions is a child of three, whose young age strengthens the idea of inherited immunity; another is a man of around 45, and therefore born c. 1615, well before any post-Columban European settlement. The only credible solution that has been advanced for this immunity to TB is that there had been a substantial influx of European genes.

The hypothesis is that significant numbers of Vikings intermarried with the Narragansett, producing a gene pool which had some immunity to tuberculosis. Sometime around the mid seventeenth century an early encounter between the Narragansett and Europeans introduced tuberculosis, which as a result of their genetic protection caused a slow death for the infected Narragansett, giving time for bone lesions to form on many of the individuals.

That the Narragansett tribe was unusual is well attested. Giovanni da Verrazano in 1524 provides both the first and the clearest description of the tribe, in which he contrasts it with other Native American peoples he had encountered further south.[3] He comments on their height, taller than other peoples. This is corroborated by the cemetery, which yields one skeleton of 6 feet 2 inches, unusually tall for any Native American. He describes their skin as being light to olive, and their hair as flowing – a term he uses in contrast to the thick, straight hair of other Native American peoples he had encountered, and which may signify a thinner hair. He notes that the men had beards, while Native Americans in general do not have beards. An account of the language and culture of the Narragansett is found in Roger Williams' 1643 'Keys to the Indian Language', which is effectively a dictionary of Narragansett. The assertion that Norse words can be found in their language needs further work – perhaps as someone's doctoral thesis – though an initial impression is that the area is promising. Thus there is the place-name element -sett, found in many dozens of names in New England including Massachusetts, which cannot be clearly linked to any Native American language. Phonologically a link with the Germanic -sted/-stat is plausible – the meaning therefore is place, perhaps a permanently settled place rather than an aboriginal camp. The place names in -sett do seem to correspond with settlement sites. There are other features which might support the idea that the Narragansett have a Viking heritage. The organisation of their cemetery with regular rows is uncharacteristic of a Native American burial site, though standard for a Viking site; similarly, the deep level of burial is unusual for Native Americans but common for Vikings. The Narragansett had developed a sophisticated monetary system using what were, in effect, coins – called 'wampum'. While many Native American groups adopted a comparable system as the Europeans spread across America, the Narragansett seem unique in having such a system in place before the Europeans arrived. Along with money was a fully developed counting system, with Williams reporting that their number system went at least as far as 100,000. Numbers up to this level are of little use without knowledge of arithmetic; presumably they had this, too.

The Narragansett are a North American people, but possibly a people who have had substantial genetic exposure to the Vikings. It is plausible that Leif Eiriksson's descendants live on in Rhode Island, and plausible that DNA testing on members of the tribe alive today will one day find proof of such ancestry. The case of the Narragansett gives a simple answer to the question 'what happened to the Vikings in America?' – they are still there.

The Newport Tower

The structure known as the 'Newport Tower' deserves far more investigation than it has so far received. At the moment it is simply another unconfirmed possible indicator of Viking presence in North America, a frustrating building without proof and with academic caution tending to dismiss all indicators that it may be Viking. Given the significance of establishing it as Viking it is unfortunate that more work has not been carried out.

Situated in Newport, Rhode Island, the tower overlooks Narragansett Bay – the area being home of the Narragansett Indians with their apparent European genetic heritage. The tower is certainly old, first mentioned in a colonial document of 1665, but it is a big leap from this date to the Viking Age.

What has been preserved is a circular tower structure some twenty-eight feet high, and supported on eight pillars. The whole is built from dry stone, with walls around three feet thick, though mortar has been added at many different dates, presumably in association with repairs. There is a covered area on the ground level, with an internal diameter around 18 feet, and there would once have been a room above of comparable size with a single, small window and a fireplace. The structure looks like nothing else in America, and lacks exact parallels in Europe.

The simplest explanation for the building is that it was constructed by some of the very first colonists of Rhode Island, and may have been associated with the colonial governor, Benedict Arnold, who owned the land on which the tower stands from 1661. It was mentioned in his will as 'my stone-built wind mill', and a plausible assumption is that it was an early windmill for the colony. As a windmill the design is most peculiar – it may be noted that some have seen parallels with an English windmill of the seventeenth century, the Chesterton Windmill in Warwickshire, but the parallel is not close.

That Arnold used the building as a windmill is in no doubt – for that matter we know of other uses for the building at different times, including a powder store. What is in doubt is whether he or his fellow colonists built it, or whether they found the structure there and merely repaired and adapted it. As early as 1837 Danish archaeologist Carl Christian Rafn in *Antiquitates Americanae*[4] proposed that it was a Norse building, and a lively debate has continued since then. Those who favour a pre-colonial origin for the building suggest it was modified or repaired by Arnold and the first colonists but not built by them. Thus in 1942 Philip Meanes wrote a then-definitive study of the tower and concluded that Arnold had not built it 'from the ground up'. Among the critics the language used has frequently been far from scholarly. For example, one of the leading opponents of the Norse theory, William S. Godfrey, reported in his PhD thesis (Harvard, 1951) that in an excavation he had been able to find no objects earlier than the seventeenth century, and that those who suggested the building was anything other than early colonial were 'crackpots', 'pygmies', 'zealots' and 'the lunatic fringe'. The language today tends to be more measured, but the underlying views are much the same. It is the established view that the building dates from the early colonial period, and anyone who dissents from this view is treated as some modern-day heretic.

Yet there are some most serious objections to the building being from the early colonial years. The work required to move such a quantity of stone for the construction of walls three feet thick is substantial, particularly as the stone does not occur in the immediate vicinity but at the bottom of a hill at the edge of the bay. The construction is unnecessarily elaborate for a windmill, and its most unusual design lacks structural integrity – indeed, it looks as if it should fall down. Early colonists generally built windmills of wood and to a more or less standard design, and were keen to expend as little time and effort as possible in their construction. While there is no absolute reason why the first settlers of Rhode Island should not have put a very great effort into constructing this dry-stone building it does seem an odd thing to do. Add an innovative design, and then a fireplace – an unusual feature of windmills, in view of the fire risk to dry corn and flour, though admittedly not unknown – and the idea that they built such a structure is most surprising.

Suzanne Carlton, a practising architect, has brought new information to the debate. She has quantified the building materials, with the following results:

450 tons of granite, selected and prepared (available locally)
6 tons of lime (from shells, washed, burnt and mixed with clay)
46 tons of sand (from the beach)
4 trees 60 feet high and 5 feet around, plus other trees for smaller timbers.

The building team would have needed to be around 16 men, including several skilled men, and the construction would have taken around a year. This is a very major outlay of labour for a new colony with a tiny workforce, expended for a building which is without an obvious purpose. There are no comparable stone-built constructions from seventeenth-century New England precisely because the labour outlay in making such a building is so high.

Dry-stone buildings are difficult to date anywhere in the world. The basic techniques used are to compare with similar buildings for which there is a date, or to date tools discarded around the foundations. Neither technique has helped much with the Newport Tower. There is no building generally acknowledged as directly comparable. Carbon-14 dating is not possible on the stones themselves, but it can be carried out on the mortar. Tests in 1992 found a cluster of dates, most within a range that they express as 1635 to 1698 – around the time of the ownership of Governor Benedict Arnold. However the full range of dates discovered range from 1410 to 1930. The later dates are readily explained as more recent repair work, but even one date prior to the seventeenth century is a startling find. A single undisputed date from as early as 1410 would, of course, place the tower firmly in the pre-Columban period.

In fact the dispute about this date has been loud. The radiocarbon dates have been criticised on the grounds that the sample tested was too small, that there was poor precision in some of the work, that there was poor control for the interference of modern absorption of carbon dioxide by the mortar, and that the group's initial hypothesis that all the mortar was of the same age was wrong. In short the dates must be wrong, therefore there is shoddy archaeology. It is hard to avoid a sense that there is circularity in the reasoning: a date such as 1410 is assumed to be wrong, therefore in itself it proves sub-standard work. The obvious solution of redoing the tests with newly obtained mortar samples has not been carried out. Indeed scientific investigation of the Newport Tower appears to have gained the academic respectability of looking for the Loch Ness Monster. Yet even those most critical of the Tower being a pre-colonial construction feel it is necessary to pull their punches, and do not dismiss this absolutely. A characteristic recent statement is found in a news conference report made in December 1995 based on four years of research by Danish and Finnish experts, the City of Newport, and the Rhode Island Preservation and Heritage Commission. They concluded that there is a '95% probability' that the tower was constructed in the late seventeenth century. Even the critics give a 5 per cent chance that the building is pre-Colonial.

Most recently an archaeological investigation of the area surrounding the Newport Tower has been carried out by the Chronognostic Foundation,[5] an

Arizona-based research firm. They have found remains of buildings close to the tower dating from the seventeenth century, but nothing earlier. That there were early colonial buildings in the vicinity of the tower fits neatly with use of the tower itself in this period, but otherwise does not carry forward the question of the date of building.

Comparable buildings can be found in Europe, though they are mediaeval rather than seventeenth-century. Two seem particularly close. The first is Orphir Round Church in Orkney. This shows a remarkable similarity with Newport in terms of the style of building, which arguably can only reasonably be explained in terms of a common construction tradition. Orphir was built around 1115, at a time when Orkney was an integral part of the Viking world. The second is the cluster of four mediaeval stone-built Round Churches on the Danish island of Bornholm. These have granite walls externally plaster covered – pargeted – as there is evidence Newport once was, a comparable window construction, and a second floor as does Newport. If the Newport Tower were in Europe it would be dated and understood within the context of such monuments as Orphir and the four Bornholm Round Churches, as a mediaeval Norse church. Greenland also has a parallel – the stone-built church of Gardar in Greenland. Gardar is a twelfth-century construction with substantial fourteenth-century changes, including the introduction of glazed windows, a feature exhibited by the Newport Tower. Newport and Gardar appear to be within the same building tradition.

There is European documentary evidence for the existence of the Newport Tower prior to the colonial age. The Italian Giovanni da Verrazano, one of the earliest explorers of the coast of North America, reported in 1524 that he has found in this location a European building which he calls variously a Norman villa and 'tolos'. The word 'tolos' is an Italianisation of Greek 'tholos', a round temple or church. In Italian usage 'Norman' was the adjective not 'from Normandy' but 'from Norway'. At face value Giovanni da Verrazano reports clearly that he has found a Norse house or church (or both?) in Newport. Gerardus Mercator (1512–94) also marks the tower on his map (published 1595, after his death). Finally, it has been pointed out that the unit of measurement for construction of the building appears to be not the English foot (used by the early colonists of Rhode Island) but the Norse foot of twelve and one-third inches. There has also been a suggestion that the unit may be the Scottish ell (of 37 inches), though as the ell is based on the Norse foot (and is exactly three Norse feet) this is more or less the same statement.

We are lacking evidence to prove beyond doubt that the Newport Tower is a Viking construction. Carbon-14 dating is disputed; no tool or similar instrument from the pre-colonial age has been found around the foundations; Verrazano's notes are brief. Scholarly caution argues against asserting that the tower is a genuine and well-preserved Viking building, yet there is much support for the idea that it is in origin something other than an early colonial windmill. Verrazano saw something there which he thought to be a European building, and no Native American construction could be so misidentified. Mercator believed there was something there. And while Arnold's contemporaries certainly carried out extensive work on the tower, this is compatible with repairing rather than rebuilding. A strong case can be made for considering the Newport Tower as a mediaeval Viking round church on the New England coast of the USA – yet until evidence can be produced which permits of no doubt whatsoever the academic world will not accept this.

Where Will We Find the Vikings Next?

Where should we expect in the future to find traces of the Vikings? If nothing else an answer to this question might provide some amusement for readers in future generations. The underlying view is that we should be actively looking for Viking traces. We have found a major settlement in Newfoundland, and traces through much of the far north of America, enough to give grounds to expect much more. Clearly the area is immense. However, several specific areas do suggest themselves:

> • North-west Greenland, around 77° north. The Vikings visited this area every year, and presumably had some form of seasonal settlement as evidenced by Viking remains across the bay on Ellesmere Island. While the climate is severe and the polar night challenging, the location is even so habitable year-round, as for many centuries the Polar Inuit have demonstrated. If it could be done, then the likelihood is that the Vikings did it – my belief is that sooner or later Viking archaeological remains will be found in the vicinity of Thule. I also see no reason why such a settlement, or a settlement on Ellesmere Island, would have died out with the failure of the Eastern and Western settlements. In the eighteenth century Hans Egede believed that he would find Norse living in Greenland, apparently basing

his belief on something more recent than the sagas. He found none, but neither he nor the Inuit he spoke with ever visited the Thule area. Just possibly a Viking settlement survived even then in the far north.

• Canadian High Arctic. The area is immense and basic survey-ing and mapping in many cases have still not been carried out. Archaeological investigation has hardly started. That we have already found Viking remains with so little investigation sug-gests that there is much, much more to be found. There is an ultimate westward barrier in the multi-year ice, and Victoria Island surely represents the furthest west that any Viking traces could possibly be found. Yet almost anywhere in the High Arc-tic that had open water access in the summer months – which is most of the High Arctic – we can reasonably expect to find traces of the Vikings.

• Hudson Bay. The lure of timber and the relatively short journey – relative to a trip to Norway – would have made the south-western shore of Hudson Bay attractive to the Vikings. We should find traces there, though probably summer settle-ments only. The winters on Hudson Bay are extreme – more so than Greenland – and over-wintering or permanent settlement would not have been attractive. Given the exploring zeal of the Vikings it is likely that some penetrated the rivers south from Hudson Bay, and Viking archaeological finds from the centre of the North American continent must be a possibility.

• Finally, Vinland. While the finds at L'Anse aux Meadows demonstrate Viking presence on the American continent, Newfoundland is not Vinland. Rather, it is a transit point for voyages from somewhere further south to Greenland. From Newfoundland the vast estuary of the St Lawrence River is within easy reach. So too is the coast of New England. In view of the presence of an indigenous population in North Amer-ica it is most likely that the Vikings would have sought to es-tablish settlements in defensive locations, particularly islands. Aquidneck Island, site of today's city of Newport in the state of Rhode Island and the location of the Newport Tower – fits the requirement, as do for example Martha's Vineyard, Nantucket

Island and many smaller islands in the modern states of Maine, Massachusetts and Rhode Island.

While the sagas recount stories from around 1,000 years ago, there is no necessity for Viking remains in the Americas to be this old. They may certainly be expected for the whole of the period of Viking Greenland, so right up to the time of the first Columbus voyage just 500 years ago. There is no absolute necessity for the cessation of Viking Greenland to have ended all Viking involvement in the New World. I am not suggesting a continuous presence in America from the time of Leif Eiriksson to the present day – though some writers have, with Martha's Vineyard the preferred location.[6] I am, however, suggesting that we need to be open-minded, and that finding evidence of Nordic people in the New World before and after Columbus is perfectly possible.

The Vikings Named America!

There are reasons why every place on the globe is called what it is.

Often we know little about the origins of a name. For example, Canada is supposed by some to be called Canada after a hypothetical map in which the northern part of the continent was labelled in an unspecified Spanish dialect 'aca nada', supposedly meaning 'there is nothing there'. Many Canadians seem to find this amusing, and treating it as a joke is about all this unbelievable derivation deserves. Alternatively, it is supposed that Jacques Cartier and some of the early settlers of Canada were met in 1535 on the St Lawrence River by a group of indigenous people. They asked the name of the land, presumably speaking English or French, and received the reply in Huron–Iroquois: 'kanata', meaning 'this way to the village'. By some poorly explained process this word for village came to be applied to the whole of Canada. There must be a reason why Canada is called Canada, but we can be almost completely sure that neither of these explanations is correct. The honest answer is that we really don't know why Canada is called Canada.

On the other side of the Atlantic there is similar uncertainty. The name England comes from English – it is quite simply the land of the English. But a meaning for English is long lost. Similarly Scotland is the land of the Scots, though why the Scots are called Scots is not known. We're on stronger ground with Wales, the land of the Welsh. Welsh is a straightforward Old English word, and it means slave. Wales was called by the English the land of the slaves – so no wonder that today the people of Wales prefer their country to be known by its name in their own Welsh language – Cymru. The name Britain has been around for a very long time. In this case there is no known origin for the name, but this didn't stop writers of an earlier age inventing an origin, and creating a foundation myth. To Geoffrey of Monmouth and to the mediaeval world, Britain was named after Brutus, a Prince of Troy who fled the city following its destruction at the hands of the Greeks, and founded a new home for himself in what we now call after him the British Isles. There is no likelihood of truth in this story but so strong is the need to find an origin for names that a whole myth cycle was created around it: the fictitious person of Brutus and his supposed Trojan origin in Anatolia, his voyage through the Mediterranean and out into the Atlantic, and his conquest of a great island which he named Britain after him.

America is a name as much in need of an origin as Canada or England or Scotland or Britain. The story which has found its way into the history books and which is still taught in American schools is that America takes its name from an explorer called Amerigo Vespucci. Of course this is not correct. It is a foundation myth comparable to the naming of Britain after Brutus.

Amerigo Vespucci is a real enough figure. An Italian born in Florence around 1451 he moved to Seville in 1492, and in the years from 1497 to 1504 took part in four Spanish voyages to the New World, possibly leading the last of them. He was therefore one of the early explorers who followed Columbus across the Atlantic, and the voyages he took part in made discoveries in South America and in the southern Caribbean. He never set foot in the present area of the USA. Vespucci's role in history is as a rather minor figure in the exploration of the continent. The Europeans of Amerigo Vespucci's time were clear that the New World had been 'discovered' by Christopher Columbus, and if that land was to be named after anyone it would have been after Columbus. Amerigo Vespucci as the origin of the name America is not credible; as much a myth as the origins proposed for Canada, or the mythical origin of Britain. Whatever the origin of the name America might be, we can be sure that this is not it.

The origin of the myth of Amerigo Vespucci comes from historians' accounts based on a map produced by a German cartographer, Martin Waldseemuller, and dated 1507, which shows the New World and gives the name as America, writing the word America roughly in the area of present-day Brazil.[7] In a marginal note Waldseemuller links the name America with Amerigo Vespucci. His motive seems to be desperation. The format of the notes on his map required him to explain the origins of the names of all the continents, something that he does with conventional accuracy for the Old World continents of Europe, Africa and Asia. Yet he clearly has no idea of the origin of America, and he grasps at a straw by linking it with the name of an explorer he has heard of. Waldseemuller makes a mistake; whatever the reason for calling America by its name, this cannot be it.

Other ideas for the origin of America have been proposed. One just about plausible is that America is indeed named for a man, but after Richard Ameryke, the name of the Bristol tax collector and civil servant of the English king Henry VII who handled the funding and administration of Jean Cabot's first voyage to America. As far as the English court and civil service were concerned the project was linked not with Jean Cabot, the hired captain, but rather with Richard Ameryke, the civil servant responsible for administering the project. There have also been suggestions that the name is an Old Norse phrase meaning either 'far kingdom' or 'west kingdom', in my view linguistically untenable as well as nonsensical.

However, I believe there is a plausible Viking origin for the name which should be considered. The clue comes from the way in which the Vikings used names. Thus for example the name Norway is a simple description – it means the north coast. It was the coast the Vikings sailed up when travelling north, towards the summer hunting grounds of the Scandinavian Arctic. West across the sea were the islands of the Faroe Islands. When the Vikings arrived they found sheep running wild over the islands and in great numbers. The Vikings named the land for its dominant feature, 'Faroe Islands' means simply 'the sheep islands'. North from the Faroe Islands is Iceland. The Vikings arriving from the Faroe Islands were met with the vast Vatnajokul glacier, ice visible well out to sea. Iceland was a simple, factual description of this dominant feature. Iceland seems to have been an unfortunate choice of name because it does seem to have deterred settlers, a state of affairs that the Vikings themselves remarked upon. When land was discovered to the west there was an incentive not to repeat the mistake, and so Greenland received its attractive name. Yet the name is more than just a piece of Viking propaganda. The coasts of Greenland are spectacularly green, with lush sedge meadows that stretch from the sea to the interior ice cap. For Vikings arriving from Iceland, a land with thin soil, few meadows and little grass, 'Greenland' was a simple factual description.

West of Greenland the Vikings made landfall in the New World. Three names they used have been preserved. Helluland was used of the northern part of the New World. The name means slab-land, a description of a land of bare, ice-scoured slabs of rock. Markland to the south means forest-land. South of Markland was Vinland, meaning fertile-land. The underlying principle used in all these place names is simple physical description.

There is one name that the Vikings applied to many lands they visited – 'merki'. The primary dictionary meaning is a boundary, a wide expanse of land, a frontier. In particular it signified to the Vikings and to other Germanic peoples speaking cognate languages an area of unfarmed land, a land beyond the area they had settled, a border land, a land 'beyond the pale', over the border. Perhaps the closest single word in modern English which expresses this concept comes from Australia: outback. To past generations of Americans an equivalent was simply 'the west', the frontier beyond the first colonies on the east coast. The name 'merki' was very common throughout the Germanic lands of northern Europe. Thus in England the unfarmed, unsettled area of the interior was called in the English dialect 'Mercia'. The name lives on today not as an administrative unit but as a regional term used by several English Midlands media and utility companies.

When the Vikings arrived anywhere at the edge of their range they would have used the name merki, not as a specific name for a specific land, but simply as a description for the type of land. We can be sure that this everyday geographical term in the Old Norse language was used by the Vikings for America.

There is a similarity of sorts between 'merki' and 'America', but plenty of room for coincidence. It could not be asserted that just because merki and America are similar they must be linked. Etymology does not work that way. However there is a discipline which enables the problem to be addressed – philology – which concerns itself particularly with language change, including etymology. Philology has as its fundamental idea the neogrammarian hypothesis, that language change is governed by rules which may be precisely described, and which admit of no exceptions. It is possible therefore to compare words in related languages, or in the same language at different dates, and say something about whether they really are or are not related, something which goes beyond merely noting a general similarity.

An example from English illustrates how philology operates. We know that as a rule, one without any exceptions whatsoever, any Old English word which contains a diphthong lost that diphthong as the language developed into Middle English, and took in its place a monophthong. So Old English *chiese* we can say for sure must lose the diphthong *ie* and replace it with a single vowel. And we can further say as an absolute rule that when the diphthong is *ie* the vowel will be *e*. And when the diphthong is pronounced long – as it is in *chiese* – the resulting vowel will be long, which in our spelling convention is *ee*. So *chiese* by application of rules must become *cheese* – which it does. *Chiese* is the Old English word for *cheese*, and even if somehow we didn't know the modern English word we could work it out from the Old English original by applying rules. Using rules we can project the forms of words forward with much confidence, and we can go backwards with a measure of success. Thus we have now worked out that the word for *cheese* in Indo-European, the postulated first language of the European and Indian peoples, is *kasi*. This word changes in the earliest forms of Germanic according to exactly describable rules to *kaesi*. Still following rules *kaesi* becomes *kiesi* and *chiese*, then *cheese*. If we have the rules worked out and we know that the Indo-European form is *kasi* then we can work out that the Modern English form will be *cheese*.[8]

So what can we say about *merki*? Quite a lot, in fact. First of all the word was used throughout the Viking world, with different forms in different dialects. *Merki* is the West Norse form, used in Iceland, Greenland, and by the Vikings who found the New World. In East Norse – the language of Denmark – it is found as *maerke* and *mirke*. In England the same word is found as *mierce* and *mercia*. These words are cognate, effectively the same word but with differences in pronunciation. A Norwegian Viking would have said *merki*, his Danish Viking companion *maerke* or *mirke*, and an Englishman *mierce* or *mercia*, and they would have perceived these differences as no more than different accents.

The English form *mierce* developed through rules that have been worked out. *Mierce* loses its diphthong and becomes first *merce*, then by the application of separate processes becomes next *merch* and then *march*, the basic modern English form of *mierce*. Certain English dialects favoured *k* to *ch* giving *mark*. The word still hangs on in English in the term *march* for a border land – as in the Welsh Marches. 'Mark' can also be found as a word for a territory or area of land, though it is now archaic. A familiar form is *landmark*, originally something which showed the boundary of a territory.

The Old Norse *merki* is subject to a different set of rules, doesn't have a diphthong to lose, but it does have an awkward -*rk*- consonant cluster. This is subject to a special change, metathesis, by which sounds have their positions within a word swapped around. Metathesis is very common in all languages.[9] No-one's tongue likes dealing with clusters of consonants. An example from English is the old word *brid*, where the tongue was confronted with the initial two consonants. Of course we can manage this in English – after all there are plenty of words starting *br-* – but in linguistic terms we are all lazy and seek to avoid exercise for our tongues wherever possible. By a regular process of metathesis the Old English *brid* becomes modern English *bird*.

Just the same process – metathesis – applies to the Viking name *merki*. The consonant cluster was broken by bringing the *-i-* forward to give *merik*. Thus regular processes mean that the Viking word for outback, and which the Vikings applied to the New World, must become by one route in English *march* and *mark*, and by another route in the Scandinavian languages *merik*.

Merik, of course, is not America. The initial A- is a feature of Romance philology, particularly in Spanish. It is intrusive, a modification of a name as Spanish speakers assimilated an alien word into their language. A Spaniard using the Viking name *Merik* would tend to form *Amerik*. The final vowel is again a Romance feature – *Amerik* becomes *Amerika*. From this to *America* is purely a convention of spelling.

This is not a proof that America is a Viking name. However if it is a coincidence, it is a remarkable one. A name that the Vikings would have used to describe America when brought forward to fifteenth-century forms of Norse and adopted by Romance speakers gives America, exactly the name that the Spanish gave to the New World. At the very least it is a plausible derivation. It must be preferred to derivation from the name Amerigo Vespucci. It is far better than the weak derivations proposed for Canada or Britain.

On the evidence that we have, it is most likely that it is the Vikings who could have named America!

The Impact of Viking America

In this book we have seen the impact of the Vikings on America. It investigates just how far they travelled, where they settled and the effect they had on the land they settled. It examines too the knowledge that Europe had of the New World before Columbus.

Above all there is an awareness that the Vikings matter. The Vikings are the European discoverers of America – not Christopher Columbus. Certainly they settled there, probably they left their genes there, certainly they traded North American goods back to Europe, and even provided the sea routes which enabled Columbus and the renaissance European explorers with the means to get to America. Plausibly the Vikings even named the land. Their contribution was immense, yet it has been marginalised. In working on this book I have felt there is a spirit of disinformation in the records of Europe and in much modern writing, almost a conspiracy to marginalise the Vikings' contribution. Europe has wanted to forget the Vikings, and even today the world is slow to accord the Vikings their central role.

While the contribution of the Vikings to American history is enormous, it is not adequately recognised. Typical of this marginalisation is the lack of consideration that the Vikings may have named America. The etymology advanced here is not complicated, and it should have been suggested a century or more ago. It should not be that a case now has to be advanced for what is, in effect, a new theory. Whether the theory is right or wrong, in the absence of any other information, it is the Vikings who are the most likely people to have named America.

We need to move on from the Columbus myth. We need to replace the language of Columbus as discoverer of America with the language of Columbus confirming for the Spanish monarchs the existence of America. As a counterbalance to Columbus, the achievement of the Viking expansion across the North Atlantic has been told in this book. Likewise the story has been told of the three great Viking steps onward from Greenland – to Vinland, to Ellesmere Island and to Hudson Bay. Archaeology and genetics provide exciting insights, but the main thrust of this story is also told in European archives, and the Viking role should have been accepted even without the recent corroboration of archaeological evidence.

Future researchers need to look in more detail at the interaction between the Vikings and the American peoples they met, particularly the Inuit, for here seems to be a key to understanding both Viking and Inuit expansion. The arrival of the Inuit post-dates the Viking colonisation, and it may well be that the Inuit arrival was supported by the presence there of the Vikings. The Ellesmere Island Viking settlement presumably coexisted with the Inuit, and if this settlement indeed survived the destruction of the Greenland colony then the support of the Inuit there is likely to be key. In many of the lands the Vikings visited the Inuit either held sway or followed. Baffin Island, most of the High Arctic, Labrador and the northern tip of Newfoundland were all occupied by Inuit. It may well be no coincidence that the Viking way-station of L'Anse aux Meadows later became Inuit territory. The Hudson Strait and much of the shores of Hudson Bay are again Inuit areas. The Vikings found a way of coexisting with the Inuit, perhaps of cooperating. Elsewhere in America the Vikings came across Native Americans from many different tribes representing many languages and ethnic groups. The evidence suggests attempts at trade, but little success. Rather there is conflict, from which the Vikings seem to have been the losers.

Future researchers also need to look at the European misinformation about the Vikings in America, to the extent that we must feel we are unearthing a cover-up, even a conspiracy. Hiding Greenland and America was of commercial benefit to Denmark. Subsequently the deception of presenting Columbus as the discoverer of America was of enormous benefit to Spain and to the papacy. Today mediaeval and fifteenth-century politics should be set aside, so that we can review the true European discovery of America.

Five hundred years before Columbus the Vikings reached America. It is the Vikings, not Columbus, who start the European history of America.

Legacy of Heroes

Not only are the Vikings the first settlers of America, but they lived their lives in a curiously modern, American manner, almost in accordance with what we today think of as the American dream.

Europe on the eve of the Viking Age was a brutal, feudal society with scant personal freedoms. The labourers at the bottom of the social structure, while called serfs, were in reality slaves. The classes above were bound to their superiors, and ultimately to a king whose power was absolute. During the years of the Viking expansion the structures in Europe worsened as petty despots and the popes consolidated their power, so that by the fourteenth century the vast majority of Europeans were living in a state of subjection. Europe was not a nice place to live.

Scandinavian society was not free from these class divisions, yet there was some modification. The terms *jarl*, *karl* and *thrall* sum up the fundamental feudal authoritarian structure. The farms of Scandinavia would not have functioned without their slave labour, the thralls. Above them were the freemen, the karls or farm-owners, while the pyramid was topped by the jarls, the rulers, who were as tyrannical as any in Europe. Yet the reality of remote communities within Scandinavia promoted modification of this social distinction. Karl and thrall lived and worked together. The position of the farm owner was ultimately defended by law, and there were draconian penalties for thralls who did not keep to their place, but on a daily basis a farm could only function when the thralls were motivated to do their work, and accepted the leadership of the karl. Karl and thrall ate the same food, sheltered under one roof, and in the many skirmishes between rival groups karl and thrall fought together. Difficult geography meant that the jarl was a distant figure, not impacting on everyday life. The jarl led the army, but his army was in effect of volunteers. In this was the start of a different, more modern, method of social interaction.

It was on the sea routes of the North Atlantic that a new Viking social structure developed, characterised by personal freedom and independence. The pioneers who settled the stepping stones of the North Atlantic started with a common experience – a long sea-voyage in an open boat. No amount of reference to supposed Viking hardiness or the high quality of Viking woollen clothes can take away the simple facts that such journeys were cold, wet and miserable, in over-crowded, leaking boats which needed continual bailing. The experience brought people together.

It is in Iceland that Europe develops its first true democratic institutions. Democracy is, of course, a Greek concept. Yet Athenian democracy had not survived in Athens, and had left no direct legacy in the Mediterranean. It is in Iceland that the Vikings established Europe's first enduring democracy, and one which still exists today in an unbroken tradition, so that today's prime minister of Iceland is truly the direct successor of the first Viking law-speaker and presides over a legislature which has its roots in the first Icelandic parliament in Thingvellir. It is perfectly easy to criticise the early Icelandic democracy – for example, it was based on a household suffrage rather than a universal suffrage, and was an annual event rather than in more or less permanent session – yet it was also the very best that could be achieved 1,000 years ago, and much better than the undemocratic governmental systems endured by most of the world's people even today. The Vikings were truly democrats.

For many Vikings the motivation for voyaging the North Atlantic was simply the preservation of their lives. This is recorded, for example, in the case of Eirik the Red and his followers, who would have been executed as outlaws had they stayed in Iceland, and so were thereby prompted to settle Greenland. Doubtless similar stories lay behind many of the migrations west across the Atlantic.

There was also a desire for liberty, along with an appreciation of personal responsibility for one's actions. There was no-one to help if a Viking ship ran into problems in the middle of the Atlantic. The farmsteads in the Faroe

Islands, Iceland and Greenland, the settlements in North America, were isolated and dependent on their own resources for survival. Freedom, and the pursuit of this freedom, drove the first Viking settlers west to America.

Yet it seems to me to be wrong to regard the Vikings who crossed the Atlantic simply as refugees seeking freedom in a new world. Rather they were excited by what they did, happy to be living in accordance with the spirit of heroism that was their ethical code. The rigours of a transatlantic voyage in an open boat are substantial, yet everything that we see in the sagas is that the Vikings embraced these challenges, and took pleasure in their achievements. In the experience of the North Atlantic voyages the Vikings lived life to the full. They lived without the hierarchies of kings and courts, without taking much notice of papal authority, asserting rather the equality of all, women and men. Their lives as set out in the sagas demonstrate belief in a personal ethical code derived from direct, personal experience of the divine, and with little reference to dogmas, whether Christian or pagan. In reading the sagas, even with all their bloodshed and suffering, there is a spirit of joy in being able to live life, take decisions, embrace the moment.

In the Vikings, America finds its first European settlers. Most fittingly these first European settlers in America were people searching for what we know today as the American dream: life, liberty and the pursuit of happiness.

Appendix 1

A Note on Methodology

The ideas found in this book derive from several distinct disciplines. The approach is therefore of necessity multi-disciplinary, and to complement this, methodologies are derived from more than one discipline.

The unifying methodology of this book is the multi-method approach,[1] which has gained popularity in recent years within the social sciences and is beginning to be applied more widely. A question may be approached using several methodologies or several bodies of evidence, each of which has distinct flaws which throw doubt on the validity of the conclusion. When several different methodologies can be found which yield the same conclusion then that conclusion assumes a greater degree of validity than could be given by one method alone. The metaphor of a three-legged stool is sometimes used – with one or even two legs it falls over, but with three legs it stands up.

Historical method is fundamental to this book. Events discussed are related to the sources from which our knowledge of those events is derived. While I have made much use of the interpretations made by experts in their many and varied specialist areas, ultimately the events are rooted in a primary source to which a degree of credence may be attached. Discussion of events from literary sources, particularly the sagas, takes account of the methodology of literary criticism. Ideas which derive from language are influenced specifically by the neo-grammarian philological method, though the general approach is familiar to descriptive linguists. My approach to archaeology, genetics and ethnology is as an interested non-specialist. Historical method alone cannot give all the answers to questions about the Vikings in America. Literature presents us with a series of events around the lives of Eirik the Red and Leif Eiriksson, clearly a limited approach. Language, archaeology, genetics and ethnology all have something to contribute. Taken together these disciplines and the methodologies they offer provide the framework for the story told here.

The style of this book is as a continuous narrative free from a heavy critical apparatus. Researchers will readily find corroboration for factual material in major libraries or online. My contribution has been to put the whole together. There is little here that is original or primary research, save for the etymology proposed for 'America'.

There are many gaps in the story of Vikings in America, and the best that can be done with the gaps is to offer hypotheses. Once the question is formed then someone, somewhere may be able to find a methodology to provide an answer. *Vikings in America* is a key story in the development of both Europe and America, and it needs much more work by a host of scholars. We need to move on from unproductive reworking of such disputes as the Vinland Map, Kensington Runestone and Newport Tower – for until there is new evidence one way or the other we just don't know about these. Rather we need academic and public acceptance that the Vikings were in North America in large numbers and for a long time. We need to accept that we should be able to find traces of the Vikings, and actively search for them.

Appendix 2

Bishops of Greenland

Eirik Gnuppson 1112–24?
Arnald 1124–52
Jon Knutr 1152–88?
Jon Smyrill Sverrifostri 1188–1209
Helgi 1212–30
Nicholas 1234–42
Olaf 1247–80
Thord 1289–1314
Arnni 1314–48
Jon Eiriksson Skalli 1343–50s?

From 1124 all had their bishopric at the cathedral of St Nicholas, Gardar, modern Igaliku, in the Eastern Settlement. Eirik Gnuppson's bishopric was at Sandnes. The list contains several gaps when there may have been bishops appointed whose names are not remembered. Bishop Nicholas was in Norway 1234–40, leaving Greenland effectively without a bishop. From 1343–48 Greenland appears to have had two bishops. The bishopric of Greenland was founded as part of the archdiocese of Hamburg-Bremen; later it was part of the archdiocese of Nidaros.

Appendix 3

Mediaeval Kings of Norway

Harald Fairhair (*c.* 890–*c.* 930)
Eirik Bloodaxe (*c.* 930–34)
Håkon the Good (934–61)
Harald Gråfell (961–76)
Haakon Jarl (976–95)
Olaf Tryggvason (995–1000)
Svein Forkbeard (999–1015)
Olaf Haraldsson (Saint Olav) (1015–28)
Knut the Great (1028–35)
Magnus the Good (1035–47)
Harald Hardrade (1046–66)
Magnus Haraldsson (1066–69)
Olaf Kyrre (1066–93)
Håkon Magnusson (1093–94)
Magnus Barefoot (1093–1103)
Olaf Magnusson (1103–10)
Øystein Magnusson (1103–23)
Sigurd Jorsalfar (1103–30)
Magnus the Blind (1130–35)
Harald Gille (1130–36)
Sigurd Slembe (1135–39)
Sigurd Munn (1136–55)
Øystein Haraldsson (1136–57)
Inge Krokrygg (1136–61)
Håkon Herdebrei (1157–62)
Magnus Erlingsson (1161–84)
Sigurd Markusfostre (1162–63)
Eystein Meyla (1174–77)

Sverre Sigurdsson (1177–1202)
Jon Kuvlung (1185–88)
Sigurd Magnusson (1193–94)
Inge Magnusson (1196–1202)
Håkon Sverreson (1202–04)
Guttorm Sigurdsson (1204)
Inge Bårdsson (1204–17)
Erling Steinvegg (1204–07)
Filippus Simonsson (1207–17)
Håkon IV Håkonsson (1217–63)
Skule Bårdsson (1239–40)
Magnus Lagabøte (1263–80)
Eirik Magnusson (1280–99)
Håkon V Magnusson (1299–1319)
The Union of Sweden and Norway (1319–43)
Magnus Eiriksson (1319–43)
Håkon VI Magnusson (1343–80)
The Union of Denmark and Norway (1380–96)
Olav IV Håkonsson (1380–87)
Margaret I (Margrete I) (1387–89)
Eric VII of Pomerania (1389–1442)
The Kalmar Union (1397–1536)
Denmark, Norway and Sweden (1397–1523)
Christopher III of Bavaria (1442–48)
Carl I (Karl Knutsson Bonde) (1449–50)
Christian I (1450–81)
Hans (1481–1513)
Christian II (1513–23)

The Norwegian king list contains many examples of two men claiming the throne, and both reigning over part of Norway during a period of civil war. Norwegian kings frequently ruled neighbouring countries. Thus Knut the Great – Canute – was King of Norway, King of Denmark and King of England.

Bibliography

General Sources for the Vikings

Alan, Tony, 2004, *The Vikings – Life, Myth and Art*, Barnes and Noble, New York

Binns, Alan, 1980, *Viking Voyagers – Then and Now*, Heinemann, London

Cotterell, Arthur, 1999, *Norse Mythology*, Sebastian Kelly, Oxford

Ellis Davidson, H.R., 1979, *Gods and Myths of Northern Europe*, Penguin, Middlesex

Foote, Peter G., and Wilson, David M., 1974, *The Viking Achievement*, BCA, London

Gordon, E.V., 1974, *An Introduction to Old Norse*, Oxford University Press, Oxford

Graham-Campbell, James, and Kidd, Dafydd, 1980, *The Vikings*, British Museum Publications, London

Guerber, H.A., 1929, *Myths of the Norsemen from the Eddas and Sagas*, George G. Harrap & Co, London

Hagen, Anders, 1966, *The Viking Ship Finds*, Universitetets Oldsaksamling, Oslo

Jones, Gwyn, 1984, *A History of the Vikings*, Oxford University Press, Oxford

Linklater, Eric, 1955, *The Ultimate Viking*, Macmillan, London

Magnusson, Magnus, 1979, *Viking Hammer of the North*, Orbis Publishing, London

Magnusson, Magnus, 1980, *Vikings!*, Bodley Head, London

Musset, Lucien, 1951, *Les Peuples Scandinaves au Moyen Age*, Presse Universitaires de France, Paris

Orchard, Andy, 2002, *Cassell's Dictionary of Norse Myth and Legend*, Cassell, London

Sweet, Henry, 1895, *An Icelandic Primer*, Oxford University Press, Oxford

Wilson, David, 1971, *The Vikings and their Origins – Scandinavia in the First Millennium*, BCA, London

Viking Shetland

Balneaves, Elizabeth, 1977, *The Windswept Isles – Shetland and its People*, John Gifford, London

Davis, Graeme, 2007, *The Early English Settlement of Orkney and Shetland*, John Donald, Edinburgh

Leirfall, John, *West Over Sea – Reminders of Norse Ascendency from Shetland to Dublin*, The Thule Press, Shetland

Linklater, Eric, 1965, *Orkney and Shetland*, Robert Hale, London

Livingstone, W.P., 1948, *Shetland and the Shetlanders*, Nelson, London

Palsson, Hermann and Edwards, Paul, 1987, *Orkneyinga Saga, The History of the Earls of Orkney*, Penguin Books, London

Viking Faroe Islands

Kjorsvik Schei, Liv, and Moberg, Gunnie, 1988, *The Faroe Islands*, Birlinn, Edinburgh

The Royal Danish Ministry of Foreign Affairs, 1959, *The Faroe Islands*, Copenhagen

Williamson, Kenneth, 1948, *The Atlantic Islands – The Faeroe Life and Scene*, Collins, London

Williamson, Kenneth, and Morton Boyd, J., 1963, *A Mosaic of Islands*, Oliver and Boyd, London

Viking Iceland

Bjorn Thordarson, 1953, *Iceland Past and Present*, Hlathbuth, Reykjavik

Davis, Graeme, 2004, *A Brit in Iceland*, Shakespeare Centre Press, Newcastle

von Linden, Franz-Karl, and Weyer, Helfried, 1974, *Iceland*, Almenna Bokafelagith, Reykjavik

Magnusson, Magnus, 1992, *Iceland Saga*, Bodley Head, London

Smiley, Jane, 2000, *The Sagas of Icelanders*, Penguin Viking, New York

Sveinbjorn Johnson, 1930, *Pioneers of Freedom – An Account of the Icelanders and the Icelandic Free State 874–1262*, The Stratford Company, Boston, Massachusetts

Viking Greenland

Garnett, Eve, 1968, *To Greenland's Icy Mountain – The Story of Hans Egede, Explorer, Coloniser, Missionary*, Heinemann, London

Hertling, Birgitte, 1993, *Greenlandic for Travelers*, Atuakkiorfik, Nuuk

Malaurie, Jean, 1982, *The Last Kings of Thule*, Jonathan Cape, London

Ministry of Foreign Affairs of Denmark, undated, *Greenland Arctic Denmark*, Copenhagen

Stefansson, Vilhjalmur, 1943, *Greenland*, George G. Harrap & Co, London [arguably the best book on Greenland ever written]

The Royal Danish Ministry of Foreign Affairs, undated, *Greenland*, Ringkjobing

Viking High Arctic

Alexander, Bryan and Cherry, 1996, *The Vanishing Arctic*, Cassell, London

Baird, Patrick D., 1965, *The Polar World*, Longmans, London

Banks, Mike, 1957, *High Arctic*, J.M. Dent and Sons Ltd, London

Beatie, Owen and Geiger, John, 1992, *Buried in Ice*, Madison Press Books, Toronto

Confrey, Mick and Jordan, Tim, 1998, *Icemen – A History of the Arctic and its Explorers*, Boxtree, London

Fiennes, Ranulph, 1995, *To the Ends of the Earth*, Mandarin, London

Hodgson, Stuart, 1976, *Stories from Pangnirtung*, Hurtig, Edmonton

Illingworth, Frank, 1951, 'Wild Life Beyond the North', *Country Life*, London

Miles, Hugh and Salisbury, Mike, 1985, *Kingdom of the Ice Bear*, BBC, London

Mueller, Fritz, 1981, *The Living Arctic*, Methuen Publications, Ontario

Nansen, Fridtjof, 2002, *Farthest North – The Exploration of the* Fram *1893–1896*, Birlinn, Edinburgh

Norman Smith, I. (ed.), 1964, *The Unbelievable Land*, The Queen's Printer, Ottawa

Officer, Charles and Page, Jake, 2001, *A Fabulous Kingdom – The Exploration of the Arctic*, OUP, Oxford

Schledermann, Peter, 1997, *The Viking Saga*, Weidenfeld and Nicolson, London

Shackleton, Edward, 1936, *Arctic Journeys*, Hodder and Stoughton, London

Stefansson, Evelyn, 1945, *Within the Circle*, Charles Scribner's Sons, New York

Weems, John Edward, 1967, *Peary –The Explorer and the Man*, Houghton Mifflin Company, Boston

Young, Steven B., 1976, *To the Arctic – An Introduction to the Far Northern World*, Wiley, New York

Viking North America

The Arni Magnusson Institute, 2000, *New Lands New Faith – Christianity and the Vinland Voyages in Mediaeval Manuscripts*, Reykjavik

Harris, Leslie, 1968, *Newfoundland and Labrador – A Brief History*, Dent & Sons, Canada

Hodding Carter, W., 2000, *An Illustrated Viking Voyage*, Pocket Books, New York

Ingstad, Helge, 1969, *Westward to Vinland*, translated from Norwegian by Erik J. Friis, Book Club Associates, London

Lomax, Judy, 1992, *The Viking Voyage – With Gaia to Vinland*, Hutchinson, London

Magnusson, Magnus and Palsson, Hermann (translators), 1978, *The Vinland Sagas: The Norse Discovery of America*, Penguin, London

Wahlgren, Erik, 2000, *The Vikings and America*, Thames and Hudson, London

Before and After the Vikings

Ambrosini, Maria Luisa, 1996, *The Secret Archives of the Vatican*, Barnes and Noble Books, New York

Cary, M., and Warmington, E.H., 1929, *The Ancient Explorers*, Methuen, London

Evans, Admiral Sir Edward, 1946, *British Polar Explorers*, Collins, London

Fitzpatrick-Alper, Ann, 1991, *Forgotten Voyager – The Story of Amerigo Vespucci*, Carolrhoda Books, Minneapolis

McGhee, Robert, 2002, *The Arctic Voyages of Martin Frobisher – An Elizabethan Adventure*, The British Museum Press, London

Mowat, Farley, 1998, *The Alban Quest – The Search for a Lost Tribe*, Weidenfeld and Nicolson, London

Simpson, Colin, 1967, *The Viking Circle*, Hodder and Stoughton, London

Sinclair, Andrew, 2004, *The Sword and the Grail*, Birlinn, Edinburgh

References

1 Vikings to America

1. A forceful criticism of forged Viking artefacts and curious theories is contained in the chapter "Buckram Vikings" in Wahlgren (1986): "Let oddball deviancy be taken for what it is. Seen with the humour it deserves the occasional hoax, the inevitable daffy theory, help to give us perspective on the equivocal human condition" (p. 120). While undoubtedly right to warn against the strange theories and forgeries which seem to gather around the topic of Vikings in America it has to be noted that the twenty or so years since the publication of Wahlgren's book has seen evidence appear which supports theories which Wahlgren may have seen as "daffy".

2. The idea of Vikings in California is promoted by numerous web sites, including an eBook *The Last Viking* by John N Harris (1999) at *http://www.spirasolaris.ca*. Here Vinland is identified with California. Evidence is in my view very thin indeed, though not totally lacking. Certainly the evidence is too slight to persuade me that the Vikings managed voyages through the ice-choked North West passage and Bering Straight. Unless some unexpected, strong, new evidence should come to light I do not see how this theory can be upheld. A Knights Templar colony in the New World on Viking foundations is a staple of much of the extensive popular writing around the Templars. An example is Steven Sora's *The Lost Colony of the Templars, Verrazano's Secret Mission to America* (2005). These ideas need evidence if they are to be taken seriously.

3. The Vikings fought for the Byzantine emperors at least from the early tenth century. A Viking bodyguard was adopted in 988AD by Byzantine Emperor Basil II, with an initial strength of 6,000 Vikings, later formalised as the Varangian Guard. Over four centuries in countless battles throughout the Mediterranean region the Varangian Guard became famed for its unswerving loyalty, for its military excellence, and for its brutality.

2 Stepping Stones to America

1. "Ohthere sæde his hlaforde, Ælfrede cyninge, thæt he ealra Northmonna northmest bude" – Othere told his lord, King Alfred, that he of all the North Men lived the furthest north.

2. The two major sources of information for Viking ships are the two Viking ship museums: *The Viking Ship Museum*, Roskilde, Denmark, and *The Viking Ship Hall*, Oslo, Norway. Several replicas have been built and sailed on routes known to have been used by the Vikings, including the North Atlantic.

3. A description of the fleet of Sweyn Forkbeard on a visit to Normandy in 1013 from *Encomium Emmae Reginae* (otherwise known as *Gesta Cnutonis Regis*), an encomium written around 1041 in honour of Queen Emma of Normandy.

4. The first historical use of the name Pict is of course later, but it has long been conventional to use the name Pict for the people who built the brochs.

5. The Irish discovery of the Faroe Islands is firmly accepted in the Faroe Islands, and was a subject of a 1994 Faroese Post Office commemorative stamp. The archaeological record shows oat pollen from 650 AD, demonstrating that the islands were inhabited from at least this time. The Irish seem to be the only candidates.

6. Sigmundur Brestisson's story is told in *Faereyinga Saga*. He brought Christianity to the Faroe Islands in AD 999 by the expedient of offering the head man of the Faroe Islands the choice between beheading or accepting Christianity. In a subsequent fight Sigmundur supposedly escaped death by swimming from Skuvoy to Suthuroy islands (an improbable if not wholly impossible distance in view of the cold waters), only to be murdered on his arrival in Suthuroy.

7. The story of the voyage to Thule Ultima is from Diodorus Siculus (book V), itself a restatement of now lost work by Timaeus and from an informant Pytheas of Marseilles. The voyage is often called Pytheas's voyage, though there is no reason to think Pytheas himself made it – rather he reported on it. Scholarly reflection on the story has yielded remarkably little to add to the bare outline of the narrative. Writers have been consistent in reflecting admiration for the achievement of the Pytheas voyage.

8. The large coracle which was used for sea voyages is sometimes called a *currach*, with the name *coracle* reserved for the single person boats used on rivers and lakes. However *currach* does not have wide currency, and I have used *coracle* throughout.

9. Floki Vilgertharson's use of ravens as a navigational aid is recorded in *Landnamabok*. The story has become a staple of Icelandic story-telling, earning Floki the nickname "Ravens Floki". Stories also develop the theme of the different views on the worth of Iceland held by Floki and two of his

crew. While Floki is reported as seeing Iceland as wholly worthless, Herjolf regarded Iceland as having good and bad qualities, while Thorolf pronounced the Nordic equivalent of a land flowing with milk and honey – he said that there was butter on every blade of grass. By this statement Thorolf won himself a nickname – Butter Thorolf.

10. *Landnamabok* records by name the 435 original settlers of Iceland, along with many of their descendants, giving a total of more than 3,000 named individuals and around 1,400 named settlements. It is readily available online both as Icelandic transcription and translation into English and other languages.

11. News and findings of DECODE genetics are on their website at *http:// www.decode.com/*

12. The now classic account of Thingvellir and Icelandic democracy is Sveinbjorn Johnson's *Pioneers of Freedom, An Account of the Icelanders and the Icelandic Free State 874-1262* (Boston, The Stratford Company, 1930), produced to celebrate the one thousandth anniversary of the founding of the Althing.

13. The major source for the Norse pantheon is the *Elder Edda* of the Codex Regius. There is an enormous literature of secondary works and of retellings of tales of the Norse gods.

14. Much of the information about Eirik the Red comes from the saga which bears his name.

3 The Greenland Base

1. J Arneborg, J Heinemeier, N Lynnerup, H L Nielsen, N Rud, and A E Sveinbjornsdottir, *Change of Diet of the Greenland Vikings Determined from Stable Carbon Isotope Analysis and 14C Dating of Their Bones' Radiocarbon* (University of Arizona, 1961).

2. Reginald Heber (1783-1826) was Anglican Bishop of Calcutta and author of many hymns. His reference to Greenland in his 1819 hymn reflects the prejudices of his age rather than knowledge of the land described, and it may well be that his other geographical references are equally suspect. Notwithstanding he has provided what is probably the best known missionary hymn, starting:

> From Greenland's icy mountains, from India's coral strand;
> Where Afric's sunny fountains roll down their golden sand:

From many an ancient river, from many a palmy plain,
They call us to deliver their land from error's chain.

3. A discussion on sailing directions is found within James Robert Enter-line's *Erikson, Eskimos, and Columbus: Medieval European Knowledge of America* (John Hopkins University Press, 2002).

4. The English translation of *Speculum Regale* is L. M. Larson's *The King's Mirror (Speculum regale – Konungs skuggsjá)*, Scandinavian Monographs 3, New York, 1917, while the standard edition is by Ludwig Holm-Olsen, *Konungs Skuggsjá*, (Oslo, Norsk Historisk Kjeldeskrift-institutt, 1983).

5. Between the fall of Rome and the Italian Renaissance there are several instances of learning flourishing in Europe, including the Golden Age of Northumbria, King Alfred's Wessex and the Carolingian Renaissance. The Northern Renaissance in Iceland differed from these in that literacy and learning were relatively widespread rather than confined to a small group of literate monks.

6. *Heimskringla* begins "Kringla heimsins, sú er mannfólkið byggir..." – "The orb of the world on which mankind lives..." The title derives from the first two words. Heimskringla sub-divides into many sagas, often referred to as if independent works. This opening is from *Ynglinga Saga*.

7. Otherwise known as Jon Rauthi, archbishop of Nidaros (1268–1282).

8. The 1362 Oraefajokull eruption destroyed the neighbouring farm land, an area subsequently renamed Oraefi after the volcano, which has in turn entered the Icelandic language to mean "wasteland". Huge amounts of tephra were ejected, with resulting climatic disruption caused by the ash.

9. The official *Life of Hans Egede* by Louis Bobe (Rossenkilde and Bagger, 1952, both Danish and English editions) is the ultimate source of material here on Hans Egede. However Eve Garnett's *To Greenland's Icy Mountain* reworks much of the material in a format which is far more attractive to read. The story of Egede's mission to Greenland, a land then almost unknown in Europe, provides an interesting parallel with the fortitude and courage of the first Viking settlers. As well as missionary he was explorer and coloniser, while in his interaction with the Inuit Greenlanders he showed himself to be first an able linguist, then a sympathetic friend. His tombstone in Copenhagen provides an appropriate tribute which translates as: "An honour among Christians, a light to the heathens, famous in Norway, revered in Denmark, but in Greenland immortal".

10. It is important to find appropriate balance and scholarly distance when discussing the Zeno Voyages. On the one hand the book and the map were

of enormous influence in determining European views of the North Atlantic, and if nothing else they made the Mediterranean world aware that there was a North Atlantic region and there were lands within it. On the other hand the account is garbled throughout, and has become the plaything of those who want to advance theories unsupported and unsupportable. There is absolutely no shred of academic respectability in the assertions that they concern a voyage made by Henry Sinclair, Earl of Orkney.

11. Brian Smith, "Earl Henry Sinclair's fictitious trip to America", *New Orkney Antiquarian Journal*, vol. 2, 2002.

4 Vikings to Vinland

1. An extensive account of Maeshowe is offered by Colin Richard's *Dwelling Among the Monuments: The Neolithic Village of Barnhouse, Maeshowe Passage Grave and Surrounding Monuments at Stenness, Orkney* (2005, McDonald Institute Monographs). Bruce Dickens' *The Runic Inscriptions of Maeshowe* (1930) remains popular.

2. The most widely read of the early translation was James Russell Lowell's poem "The Voyage to Vinland" published within his anthology *Under the Willows and Other Poems* (1868).

3. The historical outline of Gudrid's remarkable life is readily available in numerous Viking histories. It has inspired the novel *The Sea Road* by Margaret Elphinstone (2000), considered one of the 100 best Scottish books of all time (*List* magazine).

5 Viking Exploration of the High Arctic

1. *The Viking Saga* by Peter Schledermann (Weidenfeld & Nicolson 1997). A more academic approach to the topic is within Peter Schledermann's *Crossroads to Greenland: 3000 Years of Prehistory in the Eastern High Arctic*, published by the Arctic Institute of North America of the University of Calgary (1990)

2. The Inuit resettled to Grise Fiord call it *Aujuittuq*, meaning "the place that never thaws". The modern settlement was established in 1953 with eight Inuit families who were promised homes, good hunting and the option to return to their previous homes on the Ungava Peninsula should they wish. In fact the homes were not built, the hunting available in the vicinity of Grise Ford unfamiliar to the Inuit from more southerly locations (who

found it hard to adapt), and when they requested a return to their previous homes, Canada reneged. A 1993 Canadian government hearing received the report *The High Arctic Relocation: A Report on the 1953-55 Relocation* by The Royal Commission on Aboriginal Peoples and in compensation made a settlement payment of C$10,000,000.

3. Dr Frederick Cook's claim to have reached the Pole in 1908, a year before Peary, is not now widely accepted. Cook was later convicted and imprisoned for fraud, and his poorly-supported claim to have reached the Pole does indeed appear to be another fraudulent statement. Peary's claim has been disputed on the grounds that his final dash for the pole was achieved with the benefit of some remarkably fast speeds in the final marches both to and from the pole, that he did not have a navigator with him, and because the exploit for long appeared unsupported by expedition diaries. However his diaries emerged in 1986 and are considered consistent with the reported story (and indeed replete with pemmican stains). In 2005 a team led by Tom Avery recreated Peary's route to the Pole using similar equipment, and made a journey time five hours faster than Peary's, proving that Peary's journey time, once considered suspect, is in fact possible. The balance of probability does seem to be that Peary reached the Pole just as he stated – in his own words "April 6, 1909, I have today hoisted the national ensign of the United States of America at this place, which my observations indicate to be the North Polar axis of the earth, and have formally taken possession of the entire region, and adjacent, for and in the name of the President of the United States of America". Peary's navigational readings made in the absence of a specialist navigator are likely to have been accurate to within about five miles, which most commentators seem to feel is near enough to claim a visit to the Pole.

4. Walker O Smith, *Polynyas: Windows to the World*, (Volume 74, Elsevier Oceanography Series, 2007).

5. J. H. Freese, *Photius' Excerpt of Ctesias' Indica*, 1920.

6. The seven unicorn tapestries in The Cloisters (Metropolitan Museum of Art) New York are:

　　1. The Start of the Hunt
　　2. The Unicorn Cleanses the Stream of Poison with its Horn
　　3. The Unicorn Leaps into the Stream
　　4. The Unicorn Defends Himself
　　5. The Unicorn is Tamed and Betrayed by the Maiden
　　6. The Unicorn is Killed and Brought to the Castle
　　7. The Unicorn in Captivity.

The sequence tells the story of the unicorn hunt, where the unicorn is killed not through the skill of the hunters but by the maiden's betrayal. The unicorn is killed in the sixth tapestry and resurrected in the seventh, stressing the role of the unicorn as a metaphor for Christ.

7. K McCullough and P Schledermann, "Mystery cairns of Washington Irving Island", *Polar Record* (vol 35, no.195, Oct. 1999).

8. Edward Moss, *Shores of the Polar Sea, A Narrative of the Arctic Expedition of 1875-6* (London: Marcus Ward, 1878).

6 Viking Hudson Bay

1. E C Coleman, *History of the Royal Navy and Polar Exploration: From Franklin to Scott* (Tempus Publishing 2006).

2. Rachel A Qitsualik and Sean A Tinsley, *Qanuq Pinngurnirmata: Inuit Stories of How Things Came to Be* (Inhabit Media 2009).

3. Paul Malkie, *Leif Eriksson: The Man who Almost Changed the World* (TV documentary, 2000).

4. Farley Mowat, *The Alban Quest The Search for a Lost Tribe* (1999).

5. Douglas MacKay, *The Honourable Company; A History of the Hudson's Bay Company* (Indianapolis: Bobbs-Merrill, 1936).

6. An alternative explanation would be that the rune-stone writer expected to be killed, and was writing for posterity.

7 Vikings and Inuit

1. Sources for Greenlandic pre-history include Therkel Mathiassen's *The Eskimo Archaeology of Julianehaab District: With a Brief Summary of the Prehistory of the Greenlanders*, (C.A. Reitzel, 1936); Mareau S. Maxwell's *Prehistory of the Eastern Arctic* (New World Archaeological Record, Academic Press Inc, 1985); Peter Schledermann's *Crossroads to Greenland – 3000 Years of History in the Eastern High Arctic* (Arctic Institute of North America of the University of Calgary, 1990).

2. George Francis Lyon (1795-1832) explored first in West Africa, where he sought (without finding) the city of Timbuktu, and subsequently took part in the search for the North-West Passage. He had a genuine interest in what he termed the "natives", learning Arabic to assist his West African exploration and being tattooed by the Inuit when in the Arctic. His own

account of his Arctic experiences is published in two volumes: *The Private Journal of Captain G.F. Lyon, of* H.M.S. Hecla, *During the Recent Voyage of Discovery under Captain Parry* (1824) and *A Brief Narrative Of An Unsuccessful Attempt To Reach Repulse Bay In* His Majesty's Ship Griper, *In The Year MDCCCXXIV* (1825).

3. Key texts on Inuit history and language include: Ishmael Alunik, *Across Time and Tundra: the Inuvialuit of the Western Arctic* (Vancouver, Raincoast Books, 2003); Georges-Hébert Germain and David Morrison, *Inuit: les peuples du froid*, (Montréal, Musée canadien des civilisations, 1995); Gillian Robinson (ed), *Isuma Inuit Studies Reader: an Inuit Anthology*, (Montreal, Isuma, 2004); Renée Fossett, *In Order to Live Untroubled: Inuit of the Central Arctic, 1550-1940*, (Winnipeg, University of Manitoba Press, 2001); Louis-Jacques Dorais, *La parole inuit: langue, culture et société dans l'Arctique nord-américain* (Paris, Peeters, 1996).

4. Nellie Cournoyea, Richard G. Condon, Julia Ogina, *The Northern Copper Inuit: A History* (University of Oklahoma Press,1996, in Civilization of American Indians).

5. Jean Malaurie's *The Last Kings of Thule* (London, 1982) is a starting point for much relating to the Thule Inuit.

6. An account of Peary's discovery of the Cape York meteorite is in John Edward Weems, *Peary the Explorer and the Man* (Boston, 1967).

8 Memories of Vikings in America

1. The idea that Columbus visited Iceland was first proposed in J. K. Tornöe's *Columbus in the Arctic?* (Oslo, 1965).

2. James Robinson, *The Lewis Chessmen*, (London, 2004, The British Museum Press); N. Stratford, *The Lewis Chessmen and the Enigma of the Hoard* (London, 1997, The British Museum Press).

3. The Secret Archive of the Vatican has its own website, *http://asv.vatican. va/*, which includes some general information about the archive and the documents, but neither a catalogue nor access information. The Secret Archive is separate from the Vatican Library, whose website is at *http://www. vaticanlibrary.va/*. In theory it is possible for scholars to gain access to the Vatican Library, though as the website expresses it "At present, all of the Library's collections are unavailable for consultation" (2009). Closure of the library will continue at least until summer 2010.

4. Sean McGrail, *Boats of the World From the Stone Age to Medieval Times* (OUP, 2004).

5. Writing about John Dee is extensive. A recent overview is offered by Benjamin Woolley's *The Queen's Conjuror: The Science and Magic of Dr. John Dee, Adviser to Queen Elizabeth I* (New York: Henry Holt and Company, 2001). His contribution to the creation of the British Empire is discussed in Nicholas Canny's *The Origins of Empire, The Oxford History of the British Empire Volume I*, Oxford University Press (1998).

6. The major primary source for the voyage of the *Mayflower* and the establishment of the Plymouth colony is the account of William Bradford *Of Plimoth Plantation*, written 1620-1647 (and with the spelling *Plimoth*) though describing events from 1608. The most accessible edition is that by William Bradford and William T Davis (1908) with the title *Bradford's History of Plymouth Plantation, 1606-1646*. Numerous modern accounts of the Mayflower and the Colony exist, including Nathaniel Philbrick's *Mayflower: A Story of Courage, Community, and War*, (Viking, 2006).

9 Legacy of Vikings in America

1. The Narragansett Indian Tribe's website is at *http://www.narragansetttribe.org/*. The tribe now has around 2,500 members in Rhode Island, and is associated with an additional 2,500 members of related Mohegan tribes in Connecticut and Long Island.

2. R E Wodehouse, "Tuberculosis in North American Indians" *Canadian Medical Association Journal* 1926 June; 16(6); C W McMillen, '"The red man and the white plague": rethinking race, tuberculosis, and American Indians, ca. 1890-1950', *Bulletin of Historical Medicine*, 2008, Fall:82(3).

3. The primary source for Verrazano's voyage is "Voyage of John de Verrazzano, along the Coast of North America, from Carolina to Newfoundland, AD 1524", *Collections of the New York Historical Society, Second Series, 1841, Volume 1*, pages 37-67. Verrazano's reputation as the explorer of coast including New York was long obscured, and the decision to name a New York bridge after him – the Verrazano Narrows Bridge – was controversial, and only happened because of extensive lobbying from the Italian Historical Society of America. The spelling Verrazano is now standard for his name, replacing the earlier Verrazzano.

4. Charles Christian Rafn, *Antiquitates Americanae Sive Scriptores Septentrionales Rerum Ante-Columbianarum in America* (Copenhagen, 1837).

5. The Chronognostic Research Foundation is a non-profit corporation interested in historical and archaeological investigation.

6. A runic inscription on Norman's Island off the coast of Martha's Vineyard was "discovered" in 1926 and read "Leif Eiriksson MI" (ie 1001). It is now generally dismissed as there is a report of a Norwegian cook working in the area having carved it in 1913. Additionally it is most unlikely that the runes would survive around a thousand years (the rock is sea-covered at high tide), and because the use of Roman numerals for dates was not usual in Scandinavia at this time. It is of course possible to make a case of sorts for Viking presence from the evidence of the *Vinland Sagas* – Martha's Vineyard fits the description of mild winters, self sown corn and wild grapes. J R L Anderson's *Vinland Voyage* (1966) theorises that Native Americans living in Martha's Vineyard called the area Vinland, and when explorer Bartholomew Gosnold visited the area in 1602 he took a modified form of the native name, added the name of his daughter who had died in infancy and whom he wished to commemorate, and produced Martha's Vineyard.

7. Waldseemuller's 1507 map *Universalis Cosmographia* is the only source for the link between the name America and Amerigo Vespucci. The key phrase is "... ab Americo Inventore ... quasi Americi terram sive Americam" which translates "... from Americo the discoverer ... as if it were the land of Americus, thus America". Waldseemuller is clearly struggling in his misspelling of Amerigo and his erratic declension, as the continent's name is not Amerigo, Americo or even Americus but a wholly inexplicable America. Waldseemuller appears to have thought again about this dubious derivation, for in his 1513 re-issue of the map he removes both it and the name America. The one copy of the 1507 edition surviving today was discovered in 1901 by Joseph Fischer, curiously the man who has been proposed as a possible forger of the Vinland Map. There are however no grounds for considering the 1507 Waldseemuller map to be a forgery.

8. Alistair Campbell, *Old English Grammar*, Oxford University Press.

9. Laurence C Thompson and M. Terry Thompson, "Metathesis as a grammatical device", *International Journal of American Linguistics, 35* (1969).

Appendix 1

1. Katrin Niglas, *The Combined Use of Qualitative and Quantitative Methods in Educational Research*, (2004); J Mingers, J Brocklesby, "Multimethodology: Towards a Framework for Mixing Methodologies", *Omega*, Volume 25, Number 5, October 1997.

Index

The convention of indexing Viking and modern Icelandic names by first names has been observed here. For example *Leif Eiriksson* is indexed under his first name *Leif*, not his patronymic *Eiriksson*. Viking names and most modern Icelandic names do not contain a surname.